Postcards
from the
Schoolhouse

*Practitioner Scholars Examine
Contemporary Issues in
Instructional Leadership*

Edited by

Kimberly
Kappler Hewitt

Cherese
Childers-McKee

Elizabeth
Hodge

Rhonda
Schuhler

NCPEA Publications

National Council of Professors of Educational Administration
Ypsilanti, Michigan

Published by NCPEA Publications
The publications of the National Council of Professors of Educational Administration (NCPEA)
http://www.ncpeapublications.org

Copyright © 2013 by Kimberly Kappler Hewitt and the National Council of Professors of Educational Administration

All rights reserved. No part of this book may be reproduced in any form or by any electronic or mechanical means, including information storage and retrieval systems, without written permission from the publisher, except by a reviewer who may quote passages in a review.

Printed in United States of America
Library of Congress Cataloging-in-Publication Data

Hewitt, Kimberly

Postcards from the schoolhouse: Practitioner scholars examine contemporary issues in instructional leadership

ISBN 978-1-4675-6535-9 (pbk)

How to order this book:

NCPEA Press, a book publisher for NCPEA Publications offers *Postcards from the Schoolhouse: Practitioner Scholars Examine Contemporary Issues in Instructional Leadership* as a Print-on-Demand hard copy and as an eBook at: www.ncpeapublication.org Books are prepared in Perfect Bound binding and delivery is 3-5 business days. eBooks are available upon ordering and delivered electronically in minutes to one's computer.

Postcards from the Schoolhouse: Practitioner Scholars Examine Contemporary Issues in Instructional Leadership has been peer reviewed, accepted, and endorsed by the National Council of Professors of Educational Administration as a significant contribution to the preparation and practice of school administration.

NCPEA Publications Director and Editor   Theodore B. Creighton
NCPEA Publications Associate Director and Technical Editor   Brad E. Bizzell

"Hewitt, et al., offers insightful perspectives on the practitioner-scholar model of school leadership. Through an integration of practice with theory, *Postcards From the Schoolhouse: Practitioner Scholars Examine Contemporary Issues in Instructional Leadership* addresses powerful contemporary educational issues and offers both provocative and useful discussions reflective of our time."

Dr. Rosemary Papa, The Del and Jewell Lewis Endowed Chair,

Learning Centered Leadership, Northern Arizona University

Dedication

This book is dedicated to practitioner scholars everywhere, those hearty souls, wind-burned and chapped, worn yet indefatigable, those dogged pursuers of what is just and equitable.

Contents

Introduction	The Tension of Leadership: On Being a Practitioner Scholar *Kimberly Kappler Hewitt*	1

Part 1: Rethinking How We Serve Students

Chapter 1	Of Poetry and Math: Why Culturally Relevant Pedagogy Matters *Kathleen McCarroll Moore*	15
Chapter 2	Nuestra Voz: Exploring a Parent Engagement Model for Latino Families Through a Postcolonial Lens *Jason Alemán*	30
Chapter 3	The Tears of Tiers: A Leadership Response to Teachers' Challenges with RTI *John M. Palladino*	47
Chapter 4	21st Century Learning: Educating the Whole Brain *Daniel W. Eadens, Susan Ray, Danielle M. Eadens*, and *Katherine Shirer*	63

Part 2: Rethinking Teacher Work

Chapter 5	When Teachers Find their Voice *Barbara A. Klocko* and *Caryn M. Wells*	83
Chapter 6	A Journey Toward Distributed Teacher Leadership *Cherese Childers-McKee*	101
Chapter 7	A Postcard from Members of a PLC *Linda K. Lemasters, Michael J. Cieslak, Marguerita DeSander,* and *Jennifer Clayton*	117
Chapter 8	The District's Role in Leading Improvement: Professional Learning Communities as the Starting Point *Rebecca A. Thessin* and *Joshua P. Starr*	135

Part 3: Examining 'Right Now' Reforms

Chapter 9	21st Century Learning: The Call for Change *Diane Hill* and *Jean Maness*	158
Chapter 10	Curricular Consistency vs. Instructional Freedom: The Inherent Struggle that Exists with National Standards *Elizabeth M. Hodge* and *Rhonda C. Schuhler*	169

Chapter 11	Technology Leadership: A Digital Lever for Lasting Educational Reform *Justin Bathon*	183
Chapter 12	The Use of Value Added for Accountability and to Inform Leadership *Kimberly Kappler Hewitt*	200
Conclusion	Practitioner Scholar, Instructional Leader, Public Advocate *Carl Lashley* and *Aaron Woody*	226

Introduction

The Tension of Leadership: On Being a Practitioner Scholar

Kimberly Kappler Hewitt

This project germinated from a doctoral course on contemporary challenges in curriculum and instructional leadership at the University of North Carolina Greensboro, as reflected in the course description:

> There is a sense of urgency that surrounds the imperative to provide all children a quality education, and instructional leaders have an ethical responsibility to meet this obligation. This course explores the role of leadership as it relates to the elements of curriculum and instruction and examines contemporary global, national, state, and local challenges facing educational leaders. This course will focus on the intersection of research, theory, and practice.

In one of the first class sessions, we did an affinity activity in which students identified their views on various statements that they had culled from assigned readings regarding contemporary reform efforts. Students responded to each statement by moving to stand beside Likert identifiers (e.g., strongly support; somewhat support; somewhat skeptical; strongly skeptical) affixed to the wall, forming a sort of human Likert scale graph. One of the statements, based on Diane Ravitch's *The Death and Life of the Great American School System* (2011) was, "*Most current reform strategies are mistaken.*" Resolutely, all 12 of the students converged on the "strongly support" marker, indicating that all of them agreed with the notion that most current educational reform efforts are misguided. This was the only statement in the activity on which there was unanimity. What a striking realization: All of the students—each of whom is a school or district leader—are responsible for implementing reforms of which they are skeptical. What an uncomfortable—if not untenable—position. How do educational leaders navigate and negotiate their work as change agents when reforms that they are charged with enacting run counter to what they believe is sound and just practice? How might ethical, justice-oriented leadership occur through, around, and despite contemporary reform efforts? How can practitioner scholars leverage both extant scholarship and their own professional experience to advocate for democratic reform and resist, shift, or reframe anti-democratic and marginalizing reform requirements? None of these questions is fully answered in the chapters that follow, but you will find the work of sincere practitioner scholars as they address the obstacles and possibilities of meaningful reform in contemporary public education.

Each of the chapters, several of which were authored by advanced doctoral students in the aforementioned course, focuses on a contemporary issue in instructional leadership, and all are written from the perspective of practitioner scholars. The authors in this collection are ethically committed to just education for all students, drawing upon scholarship and embodied experience to navigate, critique, and act in ways that are responsive to the context in which they serve as leaders.

PRACTITIONER SCHOLARSHIP

The "opposition of experience and true knowledge" (Dewey, 1916, p. 262)—of practice and theory—has a long tradition in education. The concept of the practitioner scholar obliterates what Dewey (1916) decried as the "flat opposition of reason and experience" (p. 276). At the most basic or fundamental level, practitioner scholar leaders are "individuals who use theory to inform their practice and allow their reflections upon their practice to inform theory" (Horn, 2002, p. 101). Practitioner scholars engage in "critical thinking—…thinking which does not separate itself from action, but constantly immerses itself in temporality" (Friere, 1970, p. 73). These leaders are in the "now," taking action to embody the core values of practitioner scholars—community, democracy, social justice, caring, equity, and inquiry (Schultz, 2010).

We, the authors of this collection, intentionally use the phrase *practitioner scholar*, as opposed to the more commonly used phrase *scholar practitioner*, for two key reasons. First, we seek to trouble the term scholar practitioner for implicit subordination of *practitioner* and the superordination of *scholar* in the phrase. "Communication between practitioners and theorists is rooted in authority, distance, and difference, and hierarchical assumptions about theory and practice are reinforced through patterns of socialization" (Mullen, Greenlee, & Bruner, 2005, p. 5). The inequality embedded in *scholar practitioner* "privileges some types of knowledge and expertise over others, creating a hierarchy of knowing which diminishes the work of both scholars and practitioners" (Bredeson, 2006, p. 21). Mullens (2005) refers to the phrase *scholar practitioner* as an oxymoron. The binary scholar/practitioner, like theory/practice, academic/practical, and theoretical/applied, is constructed such that the former term is elevated above and over the latter. Binaries are "secret hierarchies" (Mann & Huffman, 2005, p. 68) that "serve as grids of regularity that are not only linguistic but also material (St. Pierre & Pillow, 2000, p. 4). Fusing the binary scholar/practitioner into *scholar practitioner* nonetheless reinforces the inequality of the terms. As such, we self-consciously seek to disrupt and upend this hegemony and to privilege practitioner.

During this project, we experienced the hegemony we seek to disrupt. The chapters in this book integrate the literature on the chapter's topic with the professional experiences, expertise, and wisdom of the authors. The latter was no easy task for some of the authors. At multiple points in the writing process, a number of the authors decried the difficulty of infusing their writing with their personal perspective and experiences, claiming that they had been taught—disciplined—to avoid making themselves so present in their writing but rather to invoke a more disembodied/separate/distinct/distant, "scholarly" writing style. Indeed, missing from several of the first drafts were the authors themselves—the writing divorced from the professionals penning it. This is another example of the way in which the "scholarly" has been positioned as superordinate to the realm of practice. This is unfortunate. As Nash (2004) argues, scholarly personal narrative writing is not a contradiction: "While it is personal, it is also social. While it is practical, it is also theoretical. While it is reflective, it is also public. While it is local, it is also political" (p. 29). The writing in this book rejects disembodied, "scholarly" writing and embraces an approach that weaves personal narrative and academic styles.

The marginalization of practitioner scholarship is not committed by the academy alone. Some schools and districts marginalize the scholarly work of educational leaders and frame it as dangerous or distracting. One of the original chapter authors decided to withdraw her contribution to the book after her assistant superintendent cautioned/threatened her that she had "more to lose than to gain" by writing candidly about her experiences in a turnaround school. This is a profound act of silencing and discipline (Foucault, 1977) that effectively oppresses the educational leader and withholds her contribution from the knowledge base.

Additionally, some districts may view practitioner scholarship as detracting from—instead of contributing to—the work of professionals. When I served as a district leader in an affluent school system in Ohio, a colleague and I co-authored a book for school leaders about cultivating a culture of differentiation. In order for the publication to proceed, we had to release copyright to the publisher. According to our personnel contracts, the district holds proprietorship of any scholarly or creative works we produced that were in any way related to our work in the district. In order to get the district to relinquish copyright, we were subject to an onerous process of formally requesting release of copyright, which included submitting a written argument for release; calculations of the total % of time dedicated to writing the book that fell within "work hours"; meeting with the superintendent; and then formal Board action. Throughout the process, our practitioner scholarship was not framed as part of our work as professionals or as contributing toward our work but rather as something that potentially slighted or detracted from our work. These anecdotes serve as examples of the marginalization of practitioner scholarship committed by both the academy and the field. This book itself, then, is an act of resistance to the marginalization of practitioner scholarship.

Our second reason for using the term practitioner scholar is based on the fact that the chapter authors who are acting school and district leaders see themselves primarily as practitioners and secondarily as scholars. This is not reflective of some anti-intellectual tendency amongst them. Rather, these professionals are deeply attuned to the needs and experiences of those whom they serve—the students and educators who populate the schools and districts to which they are committed. Their deeply held and pervasive commitment is clear in their speech, their actions, and their writing. The authors leverage current scholarship and engage in the production of scholarship in service to the students and educators for whom they advocate. The term practitioner scholar more aptly respects and reflects this moral responsibility. The authors are first and foremost practitioners, and I respect them for this.

Having recently transitioned from a district administrator position to the realm of higher education, I feel a lingering sense that I have absconded from the real work of reforming education—the toil, challenge, stress, and confrontations of public education leadership. While I work to convince myself that through my role as a faculty member serving practicing and aspiring educational leaders and conducting research I have the opportunity to more broadly influence reform and the educational experiences of students, I am never fully able to convince myself that I have not somehow bowed out of the real, hard work of confronting on a daily basis the "hot action of schools" (Bredeson, 2006, p. 20). While in general I feel good about the work that I did as a school and district administrator, I am nevertheless haunted by the space between the education I envisioned for students and what I was able to provide. I was never able to achieve truly equitable, democratic schooling and caring, rigorous learning experiences for all students. Maybe these are merely the self-indulged musings of an idealist. Nevertheless, I have the upmost respect for those in the field who day in and day out, year in and year out do the grueling work of improving the educational experiences of all students.

PRACTITIONER SCHOLARS AS TRANSFORMATIVE LEADERS

Practitioner scholars like the authors of this tome can come from any theoretical tradition:

> The scholar practitioner is not characterized as someone who must see things in a particular way or perform identifiable actions; instead, such leaders can be grounded in modernist or postmodernist worldviews, or have traditional, progressive, or radical perspectives on reality. From this perspective, there is no vision or "mould" that the scholar-practitioner-leader fits. (Mullen, 2005, p. 48-49)

While there may be no formal requirements regarding what a practitioner scholar needs to believe or do, much of the literature on practitioner scholars is orientated towards critical and liberatory paradigms that promote democratic schooling and social justice (Jenlink, 2010a; Larson, 2010): "The ultimate goal of the scholar-practitioner is to create school organizations that challenge the status quo and promote an environment that fosters diversity, democracy, equity, equality, and social justice in the hopes of transforming society" (Hampton, 2010, p. 192). Social justice is a key commitment of the practitioner scholar:

> Social justice encompasses freedom for all people, the fair and moral treatment of all people, and efforts to prevent and remedy socioeconomic and political inequity—especially when that inequity manifests via systemic forces (e.g., discriminatory hiring, schooling, and housing practices) and civil and human rights violations of particular groups. (Cooper, 2009, p. 697)

The practitioner scholar is committed to social justice and "is concerned with the relationship between knowledge and thought as well as power and claims of truth within the context of her or his practice. In this sense, leadership praxis is emancipatory" (Jenlink, 2007, p. 5). The practitioner scholar is engaged in reflection, critique, and action:

> The scholar-practitioner's praxis is dynamic, actionable in nature. It is self-reflective, critical, and intentional inquiry that occurs in the mirror of one's

practice. Praxis embodies ethicality, criticality, and intentionality—tempered in democratic ideas, like social justice and equity—as guiding forces in the actions taken. (Jenlink, 2010b, p. 202)

A practitioner scholar, then, is someone who goes beyond tinkering in an attempt to improve the current system—to make it more efficient and effective—to profoundly changing the way we do schooling. A practitioner scholar is a transformative leader, as opposed to a transformational leader: "Transformational leadership focuses on improving organizational qualities, dimensions, and effectiveness; and transformative educational leadership begins by challenging inappropriate uses of power and privilege that create or perpetuate inequity and injustice" (Shields, 2010, p. 564). Transformative leadership "begins with questions of social justice and democracy, critiques inequitable practices, and addresses both individual and public good" (Shields, 2010, p. 558) and "involves one's engaging in self-reflection, systematically analyzing schools, and then confronting inequities regarding race, class, gender, language, ability, and/or sexual orientation" (Cooper, 2009, p. 696). Practitioner scholars question, critique, and uncover that which is hidden:

> The scholar-practitioner must embrace a critical perspective that enables the world to be seen in ways that makes visible the injustice and inequity, as well as to interpret the critical perspective into action that is a counter narrative against the political and ideological forces that work to control or otherwise direct the educational systems along narrow agendas in opposition to the common public good. (Jenlink, 2010b, p. 203)

Further, the scholar practitioner as transformative leader must be ever focused on "leading deliberative school communities that interrogate rather than avoid the enduring inequities that undermine student achievement and mask the real issues that undermine the educational opportunity and life chances of impoverished children and youth" (Larson, 2010, p. 327). Practitioner scholars work not to reproduce the world as it is but to loosen the chains that bind it.

This positioning of the practitioner scholar as transformative leader is in response to what Giroux (1994) sees as a "crisis of leadership" (p. 33) that stems from larger social discourses of the market and defense:

> The discourse of leadership appears trapped in a vocabulary in which the estimate of a good society is expressed in indices that measure markets, defense systems, and the gross national product. Missing in this discourse is a vocabulary for talking about and creating democratic public cultures and communities that are attentive to the problems of homelessness, hunger, censorship, media manipulation, and [sic] rampant individualism and greed. (Giroux, 1992, p. 5)

This notion of being in opposition with dominant social discourses lends warlike, military overtones to the discourse of practitioner scholarship. There is a sense that the practitioner scholar leader is in a constant state of embattlement against anti-democratic forces, that the transformative leader is one who must "engage rather than retreat from the problems of democratic life and culture," (Jenlink, 2010c, p. 290), one with the "predisposition to fight for justice" (Jenlink, 2010a, p. 100).

Juxtaposed to this oppositional framing of the practitioner scholar as transformative leader is the notion that the scholar practitioner must be intensely connected to the community she serves: "The scholar-practitioner leader works within the education community, engaged in relationships with teachers, students, parents, and others that are concerned with the common public good" (Jenlink, 2010b, p. 201). The transformative leader cannot "present its own program but must search for this program dialogically with the people" (Friere, 1920, p. 105). In other words, the practitioner scholar as transformative leader does not impose her will on the school community she serves but rather works collaboratively with members of the school community to transform education. Indeed, "for the truly humanist educator and the authentic revolutionary, the object of action is the reality to be transformed by them together" (Friere, 1970, p. 75), "working in solidarity with subordinated and marginalized groups" (Kinchloe, 1999, p. 72). These

> transformative intellectuals publicly raise uncomfortable and critical questions, confront orthodoxy and dogma and 'are not easily coopted by governments or corporations, and whose *raison d'etre* is to represent all those people and issues that are routinely forgotten or swept under the rug' (Said, 1994, p. 9). (Jenlink, 2005, p. 7)

This is no easy task, as leaders must simultaneously work within the system and yet publicly critique it: "Transformative educational leaders must be able to work from within dominant social formations to exercise effective oppositional power, to resist courageously, and to be activists and voices for change and transformation" (Shields, 2010, p. 570). Clearly, there is great "difficulty and risk taking involved in transformative leadership" (Cooper, 2009, p. 698).

This is much to ask of teacher leaders, principals, and district leaders, and a number of the students in the aforementioned contemporary challenges course see transformative leadership as ideologically consistent with their positionality but as ambitious, intimidating and overwhelming in what it requires of leaders:

> It is sometimes believed to be too idealistic and too demanding and to place too much responsibility on the shoulders of educators and educational leadership for redressing global ills... These arguments are countered by those who posit that addressing issues of equity is the only way to transform education to achieve the success of all students—a goal that, although elusive, is at the heart of most current educational leadership theories. (Shields, 2010, p. 572)

Without transformative leadership, there cannot be true change, for "true change does not occur unless it is democratic change" (Hampton, 2010, p. 187). Without transformative leadership—without courageous and tenacious practitioner scholars—there will be no new tomorrows—for our students or our society.

TRANSFORMATIVE LEADERSHIP AND THE SPACE BETWEEN

The authors of this collection work within and on public education, as opposed to outside and against it. While the National Center on Education and the Economy argues that an immediate, "wholesale transformation of the system" is required" (p. 57), our authors take incremental steps toward a new way of doing education in the United States, exploring the challenges of change within the context of their schools, districts, states, and the nation. The authors recognize the immense complexities and contradictions embedded in their work as leaders and work indefatigably to do *what's best for students*, when *what's best* is often the subject of intense debate amongst internal and external stakeholders alike. Through their work, they are oriented towards and reflective on issues of race, class, gender, sexual identity, equity, and power. They recognize that "schools are sites of cultural politics that serve both to reproduce and to perpetuate the inequities inherent in gender, race, and class constructs" (Shields, 2010, p. 569), and they want to change this. Nonetheless, they will be the first to concede that there is space between their orientation towards transformative leadership and the reality that their actions are often more illustrative of transformational leadership.

When asked about their identities as transformative or transformational leaders, students in the course generally felt ideologically committed to transformative leadership but felt that most of the time their work was more accurately classified as transformational leadership. One student wrote that transformational leadership "is probably where I end up operating more than I'd like—sometimes I think we need more shaking up than this. This is easy to fall into as principal," but that transformative leadership "resonates with me—I like to challenge the status quo." In her work, she desires to be "more like" the transformative leader she envisions for herself.

Thus, despite our intentions and convictions, sometimes there is space between the leaders we want to be and the leaders we are—a disconnect between our equity-oriented commitments and our practices (Cooper, 2009):

> School leaders today can easily get caught up in the volatile winds of market-driven reform and test-based accountability, and they can quickly lose sight of what it takes to create a school community that supports the boarder learning and life needs of children and their families. (Larson, 2010, p. 325)

As such, practitioner scholars must always be vigilantly reflective and self-critical (Jenlink, 2010b). The disconnect between the leaders we want to be and the leaders we are, as well as the need for practitioner scholars to regularly self-examine, signify that practitioner scholars are always in a state of becoming and that "practitioner scholar" is less a moniker than a continual journey. Practitioner scholars are in a constant state of *becoming*.

TRANSFORMATIVE LEADERS AS BECOMING

Some of the aforementioned literature implies that professionals are only scholar practitioners to the degree that they are actively working against or undermining dominant discourses, as opposed to mediating them, both accommodating and troubling, working within and shifting/bending dominant, anti-democratic discourses. The work of the authors in this collection often reflects this latter approach and is nuanced, subtle, and long-term, as Jenlink (2010c) describes:

> All scholar-practitioners are in a state of becoming. The first requirement of a scholar-practitioner is the disposition toward self-awareness. Because of the inherent changing nature of individuals, their activity, and the larger environment in which they are embedded, understanding one's self, others, and the social environment is a project that is always under construction. Therefore, a scholar-practitioner cannot be a scholar-practitioner, but is always becoming a scholar-practitioner. (Horn, Conway, & Williams, 2007, p. 49)

A practitioner scholar "must be a student of his or her practice within the larger context of being a student of social action for the transformation of society" (Jenlink, 2007, p. 9). Contemporary practitioner scholars must be adroit at reworking education from within, of being nimble reformers who can work with stakeholders to craft learning experiences for students that will be visible as "effective" or "excellent" according to external accountability systems *and* be ethical places in which all students are valued and encouraged to do and be their best. Being a practitioner scholar means working to "meet the expectations and mandates of interest groups (i.e., federal, state, and district standards and accountability procedures) while still providing…equitable and caring curriculum, instruction, and assessment" (Horn, Conway, & Williams, 2007, p. 47).

I believe that the authors of this book feel deeply the tension between serving schools as they now are and working to make schools more just, equitable, and caring. The authors navigate the dominant discourses of external accountability and marketization of education, and they work to make their schools and districts "effective" and "excellent" by these measures. At the same time, the authors are keenly aware that increasing test scores is not equivalent to good leadership:

> There is a commonly held conception that being able to raise a school's test scores as a principal is the hallmark of effective educational leadership… Wrenching higher test scores from a group of students and teachers does not constitute educational leadership. Rather, it may constitute nothing more than the successful manipulation of a school's instructional program to comply with the wishes and pressures of educational bureaucrats and political power brokers. (Reitzug, 2010, p. 319)

Contemporary external accountability measures fall short of really reflecting what goes on in schools and instead often reify and reinforce the inequities, shortcomings, and gaps in current schools (Darling-Hammond, 2010). Nonetheless, educational leaders cannot dismiss the discourse of test-based accountability. One of the authors in this collection was told when he was placed as principal in his current building that he had until the end of the 2012 school year to raise the school's scores and meet AYP; otherwise, he would be removed from his position. Thus the ability to engage in the discourse of external accountability and attend to achievement test scores and the standards upon which they are ostensibly based is a "survival skill that permits educational leaders to retain their positions. After all, without a base from which to operate, it is difficult to engage in the work to further democratic education" (Reitzug, 2010, p. 321). Thus there is a tension amongst competing and sometimes contradictory discourses—including those of narrow, external accountability and testing and those of transformative leadership and democratic schooling—that practitioner scholars must navigate, negotiate, critique, and act upon.

Mullen (2005) argues that "any definition of the scholar practitioner concept needs to be kept open as well as problematized and considered from multiple perspectives" (p. 56). In our use of the term, practitioner scholars are those who draw upon existing research and theory as well as their own experiences and expertise to engage in inquiry and to inform their leadership in ways that promote equity and social justice. Additionally, practitioner scholars often contribute to the knowledge base at the micro or macro level, as "knowledge is constructed within and through practice" (Jenlink, 2007, p. 6).

This project itself—the act of working collaboratively to craft this book—is not only an example of practitioner scholarship but perhaps more importantly of the act of cultivating practitioner scholarship and a practitioner scholar subjectivity amongst practicing educational leaders, one that inextricably integrates both practitioner and scholar in a synergistic—instead of oppositional or contradictory—way.

IMPLICATIONS FOR LEADERSHIP PREPARATION

For leadership preparation programs, the "challenge is to prepare leaders for schools as they are while simultaneously preparing them for schools as they might be" (Reitzug, 2010, p. 320). Unfortunately, "educational leaders often lack the preparation and support needed to significantly oppose the status quo" (Cooper, 2009, p. 697).

What, then, can leadership preparation programs do to cultivate and support practitioner scholars committed to transformative leadership? It is not enough to define transformative leadership and extol its virtues and then expect students to take up the mantel of transformative leadership and embody it and be embattled by it day in and day out in some indefatigable, heroic manner that defies and denies their personal existence for the professional obligation to "fight the good fight."

It is our moral responsibility in leadership preparation programs to model transformative leadership and to "incorporate curriculum, instructional practices, and internship opportunities" (Cooper, 2009, p. 720) that support transformative leadership. We can provide illustrative case studies and teach students the skills of agency and advocacy. We can foster supportive cohort and alumni networks (Cooper, 2009) so that no practitioner scholar feels alone and isolated. We can encourage students' self-care and renewal as they do the hard work of transformative leadership. We can provide authentic opportunities for students to be agentic practitioner scholars. This project is itself an example of cultivating practitioner scholars and producing meaningful practitioner scholarship as the work of a leadership preparation program. If we can do these things, we can prepare practitioner scholars for the "schools they enter as well as for the schools we hope they leave behind" (Reitzug, 2010, p. 321).

OVERVIEW OF THIS BOOK

Practitioners, scholars, and policy makers alike would do well to listen to the articulate, reflective, thoughtful voices of the practitioner scholars who authored the chapters in this collection. Each chapter addresses a current, critical topic in curriculum and instructional leadership. In each, the authors integrate their experiences and expertise with available scholarship to provide meaningful examination of the focus topic. While chapters can be read individually or in any order, they have been arranged in ways that point to their linkages and interconnectivity.

The book is divided into three sections: Section I focuses on "Rethinking How We Serve Students"; Section II involves "Rethinking Teacher Work"; and Section III centers around "Examining 'Right Now' Reforms." Section I, "Rethinking How We Serve Students," focuses on how we mis-serve and underserve students in today's schools and what we can do about it as leaders.

In Chapter 1, Kathy Moore argues that culturally relevant pedagogy is a just and effective way to serve students marginalized by traditional, "white" approaches to education. Often, African American students perform less well on standardized tests, relegating them to "remedial" instruction that—due to low expectations and low cognitive demand—only exacerbates learning gaps. Culturally relevant pedagogy leverages the richness of student culture and links it in authentic, relevant ways to instruction. Moore shares how poetry can serve as a culturally relevant approach to effectiveness teaching math.

In order to serve students and honor their culture, educators must reach out to and partner with parents. Chapter 2, by Jason Alémán, uses post-colonial theory to illustrate how Latino parents are often marginalized, excluded, and silenced by traditional schools. He demonstrates how disrupting myths about Latino parent involvement and rethinking what parent involvement looks like can serve to promote a true partnership between schools and Latino parents. He demonstrates how these changes develop slowly over time and require extended, concerted effort on the part of leaders and Latino parents alike.

For many years, special education leadership has meant little more than assuring compliance with federal and state law regarding the placement, service, and documentation of students with special needs. In Chapter 3, John Palladino argues that ensuring compliance in insufficient and that leaders must establish a school culture that focuses on identifying student needs and appropriate resources to meet those needs. While acknowledging that the Response to Intervention framework is not unproblematic, Palladino advocates its authentic use to ensure that students' needs are met.

Chapter 4, by Daniel W. Eadens, Susan Ray, Danielle. M. Eadens, and Katherine Shirer, illustrates how educators can use brain research to rethink how we approach working with "low performing" students, especially visual-spatial learners. We can ethically reorient education away from a deficit discourse and towards a discourse that honors student differences and utilizes findings from brain research to serve students in ways that are more effective and more respectful.

In Section II, "Rethinking Teacher Work," Barbara A. Klocko and Caryn M. Wells argue for the importance of teacher leadership as a powerful and impactful form of collaborative leadership. Teacher leadership is not something conferred upon someone but rather a "voice to lead"—a voice that can impact student learning and school culture, making a school more resilient and bolstering sustainability.

Teacher leadership is generally seen as an unmitigated good in education, and this belief is so ubiquitous as to be taken for granted. In Chapter 6, Cherese Childers-McKee critically examines teacher leadership, considering issues of power, marginalization, and reproduction. She provides strategies for leaders to cultivate teacher leadership that transforms education instead of reproducing the status quo.

In Chapter 7, Linda K. Lemesters, Michael J. Cieslak, and Marguerita DeSander examine the burgeoning phenomenon of Professional Learning Communities (PLCs). Because there is a great deal of variability in what "PLC" means to people and how PLCs are structured and enacted, research on the topic of the effectiveness of PLCs has been ambiguous. Yet, as this chapter illustrates, when certain principles are followed, PLCs have the potential to enhance teaching and increase student learning. Indeed, PLCs can be a powerful way to rethink teaching—moving it away from an isolated practice and towards a collaborative endeavor that is unfailingly focused on examining and enhancing student learning.

Chapter 8, by Rebecca A. Thessin and Joshua P. Starr, follows the journey of a New England school district as it worked to make healthy PLCs a critical component of the district's commitment to doing right by students. The chapter provides a look into what it takes to implement PLCs and what they can do to change teaching and learning.

Section III, "Examining 'Right Now' Reforms looks at four reforms that are top of mind for many practitioner scholars: 21st Century learning, Common Core State Standards, technology leadership, and the use of value added data to inform leadership.

In Chapter 9, Diane Hill and Jean Maness discuss the call for change embedded in emphasis on 21st century learning. As educators, one leading a school and one leading at the district office level, the authors feel as caught up in the turmoil and ambiguity that is the transition to Common Core State Standards as other educational leaders. At the same time, they realize that this transition, one of great magnitude and breadth, is an opportunity to transform what they do as educators and how they support students in the process of 'schooling.' The authors offer support for capitalizing on this time to change through a critical study of 21st century learning based in the expectations of the Common Core State Standards.

For Chapter 10 authors Elizabeth M. Hodge and Rhonda C. Schuhler, the promise of Common Core standards is that of greater consistency, higher standards, and increased instructional quality for our students. They wonder, however, what we are sacrificing in adopting national standards. As district-level curriculum and professional development leaders charged with spearheading Common Core implementation, the authors recognize that there are benefits and pitfalls associated with this shift. This chapter reflects upon their adoption process and challenges the reader to consider the implications of Common Core standards implementation on teaching and learning.

Many educators, when they think of 21st Century teaching and learning, think of technology. In Chapter 11, Justin Bathon argues that technology leadership is just good leadership and that good leadership in the 21st Century requires leading for and with technology. Technology, Bathon contends, can be used as a catalyst for substantive and lasting change in schools. He concludes with tools and strategies that leaders can use to leverage technology for change.

While technology can serve as a catalyst for school improvement, data can provide the direction for change. In Chapter 12, I draw upon extant literature and my experience as a district administrator to explore the use of value added data to inform leadership, highlighting both its possibilities and limitations. The chapter provides real-life examples and closes with strategies for using value added data in an ethical and efficacious manner.

Carl Lashley and Aaron Woody close the collection by adroitly pulling together the key themes and compelling arguments from each of the chapters and provide a powerful vision of practitioner scholars who serve as instructional leaders for their schools and as advocates for a new tomorrow for public schools—a tomorrow focused on engaging and investing in each learner.

References

Barnett, B. G. & Muth, R. (2008). Using action-research strategies and cohort structures to ensure research competence for practitioner-scholar leaders. *Journal of Research on Leadership Education, 3*(1), 1-43.

Bredeson, P. V. (2006, Summer). Integrated doctoral programs in educational leadership: The case for preparing practitioners and researchers together. *UCEA Review*, 20-23.

Cooper, C. W. (2009). Performing cultural work in demographically changing schools: Implications for expanding transformative leadership frameworks. *Educational Administration Quarterly, 45*(5), 694-724.

Dewey, J. (1916). *Democracy and education.* New York: The Free Press.

Foucault, M. (1977). *Discipline & punish: The birth of the prison* (A. Sheridan, Trans.). New York: Vintage Books.

Freire, P. (1970). *Pedagogy of the oppressed.* New York: Continuum.

Giroux, H. A. (1994). Educational leadership and school administrators: Rethinking the meaning of democratic public cultures. In T. A. Mulkeen, N. H. Cambron-McCabe, & B. J. Anderson (Eds.), Democratic leadership: The changing context of administrative preparation. Norwood, NJ: Ablex Publishing Corporation.

Giroux, H. A. (1992). Educational leadership and the crisis of democratic government. *Educational Researcher, 21*(4), 4-11.

Hampton, K. (2010a). Transforming school and society: Examining the theoretical foundations of scholar-practitioner leadership. *Scholar-Practitioner Quarterly, 4*(2), 185-193.

Horn, R. A., Conway, T., & Williams, M. (2007). Scholar-practitioner reflections on the urban education contexts of race and social class in the current climate of standards and accountability. *scholarlypartnershipsedu, 2*(1), 45-58.

Jenlink, P. M. (2010a). Engaged inquiry: The scholar-practitioner leader's responsibility. *Scholar-Practitioner Quarterly, 4*(2), 95-103.

Jenlink, P. M. (2010b). The importance of praxis: Preparing scholar-practitioner leaders. *Scholar-Practitioner Quarterly, 4*(3), 199-206.

Jenlink, P. M. (2010c). The scholar-practitioner as a democratic person. *Scholar-Practitioner Quarterly, 4*(4), 287-291.

Jenlink, P. M. (2005). Editorial: On bricolage and the intellectual work of the scholar-practitioner. *Scholar-Practitioner Quarterly, 3*(1), 3-12.

Jenlink, P. M. (2007). The school leader as bricoleur: Developing scholarly practitioners for our schools. *NCPEA Education Leadership Review, 7*(2), 1-12.

Kincheloe, J. L. (1999). Critical democracy and education. In J. G. Henderson & K. R. Kesson (Eds.), Understanding democratic curriculum leadership. NY: Teachers College Press.

Larson, C. L. (2010). Responsibility and accountability in educational leadership: Keeping democracy and social justice central to reform. *Scholar-Practitioner Quarterly, 4*(4), 323-327.

Leithwood, K., & Jantzi, D. (1990). The relative effects of principal and teacher sources of leadership on student engagement with school. *Educational Administration Quarterly, 35*(5), 679-706).

Mann, S. A., & Huffman, D. J. (2005). The decentering of second wave feminism and the rise of the third wave. *Science & Society, 69*(1), 56-91.

Mullen, C. A., Greenlee, B. J. & Bruner, D. Y. (2005). Exploring the theory-practice relationship in educational leadership curriculum through metaphor. *International Journal of Teaching and Learning in Higher Education, 17*(1), 1-14.

National Center on Education and the Economy. (2008). *Tough choices or tough times: The report of the new commission on the skills of the American workforce.* San Francisco: Jossey-Bass.

Reitzug, U. C. (2010a). Educational leaders or compliant bureaucrats? Reflections on 'leadership' preparation. *Scholar-Practitioner Quarterly, 4*(4), 319-322.

Schultz, J. R. (2010). The scholar-practitioner: A philosophy of leadership. *Scholar-Practitioner Quarterly, 4*(1), 52-64.

Shields, C. M. (2010). Transformative leadership: Working for equity in diverse contexts. *Educational Administration Quarterly, 46*(4), p. 558-589.

St. Pierre, E. A., & Pillow, W. S. (2000). *Working the ruins: Feminist poststructural*

Part 1

Rethinking How We Serve Students

Chapter 1

Of Poetry and Math: Why Culturally Relevant Pedagogy Matters

Kathleen McCarroll Moore

African American students, commonly designated a sub-group in assessment data reports, consistently score well below their peers on standardized tests. A common practice is to provide remedial methods of instruction focused on recall and repetitive practice in efforts to increase proficiency and narrow the achievement gap. However, these practices can actually have the opposite effect, relegating struggling students to the lowest levels of engagement and thinking. This is a socially unjust arrangement that excludes low-achieving students from experiencing intellectually challenging or engaging content and limits their academic opportunities.

Mintrop and Sunderman (2009) have presented evidence that No Child Left Behind (NCLB) Legislation, purportedly enacted to narrow the achievement gap, has done nothing of the sort. In fact, their research findings indicate that the NCLB approach to education has made it even more difficult for schools with diverse student populations to reach their targeted goals due to the attendant complexity that diversity brings. Most disturbing is the practice of excluding low-achieving students from content that is intellectually challenging or engaging (Beers, 2009). Educators, policy-makers, and researchers must be mindful, when interpreting and analyzing numbers like achievement gap statistics, to look beyond the obvious. For example, we might question whether African American students' lower performance on standardized assessments is due to lack of facility with numbers, inequitable or culturally biased assessments, or teachers with low expectations and/or a lack of cultural competency.

Focusing on closing the achievement gap through minute attention to bits of skills and knowledge is wrong-headed and misses the bigger picture regarding how we can best serve students. Culturally relevant pedagogy, a term popularized through the work of Gloria Ladson-Billings, stresses the importance of linking school and culture. According to Ladson-Billings (1995a), culturally relevant teachers are able to "utilize students' culture as a vehicle for learning" (p. 161). For the past two decades, other researchers have echoed the view that a focus on culturally relevant pedagogy can serve to benefit all students regardless of their ethnic and cultural backgrounds (Berry, 2003; Tate, 1995). Culturally relevant practices can serve to broaden students' perspectives, validate their individuality, strengthen their ability to think critically, and build a united community of learners.

Culturally relevant pedagogy assumes that students come to school equipped as social beings who reflect a set of beliefs and understandings that they have developed through their experiences and exposures within their family and community. Its theoretical roots lie in the belief that learning is a socially mediated process borne of students' cultural backgrounds (Irvine, 2009). The role of education then is to make clear the connections between what the students bring to school and the curriculum that is taught so that learning is accessible and relevant. A culturally relevant teacher assumes that there are multiple ways of presenting information and scaffolding learning, building upon the students' knowledge base in meaningful ways, and providing multiple opportunities to acquire understanding. The wealth of research on this topic (Gay, 2002; Irvine, 2009; Tate, 1995) has not had the impact on practice that it should. School today looks much the same as it has for decades. One factor that contributes to this is the reliance of many teacher education programs on an outdated view of effective instructional strategies. These programs continue to contribute to a system of intellectual and cultural deprivation by promoting narrow, traditional practices that have become institutionalized and unquestioned over time. Although educational researchers such as Ladson-Billings (1995a, 1997) and Gay (2002) have written extensively about the need to incorporate culture, experience, and perspectives of ethnically diverse students into teacher preparation programs, this has often not been the case. It is up to instructional leaders to take a long, hard look at the inequities in our classrooms, in our schools, in our universities and in our nation and raise our voices for change. It is up to us to institute the reforms needed so that all our students learn and our democracy continues to thrive.

PRISM EFFECT

Consider what happens when we look through a prism. Light is reflected and refracted. Reality is transformed. We see the world differently. Looking at classroom instruction through a lens of cultural relevance can have a similar effect. Instead of delivering instruction in traditional teacher/text - centered ways, a focus on the learning needs of the individual students in the classroom can and should dramatically change the instructional strategies the teacher relies upon to build understanding.

Take math, for instance. In the typical math classroom setting, instruction moves in a linear fashion from concept to concept in a prescribed sequence. There is usually an introduction of a concept or formula, followed by a teacher and/or book explanation, sample problems, practice problems, review and correction, and then, the subsequent introduction of the next lesson in the series. Often there is little time devoted to processing the information, to posing questions and critiquing ideas through talk or through writing—practices that are necessary in building a deep understanding. Critical thinking is jettisoned in a frantic need to "cover the material."

It has been well established that school mathematics, as traditionally taught, often fails to consider relevance (Draper & Siebert, 2004; Stone, Alfeld, & Pearson, 2008). The historically traditional scope and sequence of mathematics instruction limits the opportunities for all students to thrive as mathematicians. Without the connection to life experiences, many students, particularly African American boys, struggle (Berry, 2003; Bol & Berry, 2005; Tate 1995). Real life issues can provide rich contexts for learning mathematics, serving to build motivation and pleasure in the learning process for students (Kwako, 2011). Separating math from reality can actually be harmful, convincing students that math does not matter in their lives when it, in fact, surrounds them.

Berry (2003) has written extensively on the role of culturally relevant pedagogy in the lives of student mathematicians. In an article connecting the National Council of Teachers of Mathematics standards with the relational learning styles prevalent in the African American population, he explored the advantage that analytical thinkers have when taught traditional math, and suggests that a more socially just method of instruction would make clear the connections between ideas and experiences. Focusing on these personal, cultural and relational connections to the curriculum allow students the opportunity to develop deeper understandings and build a stronger connection to mathematics.

This line of thinking was woven throughout a two-year research study I conducted with a group of elementary teachers concerned about the math proficiency of their African American students in a predominately White, suburban school district. Our work together allowed the teacher participants to gear their lesson design and instruction towards the more relationally inclined students, a practice that Berry (2003) suggests might mediate the challenges these students have with learning in a more traditional mathematics environment.

My work began, as so much research does, on a hunch accompanied by a nagging question. As a Literacy Coach in a predominately White, suburban school district, I had been supporting K-12 teachers in implementing reading and writing workshop strategies; my work included developing instructional strategies to strengthen engagement and academic achievement with continuation high school students. Most of these students at the continuation school were severely lacking in credits towards graduation; most also had extensive behavioral or academic challenges that had designated them unsuited to traditional classroom settings. It should come as no surprise that the majority of the continuation high school students were not White, nor that they struggled tremendously with math. This, unfortunately, is an all-too common phenomenon. When a colleague mentioned that all of the remedial math students at her elementary school were African-American, the proverbial light bulb went off in my head. The educational pipeline that I had been reading about for years was laid bare right in front of me.

Research continues to reveal that while mathematics is considered the gateway to higher education, statistically African American boys fall far below their classmates in math proficiency (Muhammad, 2003; Noguera, 2003; Snipes & Waters, 2005). An interesting connection between students' lower achievement and the way they are taught and tested seems to surface when we look closely. Snipes and Waters (2005) suggest that one cause of the poor math performance of African American students can be found in the disconnect that exists between classroom instruction and their home environments; the curriculum does not reflect the life experiences of these students. It seems likely then that culturally relevant methods of instruction could support African American students' ability to access math content and demonstrate their mathematical understanding.

Of vital importance in education today is the ever-widening academic achievement gap between White students and students of color, especially African American males. These students shoulder the worst of the attention and the blame for an educational crisis that produces a disproportionate number of African American youth who fall behind and fail in traditional school settings, only to be reassigned to alternative programs, or to otherwise become educational statistics. There is a current of institutionalized racism that underlies this phenomenon (Knaus, 2009; Ladson-Billings,

1999) — an acceptance that not all students will be successful in the factory-model educational system that defines the American public school system. This reality results in a lack of access and opportunity at odds with the basic tenets upon which our nation was founded — liberty and justice for all.

Tate (1995) suggests that traditional mathematics instruction acts as a gatekeeper, preventing African American students from fully participating in the world. He further argues that this phenomenon is due to the practice of tracking, relegating African American students into remedial math courses, a practice that has been shown to limit their educational opportunities, leaving them ill prepared to use mathematics in order to negotiate the complexities of the democratic process. This is confirmed by Stinson (2004), whose research exposed a strong correlation between the early identification of struggling math students and their subsequent exclusion from higher level thinking experiences and opportunities to fully practice citizenship and realize economic success.

In the book, *Black American Students in an Affluent Suburb: A Study of Academic Disengagement* (2003), Ogbu discusses the issue of academic insecurity prevalent in African American males, and he quotes a school counselor who claims that the problem of the non-learner self-image begins as early as first grade. This is borne out, I believe, in the students I have observed in elementary classrooms. Students who are not yet continuation high school students, but whose profiles suggest they one day could be, motivated me to adjust my research lens.

We shape our self to fit this world and by the world are shaped again.
(David Whyte, from the poem *Working Together*, 1997, 1-4)

Speaking with a colleague who teaches the highest level of mathematics in a high-achieving suburban school district, the subject of inequitable curricular practices surfaced as we discussed the path that students must take to enroll in those advanced courses. The path begins quite early; I realized that struggling third grade math students had a slim chance of ever following the path to calculus, although the likelihood of them following the path to low-level secondary math courses or to continuation high school classrooms was a somewhat predictable fate. Some of these students might become statistics in the educational landscape, failing to meet even the minimum requirement of high school graduation, relegating them to a lifetime of unrealized dreams. Tutak, Bondy, and Adams (2011) suggest that the goal of mathematics education is to empower students in order for them to participate fully in socially just, democratic communities. The understanding that mathematics is the gateway to higher education, and subsequently to position and power within the dominant culture, should arouse a sense of urgency in educators.

Without a firm understanding of the factors that contribute to academic achievement of our students, we are hard-pressed to make decisions that effectively combat inequity and allow all students the opportunity to have a rich experience with mathematics — to develop a math identity. Developing lessons that take this issue into account honors the work of Gutstein (2006) and Tutak et al. (2011) who have called for major pedagogical shifts that counter the more traditional teaching of mathematics that fails to take issues of equity into account.

POETIC JUSTICE

If we look at math though a prism, perhaps we could see possibilities that had previously eluded us. A new perspective could transform reality. It seems obvious that whatever we are doing in the name of remediation and support for struggling math students is not working; students continue to struggle, and the gap continues to widen. My steadfast belief that there had to be another way to reach struggling students and help them achieve success led me to assemble a group of elementary teachers who were interested in experimenting with infusing cultural relevance into their math instruction. These teachers met regularly over a two-year period to examine their mathematical teaching practices and their students' math comprehension. It was my contention that because poetry and math share similar attributes of pattern and precision, as well as symbolic representation of ideas, linking them together instructionally might provide some new insights into student learning. Thus, we began our collaboration by focusing on this question: Could poetry be considered a form of culturally relevant pedagogy?

The teachers who formed the inquiry group recognized that even their seemingly successful math students were at risk mathematically. They indicated that many students were strong in computational skills and math fact retrieval, but showed limited ability to demonstrate an understanding of the mathematics behind the algorithm. They indicated that this phenomenon was a cause of great concern; therefore, it became a major factor contributing to our study of math through the lens of poetry. Perhaps by weaving poetry and math together, content could be made more culturally relevant and benefit all students involved.

In reflecting upon their histories as learners, the participating teachers all shared a common connection to the lack of relevancy in their own experiences as math students. They discussed ways to build critical thinking skills and made a collective commitment to look for ways to foster enthusiasm and strengthen engagement in their students' study of math. Their collaborative conversations reached the heart of what was missing in their math learning and in their math teaching — the ability to bring math to life.

The first year of the study, we discovered many ways of injecting fun into our instruction. We put together a collection of picture books that had math themes, and we scoured the Internet for appropriate math videos for the students to watch that explained mathematical concepts through humor or music. We taught the students math raps and movements to accompany the words, believing that the engagement with rhyme connected to movement would translate into content comprehension. The students showed a great deal of excitement for this approach to learning math. The students seemed tremendously engaged; they learned many enjoyable math rhymes, and looked forward to math time. However, at the end of that first year, we discovered that they had not in fact shown any more mastery of their grade–level math standards than they had prior to our study. We had mistaken enthusiasm for understanding.

Equation
Someone said
that working through difficult equations
was like walking
in a pure and beautiful landscape-
the numbers glowing
like works of art.
(Caroline Caddy, 2007, 1-6)

Minton (2007) and Schmoker (2011) stress the critical connection between numbers and words, and the necessity of incorporating language literacy into mathematics instruction. Creating literate mathematical thinkers is central to the teaching of math. Because I believe so strongly in the transformative power of poetry and the connection between the similar structures and patterns found in poetry and math, I infused poetry into every session with the participating teachers the following year. I refined my definition of poetry as a form of culturally relevant pedagogy by more closely aligning the math work the students were doing to the specific strengths of the most struggling students.

The participating teachers and I discussed at length particular students as well as the general math struggles at the different grade levels. One common challenge for students was the concept of number sense, and the teachers indicated that this struggle manifested itself in different ways depending upon the grade level. We had noticed that although number sense was especially difficult for many of our African American students to grasp, they were adept at language, and loved rhythm and rhyme. Berry (2003) echoed Ladson-Billings' assertions that it is important to focus on students' cultural styles and their learning preferences when designing lessons. We agreed that this could be an interesting area of focus, since the more difficulty the students had making sense of numbers, the more drastic their struggle to make progress in math. We felt that in order to influence the students' math knowledge, we would have to be more purposeful in our selection of instructional tools. We discussed the importance of pairing the poetry with strong mathematical practices. I had been documenting changes in the teachers' attitudes toward teaching math as well as their shifting approaches to delivering instruction; I theorized that given time, these changes would result in increased student understanding. With this in mind, the focus of the study shifted, and I became much more interested in chronicling the growth in teacher competencies. Deepening their understanding would be necessary in order to support their students' growth as mathematicians.

That second year as the inquiry group facilitator, I began every session of our work together by reading a math poem, hoping that it would not only set an aesthetically pleasing tone for our meeting, but that the infusion of poetry would allow the participants to stay open to the idea of linking our math work with an exploration of poetry as a form of culturally responsive pedagogy. Toward the end of one meeting, our discussion of the challenges inherent in building number sense evolved into the struggle that students at the lower grade levels were having with the concept of zero. I had brought several math poems with me to share with the teachers; I opened the book *Number Talk* (Pappas, 1993) and read aloud the poem "Zero." It is a simple poem, but reading it caused the energy in the room to change.

Because this was a poem for two voices, the teachers wanted to hear it read that way; two participants took my book and read it the way it was intended to be read, alternating voices. At that point, the school principal, who occasionally joined our study sessions, responded to the energy in the room and suggested we try incorporating poetry into a lesson. The response was immediate, unanimous agreement. The simple act of reading a poem about a mathematical concept brought about the kind of enthusiasm that the teachers were hoping to infuse into their lessons with their students; they left the session excited about the possibilities

Zero

I am zero.	I am zero.
Some say I'm nothing.	I have no value.
I know to the contrary.	
	I'm essential.
invaluable.	
	I'm the origin on the number line.
The positive numbers are to my right.	
	The negative numbers to my left.
I'm neither negative	
	nor positive.
I'm zero.	I'm zero.
Centuries before I appeared	
	number writing was burdensome.
repetitious	confusing
I was discovered	I made the difference
	in the place value system.
Now with zero there is	
no mix-up,	
	101 looks different than 11.
Without zero	
	there would be no
place-value system.	
I am zero.	I am zero.
Add zero to any	Multiply a number
number	by me
the result is unchanged.	zero always results.
Divide a	Beware when
number by zero	dividing by me.
There is no	The result is
answer.	undefined.
I am zero.	I am zero.
I am nothing.	I am essential.

One teacher brought this idea of constructing math poems for two voices to her third graders and she reported the process back to the inquiry group at our next session:

> So what I did was I put that up on the overhead and my kids read it. I explained how you read it, so they read it back to me and we did that for a couple of days.

And then after that I said we're going to take this concept of association and let's try to do a poem with it. So we started and I just said let's look at our chart for what association is, you know, it's that grouping thing. And so the kids talked about it and they said things like you know it's organizing and reorganizing, so I took notes on the board, and then one of them said you know it's kind of like making friends, and then somebody said it's like breaking up.(laughter) So I wrote that stuff down. . . . So we came up with this poem. And I really just took it almost in the order that they gave it, so this is the poem. (Teacher A)

Teacher B volunteered to read it aloud with her to our inquiry group; Teachers A and B performed the poems that Teacher A's students had constructed as a group effort, including "Association" (see Figure 1.1). This led to a sharing of other ideas and resources that could generate this kind of math engagement. Our study of poetry as a culturally relevant pedagogical tool (Berry, 2003; Moore, 2012) helped the teachers in the inquiry group to explore their own teaching practices and attitudes towards math instruction, motivated them to work hard to build lessons to engage and excite, and most importantly, encouraged them to build deep, critical thinking skills in their students.

As we looked for poems that would help students build their engagement with math while strengthening their number sense and their ability to articulate their understanding, we continued to immerse ourselves in literature linking poetry and math (Berry, 2003; Kwako, 2011; Ladson-Billings, 1995a; Minton, 2007; Tate, 1995). That work helped us to ground our teaching in relevant scholarship and promote social justice in our classrooms.

ASSOCIATION: A Poem for Two Voices
by Teacher A's 3rd grade students

Association	**Association**
Organizing	
	Re-organizing
Grouping	
	Switching groups
Association	**Association**
Changing Groups	
	But not the big group
The all together is the same	
Association	**Association**
Breaking friendships	
	Making friendships
The big group	
	Stays the same
	With different clubs
The whole is the same	
	Exactly
Association	**Association**

Figure 1.1 A Poem for Two Voices

PATTERNS

Devlin (2011) refers to the brain as a remarkable pattern-recognizing device. One of the connections between poetry and mathematics that supported my interest in linking them in instruction was the reliance on patterns that is common to both. In American public schools, math is generally taught during dedicated math time, and poetry is taught during language arts time (often relegated to a unit of study in April during "Poetry Month"), but the subjects are comparable in many ways. Both math and poetry are often taught through formulaic approaches, a practice that often leads to misconception, confusion, and blandness. A misapplied formula without an underlying mathematical understanding or number sense can yield wildly inaccurate answers in much the same way that the poetic form can be abused when given over to forced rhyme or cloying metaphor. Both math and poetry use symbols to represent larger or more abstract concepts. Pairing the two forms made sense as a way of breaking down the walls between two compartmentalized subjects, and allowing students access to higher-level thinking.

It is often said that mathematics resembles poetry.
We argue that some works of mathematics are in fact poetry.
(James Henle, 2011, p. 94)

I thought the introduction of poetry as a means of delivering culturally relevant math instruction would be a linear process. At the time I was beginning this research, it seemed a simple and obvious equation: Poetry plus math equals empowerment. But nothing worth pursuing is ever quite as simple and straightforward as it might seem.

As the inquiry process evolved, poetry did serve the purpose of introducing a paradigm shift in the teachers' thinking. Number sense was the overarching idea that the participants were initially interested in examining, but as we worked together, the lesson design became less about numbers, and more about developing understanding and articulating thinking. I do believe this shift was due as much to the time and space allotted for our study as to the process that allowed the participants to make such meaningful growth as practitioner scholars.

The focus on poetry led to a closer examination of the language of instruction. Teachers found that introducing a focus on language and real-life equations provided the necessary connection to make the math work relevant. Although not poetry per se, our work led us to explore the idea of equations without numbers in order to build a strong conceptual foundation.

In many classrooms, students are not permitted to construct a personal understanding of the mathematics that is presented (D'Ambrosio, 2001); however, with the idea of incorporating life equations into their mathematics instruction, teachers sought to address this issue. For example, the variety of equations that surfaced in a fourth grade classroom of a participant highlights the personal connections students were making.

- TV + Patriots + Football Channel = Awesome
- Free time + Computer + Weekend – Mom = Video Games
- Rythem [sic] + Sound + mucseles [sic] + mind + tap shoes – music = Acapella (tap dancing without music. You are the music.)
- Books + low voices + quiet sounds + comfortable area = entering another world

"Moving beyond example and observation to the creation of valid proofs is the hallmark practice of mathematicians" (Johnson, Watson, Delahunty, McSwiggen, & Smith, 2011, p. 106). In an interesting study, Johnson et al. (2011) explored the way that mathematicians establish mathematical truths by creating patterns and then working to prove those patterns. This notion is evidenced by the creativity of the inquiry study groups as well as by their attempt to teach their students to represent the truth of their lives through equations, explain their reasoning, and critique the reasoning of their classmates. As the year progressed, we met often to discuss our work, design and revise lessons, study student samples, and reflect on our learning as well as that of our students. We discovered that as we became deeply immersed in this cycle of inquiry, the link being forged between mathematics and poetry was making a positive impact on student learning as well as on teacher efficacy.

PEDAGOGY

One of the challenges to the exploration of culturally relevant pedagogical practices is the inadequate attention paid to its study; many teachers are thus insufficiently prepared and ill-equipped to implement culturally relevant instruction. With limited resources and support at their disposal, many teachers' attempts at becoming culturally aware practitioners often fall short, giving way to curricular add-ons such as the occasional multicultural celebration, cursory acknowledgment of ethnic holidays, or over-simplified inclusion of cultural practices into the curriculum. In their book, *Teaching to Change the World* (1998), Jeannie Oakes and Martin Lipton describe how culturally relevant teachers can transform their classrooms into apprenticeships for democracy. Many students are adept at playing the "school game"; they can survive a lackluster educational experience, and manage to find ways to be successful. But for students who struggle, disengagement with the curriculum may become a problem of extreme proportions. Educators should not allow students to continue to lag behind when research confirms that educational achievement is the foundation upon which successful societies are built and maintained. All students need literacy, numeracy, technological, social, and political skills in order to be active participants in democracy (Ladson-Billings, 1995a). Students who struggle early in math continue to lag behind their peers and are unlikely to reach higher levels of mathematical understanding, or to participate in the type of math coursework that would allow them to have equal chances in life. Since low-level computational skills have little connection to critical thinking and mathematical knowledge, math instruction must be rigorous, robust, and accessible to all students (Tate, 1995; Devlin, 2011). Greater opportunity to advance and compete in career, college, and community environments comes from early success in algebra; it is a necessary tool for advancement in modern society.

Ernst (2002) (as cited in Stinson, 2004) identifies three domains of mathematics empowerment, which are further supported by the findings of this study: mathematical empowerment through language, social empowerment through critique, and epistemological empowerment through a growing confidence in one's own ability to learn. The participants in this study reported a transformation in their attitudes and instructional practices through their inquiry into culturally relevant pedagogy and math instruction, and they expressed a newfound commitment as advocates for change as well. Transformation can occur when educators embrace their roles as agents of change, committed to assuring that all students are provided opportunities to achieve and succeed academically (Friedland, McMillen, & del Prado Hill, 2011). Through interpretation, data analysis, and deep reflection, both the participants and I came away from the inquiry process changed for the better. Our work together impacted our attitudes and our teaching practices.

"When you know better you do better."
Maya Angelou (n.d.)

Steinberg, Empson, and Carpenter (2004) identified three specific conditions necessary for a change in teacher belief and practice: membership in a discourse community, explicit processes employed that support honest conversation and reflection, and ownership of the resulting process of change. An interesting discovery made by this research team, and one that has critical implications for groups involved in teacher inquiry, is that at the end of a cycle of inquiry, some teachers were unable to sustain or continue applying their new knowledge about teaching and learning. The research team concluded that ongoing learning through practice and collaborative study is an essential mechanism for reform.

PARALLELS

It seems as though the same narrow thinking that impedes instructional practices from addressing students' cultural needs, resulting, for example, in traditional instructional practices that routinely focus on the kinds of rote "drill and kill" exercises which do little to promote academic literacy, critical thinking, and the development of a strong intellectual identity, also succeed in too narrowly defining culturally relevant pedagogy. However, when approached as a necessary support for maximizing student potential and learning, culturally relevant pedagogy encompasses a much broader definition. The ability to view culturally relevant pedagogical practices in more expansive terms could result in a paradigm shift for educators. This work allows us to study our students, determine what cultural experiences and expectations they bring to school, and align our instruction accordingly. By connecting students' prior knowledge and cultural experiences with instructional objectives and new concepts being taught, we can bring about more socially just schooling for all our students.

I presented the example of math because, perhaps more than any other subject, it continues to be taught in a traditional manner, moving from topic to topic, often failing to consider relevance. Tutak et al.(2011) have found that culturally relevant practices have not historically been prevalent in mathematics education because of the common misconception that mathematics represents a neutral topic, impossible to make culturally relevant. Gutstein (2006) called for a major pedagogical shift to counter the prevalence of mathematics being accepted as apolitical and unconnected to issues of equity. The historically traditional perspective of mathematics has made it difficult for researchers, teacher educators, classroom teachers, and pre-service teachers to conceptualize teaching and learning mathematics for social justice (Noyes, 2009, p. 207).

Although primarily geared toward math instruction, the examples presented here serve as a model to explore within any classroom content area. The reliance on traditional instruction, worksheets, and remedial drills that define the experiences of so many African American youth raises questions regarding the morality of academic tracking and what Beers (2009) classifies as segregation by intellectual rigor. Ladson-Billings (1995b) contends that academic achievement and cultural competency should work hand-in-hand to deliver African American students from the shackles of intellectual inequity. Acknowledging that lower achievement levels of minority students are tied to the type of curriculum and instruction that they receive, more funding committed to researching the kind of pedagogy that makes a difference is needed. In addition to research funding, professional development models built on cycles of teacher inquiry and facilitated by expert others should be developed and instituted in teacher preparation programs at institutes of higher learning and in urban, suburban, and rural public school settings. Ultimately, cross-curricular models of instruction should become the norm. The time is ripe for such an endeavor; the development and subsequent adoption of the Common Core State Standards Initiative with its focus on interdisciplinary literacy may provide an opportunity to de-compartmentalize learning and to reform and reframe curriculum and instruction to ensure that all students count.

What, after all, is mathematics but the poetry of the mind, and what is poetry but the mathematics of the heart?

David Eugene Smith (2012)

References

Angelou, M. (n.d.). Maya Angelou Quotes. Retrieved from http://www.goodreads.com/author/quotes/3503.Maya_Angelou

Beers, K. (2009). *The genteel unteaching of America's poor*. National Council of Teachers of English. Retrieved from http://www.ncte.org/library/NCTEFiles/Press/Beers.pdf

Berry, R. Q. (2003). Mathematics standards, cultural styles, and learning preferences: The plight and promise of African American students. *Clearing House, 76* (5), 244-249.

Bol, L., & Berry, R. Q. (2005). Secondary mathematics teachers' perceptions of the achievement gap. *High School Journal*, 88(4), 32-45.

Caddy, C. (2007). Equation. In *Esperance: New and selected poems*. Washington: Freemantle Press.

D'Ambrosio, U. (2001). What is ethnomathematics, and how can it help children in schools? *Teaching Children Mathematics, 7*(6), 308-312.

Devlin, K. (2011, December). *The birth of algebra.* Speech presented at San Jose Tech Museum, San Jose, California.

Draper, R.J. & Siebert, D. (2004). Making sense of the mathematics and literacy instruction in a standards-based mathematics classroom. *American Educational Research Journal 41,*(4), 927-962.

Friedland, E. S., McMillen, S. E., & del Prado Hill, P. (2011). Moving beyond the word wall: How middle school math teachers use literacy strategies. *NCSM Journal*, Fall/Winter, 6-13. Retrieved from http://edwebsfiles.ed.uiuc.edu/smallurban/ chancellorsacademy/documents/pdf

Gay, G. (2002). Preparing for culturally responsive teaching. *Journal of Teacher Education, 53*(2), 106-114.

Gutstein, E. (2006). *Reading and writing the world with mathematics: Toward a pedagogy for social justice.* New York, NY: Routledge.

Henle, J (2011) "Is (Some) Mathematics Poetry?," *Journal of Humanistic Mathematics, 1*(1) Retrieved from http://scholarship.claremont.edu/jhm/vol1/iss1/7

Irvine, J.J. (2009). Relevant: Beyond the basics. *Teaching Tolerance, 36.* Retrieved from http://www.tolerance.org/magazine/number-36-fall-2009/relevant-beyond-basics.

Johnson, H., Watson. P. A., Delahunty, T., McSwiggen, P., & Smith, T. (2011). What it is they do: Differentiating knowledge and literacy practices across content disciplines. *Journal of Adolescent & Adult Literacy, 55*(2), 100-109.

Knaus, C. B. (2009). Shut up and listen: Applied critical race theory in the classroom. *Race, Ethnicity, and Education, 12*(2), 133-154.

Kwako, J. (2011). Changing the balance in an unjust world: Learning to teach mathematics for social justice. *Journal of Urban Mathematics Education, 4*(1), 15-22.

Ladson-Billings, G. (1995a). But that's just good teaching! The case for culturally relevant pedagogy. *Theory Into Practice, 34*(3), 159-165.

Ladson-Billings, G. (1995b). Toward a theory of culturally relevant pedagogy. *American Educational Research Journal, 32*(3), 465-491.

Ladson-Billings, G. (1997). It doesn't add up: African American students' mathematics achievement. *Journal for Research in Mathematics Education, 28*(6), 697-708.

Ladson-Billings, G. (1999). Just what is critical race theory, and what's it doing in a nice field like education? In L. Parker, D. Deyhele, and S. Villenas (Eds.), *Race is race isn't: Critical race theory and qualitative studies in education*, (pp. 7–30). Boulder, CO: Westview Press.

Minton, L. (2007). *What if your ABC's were your 123's: Building connections between literacy and numeracy.* Thousand Oaks, CA: Corwin Press.

Mintrop, H., & Sunderman, G. L. (2009). Predictable failure of federal sanctions-driven accountability for school improvement - and why we may retain it anyway. *Educational Researcher, 38*(5), 353-364.

Moore, K. (2012). *Finding poetic justice: how teacher inquiry impacts elementary math instruction*, (Unpublished doctoral dissertation). California State University, East Bay, Hayward, CA. Retrieved from retrieved from retrieved from http://csueastbay-dspace.calstate.edu/handle/10211.5/24?

Muhammad, S. (2003). *How to teach math to black students*. Chicago, IL: African American Images.

Noguera, P. A. (2003). The trouble with black boys: The role and influence of environmental and cultural factors on the academic performance of African American males. *Urban Education, 38*(4), 431-459.

Noyes, A. (2009). Participation in mathematics: what is the problem? *Improving Schools, 12*(3), 277-288.

Oakes, J. & Lipton, M. (1998). *Teaching to change the world.* Boston: McGraw Hill Higher Education.

Ogbu, J. U. (2003). *Black American students in an affluent suburb: A study of academic disengagement.* New Jersey: Lawrence Erlbaum Associates.

Pappas, T. (1993). *Math talk: Mathematical ideas in poems for two voices*. Seattle, WA: Wide World Books Publishing.

Schmoker, M. (2011). *Focus: Elevating the essentials to radically improve student learning.* Alexandria, VA: ASCD.

Smith, D.E. (2012, March 29). Math is the poetry of the mind [Blog post]. Retrieved from http://howtosmile.org/blog/posts/math-poetry-mind

Snipes, V. T., & Waters, R. D. (2005). The mathematics education of African Americans in North Carolina: From the Brown decision to No Child Left Behind. *Negro Educational Review, 56*(2/3), 107-126.

Steinberg, R. M., Empson, S. B., & Carpenter, T. P. (2004). Inquiry into children's mathematical thinking as a means to teacher change. *Journal of Mathematics Teacher Education, 7*(3), 237-267.

Stinson, D. W. (2004). Mathematics as "gate-keeper" (?): Three theoretical perspectives that aim toward empowering all children with a key to the gate. *The Mathematics Educator, 14*(1), 8-18.

Stone, J.R. III, Alfeld, C. & Pearson, D. (2008). Rigor and relevance: Enhancing high school students' math skills through career and technical education. *American Educational Research Journal 45*(3), 767-795.

Tate, W. F. (1995). Returning to the root: A culturally relevant approach to mathematics pedagogy. *Theory Into Practice, 34*(3). 166-173.

Tutak, A., Bondy, E., & Adams, T. L. (2011). Critical pedagogy for critical mathematics education. *International Journal of Mathematical Education in Science and Technology, 42*(1), 65-74.

Whyte, D. (1997). Working together. In *The house of belonging*. Washington: Many Rivers Press.

Dr. Kathy Moore's passion is equity through literacy, and she serves as a school district curriculum coordinator, mentor teacher, and staff developer throughout the greater San Francisco Bay Area. Kathy is a teaching consultant for the Bay Area Writing Project and an instructor in the Masters of Teaching Leadership program at St. Mary's College of California. She was honored as San Ramon Valley Unified School District Teacher of the Year in 2007 and San Ramon Chamber of Commerce Educator of the Year in 2009. Kathy holds a Doctorate in Educational Leadership for Social Justice from California State University, East Bay, an M.A. in Teacher Leadership from St. Mary's College of California, and a B.A. in English Education from SUNY Albany. She can be contacted at katydidmor@msn.com.

Chapter 2

Nuestra Voz: Exploring a Parent Engagement Model for Latino Families Through a Postcolonial Lens

Jason Alemán

Chances are that if you were my 5th grade teacher you would have thought my parents were not that involved in my educational journey. Mrs. Wiley, my actual 5th grade teacher, probably thought the same as I look back to my time in her class. She was not a bad teacher as I recall. As a matter of fact, I have vivid memories of her being very nice and offering opportunities for me to grow as a critical thinker. Yet, from an early age, I knew that my home life and school life were completely separated. I knew that what went on at my home was not understood or valued by the likes of Mrs. Wiley. Although similar in many ways, the lessons I learned from my mother and father at home had no carry over to the classroom. Whether it was my father sharing stories of his days as a migrant field worker and the related science or my mother talking with me about poetry, the lessons I learned at home stayed outside of the classroom. Mrs. Wiley, and every teacher I had for that matter, was unaware that my household held a curriculum of its own that would propel me to develop as a person and student.

While they tried as best they could, my parents also had little impact or understanding of what went on in the classroom. If only I could have written a letter to Mrs. Wiley to explain who my parents were and what they meant to my educational journey. Due to their own negative experiences with formal schooling, my parents felt as though they did not belong on the school grounds. As students whose primary language at home was Spanish, there was a great divide between expectations and norms at home and those held by school leaders and teachers. This carried over as they became parents to my siblings and me. Fortunately for me, I was able to navigate the rough terrain of a school system that failed to connect the lessons of my Latino home with the lessons of the classroom. Many of my fellow students were not as lucky as I. It is for them, and those who struggled with navigating a system that is culturally unresponsive to Latinos, that I write the following chapter.

OVERVIEW OF ISSUE

This chapter explores a culturally responsive parent engagement model for Latino families and describes how schools can utilize it to better serve their students. Along with being culturally responsive, the model presented places a strong emphasis on academic accountability for families, students, and educators involved. Recent reviews of the research on preparing pre-service teachers to work with diverse students have concluded that the cultural gap between teachers and students is growing (Ladson-Billings, 1999; Sleeter, 2001). Beyond the student, it is my belief that the gap extends to the family and community of the student as well. Sleeter (2001) adds that these same pre-service teachers tend to have little cross-cultural experience and limited visions of what multicultural teaching entails. This is no fault of the teachers themselves; rather, it shines a light on teacher preparation programs that have yet to fully embrace the importance of culture in regards to instructional best practices. This chapter will begin the dialogue of closing the gap found between Latino families and schools. While critical in nature, this chapter is not to attempt to place blame with the families or educators. Rather, my purpose is to shine a light on barriers to strong home-school relation and explore how we can better understand how schools can collaborate with Latino families for the greater good of their students.

THE PARTNERSHIP: AN INTRODUCTION

For the past six years, I have worked with Latino families on the Eastside of San Antonio, Texas. My work in the schools of a larger urban school district revolves around creating an authentic and culturally responsive bridge between schools and the community. Based in a non-profit organization, I have worked alongside principals, teachers, parents, community organizations, and businesses to rethink the parent-school-community partnership paradigm. I found this work to be as rewarding as it is complex. There is no magic wand to wave. There have been as many mistakes as there have been successes. Even as the partnership has matured and expanded, I have witnessed the dark clouds of oppression and colonialism maneuver through different phases of the partnership. As both practitioner and scholar, I believe the dark clouds can teach us as much as the rays of light that have shined on the families and schools.

In late 2005, my employer (a large non-profit organization in San Antonio, Texas) commissioned an initiative aimed to impact educational achievement in the local community. A modest budget was allotted to this new initiative with little direction or organizational governance as to *how* to impact educational achievement in the local community. I, along with another colleague, was assigned to oversee this new educational initiative. For our organization, this initiative was a major shift in the mission of the organization that historically focused on funding a large group of direct service agencies. In the Spring of 2006, two focus groups convened to brainstorm the best approach to increase academic achievement in the Latino neighborhoods of San Antonio. The focus groups consisted of parents, school leaders, higher education personnel, and civic leaders. I met with school leaders to gauge their interest in the process and seek volunteers of potential parent leaders already involved on campus. Civic and educational volunteers who were asked to participate had long-standing relationships with my organization, and had participated in previous organizational projects. At the conclusion of this initial step, the feedback from the focus groups matched that of our initial literature review on impacting educational achievement within the local community: The family-school connection was essential to the academic success of Latino students, and school leaders and teachers who reached out in a culturally responsive way were able to create a strong academic support system for students and families alike. It was decided that our initiative would focus on increasing parental involvement at a handful of schools within one urban school district. My initial thoughts were 1) How do you increase parental involvement? 2) Are the schools not already doing this? It was in this manner that a partnership was born.

In the fall of 2006, the initiative kicked off in six schools (two sets of elementary schools that fed into two middle schools. All of the partners involved from the onset were determined not to create 'another program' as they refused to give it a name/title/label. From day one, the initiative has been simply known as *the partnership*. Initially, the focus of the partnership was on engaging parents through home visits, creating parent rooms on each campus, and other family engagement projects that were directed by parents themselves. The short-term outcomes the partnership was seeking to achieve were an increase in parent engagement, family-to-family engagement, and improved student performance (all day attendance and improved behavior).

The partnership, like parental engagement itself, is a complex web of relationship-building, trust in oneself and others, and creating long-term goals while giving the necessary attention to crucial short-term goals. This chapter focuses primarily on the first three years of the partnership and the journey to better understand the connection between Latino homes and schools. In addition, this chapter aims to introduce a new model of parent engagement framed by postcolonial theory. Along with my personal journey over the first three years of the partnership, I integrate current literature on parent involvement for Latino families.

ROLE OF PRACTITIONER/AUTHOR/RESEARCHER

The transparency of the author is critical enough in our journey to better understand how schools can collaborate with Latino families that I feel it necessary to explain my role within this partnership, the composition of this chapter, and my emerging research. Since the inception of the partnership, I have found a home of (dis)comfort in what Asher (2005; 2008) describes as the hybrid identity of the Latino father. Asher (2008) explains that hybrid identities "emerge in the interstices between different cultures…when immigrant communities negotiate cultural differences in the context of U.S. schools…as they navigate the differences and discontinuities in the process of shaping an identity" (p. 13). Over my time within this partnership, I have constantly found myself at the interstices of multiple identifications that have made it difficult to arrive at a meaningful synthesis across differences (Asher, 2005). I am Latino, but I am viewed as an outsider within the parent rooms of the partnership. With my brown skin and ability to speak Spanish, it is quickly apparent to the parents I am Latino. Yet, my formal attire (required by my organization), an understanding that I have some amount of higher education, and their awareness that I have the backing/funding of a major organization drives home the notion that I am an outsider. At times I feel myself aligning with those I feel are oppressed; other times the oppressor within me appears with a wily smirk. The dangers of colonizing a group of parents were never further than a few missteps away at any given time of the process. My responsibility was found in the duality of reporting to an organization that had, in many ways, participated in the colonizing of the very communities that over time entrusted me to help facilitate the process of creating positive change in their community. Mostly, as the hybrid identity explains, I live in a state of "in-betweenness" (Asher, 2008, p. 1081) that puts my fluid identity somewhere between the hyphen (Fine, 1994) of two distinct identities in any given situation.

As a Latino father to two brown boys, this partnership, along with my emerging research, has always been more than a job duty or intellectual exercise. My life's work as a practitioner and researcher is deeply personal and cannot be confined to the traditional confines of subjectivity and neutrality. Ladner (1971) believes there is an inherent bias in social science due to the relationship between researcher and participants: "By definition, that relationship resembles that of the oppressor and the oppressed, because it is the oppressor who defines the problem, the nature of the research, and, to some extent, the quality of interaction between him and his subjects" (p. vii). It is critical, in my role as practitioner scholar, to be mindful of working the "in between" (Fine, 1994) and to be candid with you regarding my hybrid identity and the fact that it informs my ontology, practice, and scholarship.

As a practitioner scholar, I refrain from attempting to be objective which, according to Anzaldúa (2007), is a European construct aimed at separating research from our own personal experiences and feelings. Fine (1994) also believes the "social sciences have been, still are, long on texts that inscribe some Others, preserve other Others from scrutiny, and seek to hide the researcher/writer under a veil of neutrality or objectivity" (p. 73). As I am reminded by their warnings, I do not separate my, and others', personal experiences from the literature and research process. Yet in seeking this, I also acknowledge the historically determined relationships of dominance and subordination (Gandhi, 1998, p. 2) of researcher and participants. Cornel West (as cited in Gandhi, 1998) argues:

> All cultural critics who attempt to contest the operations of power within their own institutional contexts find themselves in a disabling double blind: while linking their activities to the fundamental, structural overhaul of these institutions, they often remain financially dependent on them...For these critics of culture, theirs is a gesture that is simultaneously progressive and coopted. (p. 59)

These are the words that guide my exploration of connecting Latino families with schools.

POSTCOLONIALISM – AN INTRODUCTION

Rather than overwhelm you with the extreme complexity that is postcolonial theory, my aim in this chapter is to offer a thorough introduction to the theory while connecting it meaningfully to how schools can better collaborate with Latino families. The division between the west and the rest was formed in the 19th century by the expansion of the European empires, as a result of which nine-tenths of the entire land surface of the globe was controlled by European, or European-derived, powers (Young, 2003). Young (2003) continues by explaining the entrenchment of colonization:

> Colonial and imperial rule was legitimized by anthropological theories which increasingly portrayed the people of the colonized world as inferior, childlike, or feminine, incapable of looking after themselves (despite having done so perfectly well for millennia) and requiring the paternal rule of the west for their own best interests. (p. 2)

In its purest form, postcolonialism is the historical condition marked by the visible apparatus of freedom and the concealed persistence of unfreedom (Gandhi, 1998). For the families of the partnership, the concealed persistence of unfreedom came in the form of limited physical and intellectual access to the schools, a sense of detachment from their child's educational journey and development, and belief that they offered little in the sense of being a true educational partner with school leaders and teachers. McLeod (2000) adds,

> Colonialism is perpetuated in part by justifying to those in the colonizing nation the idea that it is right and proper to rule over other peoples, and by getting colonized people to accept their lower ranking in the colonial order of things – a process we can call colonizing the mind. (p. 18)

It is vital to understand that postcolonialism is not defined as a period after a kind of colonialism; rather Stuart Hall (1999) declares:

> It is after a certain kind of colonialism, after a certain moment of high imperialism and colonial occupation—in the wake of it, in the shadow of it, inflected by it—it is what it is because something else has happened before, but it is also something new. (p. 230)

The postcolonial lens does not claim to offer clarity—a sense of righteousness following darkness. Rather, it is afflicted by the lingering effects of colonial occupation (both mental and physical). The experience of being colonized therefore signifies a great deal to regions and people of the world whose experiences as dependents, subalterns, and subjects of the West did not end with the *Brown vs. Board of Education* (1954) decision. Rather, we all—families and educators alike—find ourselves in a certain kind of colonialism that is born in the shadow of yesteryear's injustice.

EXAMINATION OF ISSUE

Within educational discourse, parent involvement is generally understood in terms of specific practices such as bake sales, fundraisers, PTA/PTO, and back-to-school nights (Lopez, 2001). The definition of parent involvement has historically been quite transparent, relegating it to a scripted role to be performed rather than to unrehearsed activities that parents and other family members routinely practice (Lopez, 2001). In Zarate's (2007) research, teachers, principals, and counselors noted parent-teacher organizations as one form of parental involvement, yet no Latino parents cited those organizations when describing various ways of participating in their child's education. Teachers and school administrators—also in contrast with Latino parents—felt that "back-to-school nights, open houses, and parent-teacher conferences were important and viable venues for parents and teachers to communicate about students' academic progress" (p. 11). The field has not, however, paid attention to non-educators' views of their role or influence as school council members in decisions regarding student achievement, or how educators and non-educators understand the transition from parent volunteerism to authentic collaboration through the organization of school councils (Stelmach and Preston, 2007). While an honorable gesture of collaboration, the integration of parents into a decision-making role, can lead to more concerns. Even when asked to participate in the schooling process, parents' incomplete understanding about the purpose of their involvement in school activities led to challenges to such partnerships (Stelmach and Preston, 2007). This was the case for all six of our schools within the partnership. There was a sense of confusion of what schools and families identified as their role and the role of their counterpart. Even with a handful of parents sitting on advisory boards of some type, there remained an incomplete understanding of their role in school policy and practice. Parents were being asked to be involved in school, but were being asked to be involved in a manner that was dictated by school leaders who were unfamiliar with the needs of the parents and families.

Over the first three years, the San Antonio home-school partnership meandered (not always in a linear fashion) through the impact and significance of the traditional, culturally responsive (Gay, 2000, 2010; Harmon, 2012; Irvine & Armento, 2001), and postcolonial paradigms in our effort to better connect schools to Latino families. Each of these approaches and its impact—intentional and unintentional—is discussed in the following pages.

TRADITIONAL PARADIGM OF PARENT INVOLVEMENT

The notion of educational achievement is associated with relationship building practices among parents, teachers, children, and schools (Chavkin & Williams, 1993; Dauber & Epstein, 1993; Epstein, 1986; Hidalgo, Siu, Bright, Swap, & Epstein, 1995; Okagaki & Frensch, 1998; Powell & Peet, 1996; Wentzel, 1998). As we began the partnership in 2006, our vision was based in this research as we attempted to build a stronger relationship between the home and school. The burning question of our partnership was, *How can we get parents to better support the school?*

The aim of increasing parent involvement in children's school is based on a wealth of research suggesting that such involvement is beneficial for children (see, for example, Fan & Chen, 2001; Hill & Taylor, 2004; Jeynes, 2003, 2005; Pomerantz, Grolnick, & Price, 2005). At the initial steps of creating a new partnership, our vision was imbedded in the Comer model (Comer, Haynes, Joyner, & Ben-Avie, 1996), which works to disperse power and distribute decision making to all relevant players. In this model, home and school relationships are framed as collaboration, with shared responsibility and action. Yet the Comer model was nowhere to be found in our initial six participating schools. There was little-to-no dialogue, much less collaboration, and no sense of shared responsibility from either the families or the schools. The six schools we entered were home to a sense of distrust that had accumulated over generations. It was clear to us that these emotions would not be redirected in a short period of time. Yet at this starting point, we began the task of building relationships one day at a time. For the entire first year of the partnership, our focus became to build relationships through authentic conversations in the parent rooms of the schools. In having these conversations, parents, school leaders, and civic volunteers realized that no other tasks/projects could be conducted prior to forming strong, lasting relationships. Over tables full of coffee and food, difficult conversations were held to build the first steps of the bridge connecting Latino families and schools. This idea of slowing the work down to simply talk, while simple in its design, was the most difficult step of the process as we navigated through the pressing needs of the community as well as the outcome expectations of a funding organization.

Graue, Kroeger, and Prager (2001) argue that this type of partnership model is based upon assumptions that are quite situated and normative. They write:

> Using relationships that exist at the level of the aggregate, policies are suggested that are not answerable to the needs of subgroups with diverse histories and resources. As a result, the partnership model implicitly reflects the power and practices of the dominant group-the white middle class that has always had strong relationships with the school. (p. 470)

This was certainly the case for the schools of our partnership as we began the journey. School policy and practice was created and implemented with little-to-no input by those who were recipients of the service. The traditional parent involvement model of the schools was discursively constructed by the dominant white middle class viewing the process as "helping those families." So entering this dynamic within the schools and community, I pondered, "What were the power dynamics of the home-school relationship and how were they hindering parental involvement"? How did the traps of colonialism impede what we were seeking to accomplish?"

Difficult conversations began the process of breaking down the walls built over generations of injustice, judgment, and de facto policy that wedged a divide between the Latino families and their schools. The situated nature of knowing makes issues of power, language, and identity a key part of interpreting the home-school relationship (Graue, Kroeger, and Prager, 2001). Only recently have researchers begun to theorize explicitly about the intersections of these identity markers upon the home and school relational events (Lareau & Horvat, 1999; Lareau & Shumar, 1996). Yet for the families of the partnership, the intersections of identity markers were well known as were the implications of race, gender, and cultural conditions. These difficult issues were the basis of a conversation amongst educators, civic volunteers, and families that took up most of the first year of the partnership. These conversations were not a supplemental piece to some larger agenda. Having these conversations *was* the agenda. In meeting after meeting, conversation after conversation, the issues of cultural and historical barriers, expectations, and belief sharing amongst Latino families and school leaders began to set the foundation for a new kind of home-school partnership.

PARENTAL INVOLVEMENT THROUGH A LATINO LENS

When asked to define parental involvement, Latino parents mentioned life participation more frequently than academic involvement (Zarate, 2007). Latino parents defined their role in participating in activities such as, "teach good morals and respect of others, establish trust with child, provide general encouragement, provide advice on life issues, and discuss future planning" (Zarate, 2007, p. 8) as their view of parental involvement. Latino parents equate involvement in their child's education with involvement in their lives. Participation in their children's lives ensures that their formal schooling is complemented with *educación* taught in the home. On the surface, *educacíon* appears to be a direct translation of the English word "education." Although they are related etymologically, the Spanish term carries with it a set of inferences and behaviors that are not referents of its English cognate (Reese, Balzano, Gallimore, and Goldenberg, 1995). Reese et al. (1995) write, "Latino parents do not spontaneously make the distinction between schooling (academics) and upbringing (morals) that is made in English. Instead, both are part of a larger whole that leads to becoming a good person" (p. 63). For Latino parents, issues such as respect for others, expressing humility and love for *familia* are as vital to success as arithmetic and science concepts. These parents view *la educación de la vida* (the education of life) to be integrated into the formal schooling conducted within the classroom. This was found to be true with the Latino parents within the partnership. School leaders and civic leaders learned that Latino parents taught their children reading, math, and science through common, everyday living situations at the home. To Latino parents, this was not parental involvement; rather, it was fulfilling their role within *la educacíon* of their children. Latino parents have been shown to have higher academic expectations for their children than White parents (Ryan, Casas, Kelly-Vance, Ryalls, & Nero, 2010), and Latino parents believed that monitoring their children's lives and providing moral guidance resulted in good classroom behavior, which in turn allowed for greater academic learning opportunities (Zarate, 2007). Hensley (in González, Moll, & Amanti, 2005), writes, "If the teacher places value on this knowledge, then the parents suddenly feel important. They feel empowered. This alone can dramatically change the climate of the teacher-home relationship" (p. 146). Weiss, Kreider, Lopez, and Chatman (2005) observed:

> Teachers' and school administrators' perceptions of parents' socioeconomic backgrounds influence how they interact with parents, and whether or not they support or reject parent strategies of involvement. All too often, school personnel treat poor parents from a deficit perspective, which becomes a barrier to family involvement. (p. xvii)

This barrier began to crumble during the second year of the partnership. The relationships formed in the first year allowed for the partnership to move to the next phase of building a bridge between the Latino families and school. Under the true direction of the parents, the partnership took on an action-oriented approach to building a stronger home-school relationship for the sake of the students, the school, and the community. Parent groups, based out of the parent room, collaborated with school leaders and teachers to influence curriculum and assessment tools. For example, local Latino leaders were integrated into writing assignments to foster knowledge of community history while enhancing mastery of English Language Arts state standards. Working with community-based organizations, the parents infused local resources to ensure that basic needs of all families were met. For example, parents organized with a local grocery store chain to provide basic school supplies for all students at the beginning of each school year. This was not charity or a handout. It was parents working with parents to better prepare children for a successful year. What this became was each and every parent taking on the responsibility of creating a healthier community.

For many teachers and administrators, parental involvement is centered on those parents that are able to attend; those who do not are seen as uncaring (Jones and Valez, 1997; Ramirez, 1996, 1997, 1999). By implication, parents of low socioeconomic standing who are unable to attend school functions are "read" as lacking the desire to be part of their children's education (Ramirez, 2003). In the second year of the partnership, these assumptions began to fade as well. School leaders learned of parents who were involved in non-traditional ways. Through home visits conducted by parents of each school, school and civic leaders were given access to a new identity of the Latino parent that was based in love and support for one's child. The role of the Latino father, in particular, was defined by his importance to *la educacion* of the child. Johnstone & Hiatt (1997) equated the lack of Latino father participation with lack of interest in their child's education, declaring it a nationwide problem. Lopez (2001) found involvement within Latino families in parents teaching their children to appreciate the value of their education through the medium of hard work. The home visits of our partnership in year two illuminated this role of the Latino father. The Latino father depicted in Lopez's (2001) study is described as having a "personal incompatibility with the school system" (p. 424). The Latino father of our partnerships shared, reluctantly, stories of oppression and hatred felt within the school as young children. The majority of the families of the partnership are 3rd or 4th generation Latino-Americans who have attempted to navigate the same school system in which their children were enrolled. These same men, now with children of their own, were deterred by their own experiences to re-enter the very same schools in a supportive role for their children. Many of these fathers spoke of a language barrier (many are monolingual Spanish speakers) that made it difficult to find comfort in a school in which the front office personnel, teachers, and staff were monolingual English speakers. For him, the Latino father of the partnership, it was a sense of personal incompatibility that made it safer to stay home rather than be a visible support in the school system.

Culturally responsive pedagogy has been referred to by many names: culturally responsible, culture compatible, culturally appropriate, culturally congruent, culturally relevant, and multicultural education (Irvine & Armento, 2001). Gay (2000, 2010) describes cultural responsive teaching as multidimensional, empowering, and transformative. She refers to culturally relevant pedagogy as the use of "cultural knowledge, prior experiences, frame of reference, and performance styles of ethnically diverse students to make learning more relevant. It teaches to and through strengths of the students. It is culturally validating and affirming" (Gay, 2000, p. 29). What did culturally responsive mean to our partnership? It meant conducting each and every meeting with simultaneous translation to ensure that English and Spanish speakers could fully participate. It meant understanding that parents worked sometimes multiple jobs to provide for their families. Because of this, all meetings were held at times that were considerate of family schedules as opposed to school schedules. As a school leader, it is critical to seek when it is best for the parents, not the school staff, to meet. For our partnership, there were two specific times that worked best for parents. The first was right after dropping students off in the morning. The second was during dinnertime. With the help of school and organizational resources, we were able to provide dinners for parents who were extremely busy, meeting the needs of their family.

Culturally responsive also meant that we as a partnership worked off the strengths of each individual and group. The strengths of the parents, such as creativity and cultural knowledge, allowed them to integrate their talents into the curriculum design of the schools. Specific cultural figures and dates were integrated into science, literature, and writing assignments for all students to connect culture with learning in an authentic way. Parents of the partnership also held the vision of creating a college awareness day that allowed for parents and students to become more aware of the process together as a family. Civic and educational volunteers provided best practices to the partnership in assuring our overall vision was evidence-based. Having said this, the progression to creating a more culturally responsive atmosphere will be an on-going process that will never fully be accomplished. For those within the partnership, becoming fully culturally responsive has been a learning journey rather than a set destination.

PARENTAL INVOLVEMENT THROUGH A POSTCOLONIAL LENS

This task of moving to a new kind of colonialism, a postcolonialism, while perhaps beneficial to the scholar and practitioner, is more often painful and humiliating to the colonized as they recover a history of race and racism (Bhabha, 1994). This became apparent in year three of our partnership. Parents, with their newfound power and understanding, exhibited what could only be defined as a collective pain. This pain took many forms that included parents lashing out at each other, holding contempt for school leaders, and struggling to understand the pitfalls of their newfound voice and power. For many who struggled with the complexity of moving onto a new type of colonialism, this pain was considered to be counterproductive to a partnership that had gained traction with the public. Tensions between the community and schools that were buried for generations shined a light on the hidden unfreedom felt amongst partners. These events in themselves could easily have derailed the partners from continuing the process of bridging Latino families and schools. Yet Bhabha (1994) believes there are two major benefits to the retrieval: first, it simply seeks to uncover the overwhelming and lasting violence of colonialism. Second, the retrieval requires that the colonized reclaim and own the images retrieved in an initial step of historical and psychological recovery. I understood that the lasting violence and destruction of colonialism needed to be uncovered and addressed. As uncomfortable as it was to go through this phase of the relationship building, I believe we all realized that this paled in comparison to the discomfort felt by Latino families for generations within the community. The discomfort of parents revisiting the harms done to them as children of these very schools was at times traumatic, but they found it necessary to ensure that their own children would not go through the same struggle. For school leaders, the discomfort in questioning their own power structure was done in the spirit of realizing that a more authentic Latino parent engagement model would only strengthen their chances of achieving academic success for their campus.

Thinking about home-school relations in terms of addressivity, in particular how school leaders address Latino parents, provides a glimpse into the basic struggle of connecting schools to Latino homes. Addressivity focuses attention on the potential links to people and status that propel individuals in activity (Graue, Kroeger, & Prager, 2001). Holquist (1990) writes:

> The world addresses us and we are alive and human to the degree that we are answerable, i.e., to the degree that we can respond to addressivity. Each one of us occupies a place in existence that is uniquely ours; but far from being a privilege, far from having what Bakhtin calls an alibi in existence. (p. 30)

What Hoquist suggests is that it is not only the address that plays a role in the notion of addressivity; rather, it is how the addressee positions himself/herself in the form of the answer or response that impacts the power of the relationship. For the parents of the partnership, the answer/response to the address, for the majority of them, implicated their existence as a submissive entity of a colonized society. This, like most aspects of the school-Latino home connection, began to change over time into an address that was more balanced and postcolonial in nature. Bakhtin (1986) explains his view of addressivity:

> When speaking I always take into account the appreciative background of the addressee's perception of my speech: the extent to which he is familiar with the situation, whether he has special knowledge of the given cultural area of communication, his views and convictions, his prejudices (from my viewpoint)—because all this will determine his active responsive understanding of my utterance, my choice of composition devices, and finally, my choice of language vehicles, that is, the style of my utterance. (p. 96)

In year three of the partnership, the issue of addressivity came to the forefront. Gone were the days of year one in which two distinct groups sat in a room and got to know each other. Gone were the days of year two in which two distinct groups made action plans to improve the well being of families, schools, and community. In year three, issues of perception, identities of the addressee and those being addressed, and viewpoints became the latest barriers to overcome. Parents had gained a sense of power, but who had given it to them and what was the perceived meaning behind the gift of power? Who was talking on behalf of the parents and who was the addressee? As the partnership grew stronger and stronger, the issues became more complicated than the basic needs addressed in year two.

Bakhtin (1986) argues that there are no such things as unique, innate ideas or experiences outside of language. He explains the construction of meaning through social interaction as built through a relationship dependent on two individuals or communities. Through language, the words become a shared experience with those receiving and offering the message. The power of language was felt throughout the partnership as year three progressed. With their newfound voice, parents pushed the foundation of the new model for Latino parent engagement further than anyone ever thought possible. No longer willing to submit as simply a subject to be addressed, the parents became a force of ideas in curriculum design, parent support systems, and ensured sustainability beyond the partnership. In year three of the partnership, parents created leadership development trainings for other parents, presented their work to district and city officials, and expanded their work to other schools within the school district. School leaders who witnessed the power of engaging Latino parents as authentic educational partners participated in peer mentorship with their fellow school leaders in local schools. By the end of year three, Latino parents were an integral part of home and school life for their children in a manner that erased the borders of home and school life. In essence, the notion of *la educacion* came to fruition for all involved.

CONCLUSION

Six years after our unheralded start, the partnership is still going strong. After year three, the partnership expanded to more schools. As of today, the partnership is in fourteen schools, has over 200 parent volunteers, and is the driving force for redefining parental involvement in the schools of San Antonio, Texas. After year three, I left my role as staff support to the partnership in order to complete my doctoral studies. Yet with a partnership such as this, one can never fully depart. I now sit on an advisory board that works to grow the partnership in a healthy manner. In the end, this partnership has been about rethinking the parental involvement paradigm by utilizing a postcolonial lens to disrupt past oppression while forging new relationships and collaborations.

IMPLICATIONS FOR PRACTICE

Weedon (2004) explains that history is crucial to the process of decolonizing identities and showing them to be complex, located and contingent, rather than fixed, authentic and true. In the absence of this historicity, identities are often based on myth and misconception. As educators, we must move beyond the myths and misconceptions of Latino families and their roles within the educational journey of their children. Authentic conversations must be conducted to break through the barriers of assumption, misconceptions, and ignorance. To do this with Latino families, school leaders must set up *platicas* (Guajardo & Guajardo, 2004) at times/locations that are convenient for the lives and schedules of parents. *Platicas*, or informal conversations, are the method through which we, as Latinos, learn and know the nature of our reality. There is no agenda set forth for these conversations. Rather there is a desire to listen, learn, and respond in a manner that is authentic to the relationship formed. When given the chance to share in a safe space and relationship, many Latino families will clearly state who they are, what they expect from schools, and what role they can play in supporting the learning process.

The role of home visits cannot be overstated within this chapter. Each summer, from the inception of the partnership, groups of Latino parents have canvassed the neighborhoods, knocking on the doors and forging new relationships. The home visit is not a solicitation of any sort; rather, the home visit is a tool to invite each parent to the parent room and to ask what would make for a better school-going experience for their children. The parent-to-parent connection is, and always has been, the first step in bridging the Latino home to schools. Within the home visits, Latino parents from the same school met with other Latino parents and stated two things: 1) Thank you for sending your children to the specific school, and 2) What can we do to help connect the school to your home in a more meaningful way? The act of Latino parents reaching out to the homes of their neighbors was the foundation of all that followed in connecting families to schools.

Crucial to the success of practice, the school leader must fully buy into the idea of Latino parents as an educational ally and asset. Without the support from school administration, all attempts to rethink the traditional parent involvement paradigm will falter. School leaders must make this a priority as opposed to another task that takes time away from other school matters. Attendance by school leadership at every meeting, every event, and every parent function communicates that this is important and worthwhile. Over the past six years of the partnership, participants have made tremendous strides in cultivating relationships between school leaders and families of the school community. Dialogue forged an authentic partnership. While the partnership has overcome many barriers throughout this journey, many still remain.

The first three years of the partnership are a roadmap to be utilized in practice to increase the home-school connection for Latino students and families. This roadmap has been created through actions (and inactions) that were fluid and specific to our unique partnership. Therefore, the roadmap has been created and presented to provide a template to be adjusted for any given situation and community. Through families owning the direction of a new landscape for healthier school relationships, schools can begin to move beyond the colonial past that has plagued the Latino community for generations.

IMPLICATIONS FOR RESEARCH

Kincaid (1998) writes about the English who conquered her Antiqua (not being that different than white settler's conquest of the Mexican who called Texas home):

> And so everywhere they went they turned into England; and everybody they met they turned English. But no place could ever really be England, and nobody who did not look exactly like them would ever be English, so you can imagine the destruction of people and land that came from that. (p. 24)

Researchers must continue to examine the impact of myths, misconceptions, and continued colonialism inside and outside of the classroom and school grounds. This chapter begins to dismantle the traditional paradigm of parental involvement while emphasizing a culturally responsive and postcolonial approach to Latino home and school relations.

Kincaid (1998) discusses a type of destruction that, at times, cannot be seen with the naked eye. The destruction is internalized by victims in a way that makes it invisible to even those closest to them. A deeper analysis of the impact of the destruction, and its impact on the parent involvement paradigm, needs to be explored.

Further research must also explore the impact of postcolonial theory on creating strong connections between Latino homes and schools. Issues of power, culture, and identity in a historical sense must be at the forefront of addressing the home-school relationship. With the promise of our partnership and its impact on exploring generations of colonialism, we must continue to research new threads of colonialism and oppression borne out of our successes.

A Letter to Mrs. Wiley

Mrs. Wiley,

I know you did not get to know my Mom and Dad, but I bet you would have liked them. My Dad worked a lot. When I was in your class, he was either sleeping or working most of the time. He had a good job at the chemical plant, but it required him to work long, hard hours, and he just could not make it to most parent meetings. Yet, I remember him coming home from work and tucking me in to bed with a story. It was my father who sparked my love for the written word. He would read to me, and then I would read to him. He also taught me how to work with tools, clean the bathroom, and take responsibility for my actions. I am not sure if you know it, but all of these things helped me in your class.

My Mom was the best too. You would have loved her; I am sure. It was she who ran the household and taught me what it meant to be a good person. It often seemed like she loved me more than life itself. She encouraged me when I was feeling down and kept me grounded when I began to stray from her vision. Mom also made sure that I understood where we came from and the importance of loving my grandmother, aunts, uncles, and cousins. We have a large, extended family, Mrs. Wiley, and they meant so much to me. She had a rough time going to school when she was a little girl and did not want her own children to go through what she did.

Mrs. Wiley, my parents were rarely at the school, but they were there for me and supported my learning in their own way. Did I wish they would go see me at school sometimes or feel more comfortable at school? Of course I did. The fact is I wish I could have felt more 'at home' when I was in your class. Maybe we can figure out a way to bring home into the classroom for next year's students. Maybe, just maybe, we can bridge my school to the home I love so dearly.

Sincerely,
Jason Alemán

References

Anzaldúa, G. (2007). *Borderlands/La Frontera: The new Mestiza* (3rd ed.). San Francisco: Aunt Lute Books.

Asher, N. (2005). At the interstices: Engaging postcolonial and feminist perspective for a multicultural education pedagogy in the south. *Teachers College Record, 107*(5), 1079-1106.

Asher, N. (2008). Listening to hyphenated Americans: Hybrid identities of youth from immigrant families. *Theory Into Practice, 47,* 12-19.

Bakhtin, M.M. (1986). *Speech genres and other late essays.* Austin: University of Texas Press.

Bhabha, H.K. (1994). *The location of culture.* London: Routledge.

Brown, Oliver v. Board of Education of Topeka, 347 U.S. 483 (1954).

Chavkin, N.F. & Williams, D. L. (1993). Minority parents and the elementary school: Attitudes and practices. In Chavkin, N.F. (Ed.), *Families and schools in a pluralistic society* (pp. 73-83). Albany: State University of New York Press.

Comer, J.P., Haynes, N.M., Joyner, E.T., & Ben-Avie, M. (Eds.). (1996). *Rallying the whole village*. New York: Teachers College Press.

Dauber, S., & Epstein, J.L. (Eds.). (1993). *Parents' attitudes and practices of involvement in inner-city elementary and middle schools*. Albany: State University of New York Press.

Epstein, J.L. (1986). Parent's reactions to teacher practices of parent involvement. *The Elementary School Journal, 86*(3), 277-294.

Fan, X., & Chen, M. (2001). Parental involvement and students' academic achievement: A meta-analysis. *Educational Psychology Review, 13,* 1-22.

Fine, M. (1994). Working the hyphens: Reinventing self and other in qualitative research. In N.K. Denzin & Y.S. Lincoln (Eds.), *Handbook of qualitative research* (pp. 70-82). Thousand Oaks, CA: Sage.

Gandhi, L. (1998). *Postcolonial theory: A critical introduction*. New York: Columbia University Press.

Gay, G. (2000). *Culturally responsive teaching: Theory, research, and practice*. New York: Teachers College Press.

Gay, G. (2010). Acting on beliefs in teacher education for cultural diversity. *Journal of Teacher Education, 61,* 143-152.

González, N., Moll, L., & Amanti, C. (Eds). (2005). *Funds of knowledge: Theorizing practices in households, communities and classrooms*. Mahwah, NJ: Lawrence Erlbaum.

Graue, M.E., Kroeger, J., & Prager, D. (2001). A Bakhtinian analysis of particular home-school relations. *American Educational Research Journal, 38*(3), 467-498.

Guajardo, M.A. & Guajardo, F.J. (2004). The impact of Brown on the brown of South Texas: A micropolitical perspective on the education of Mexican Americans in a South Texas community. *American Educational Research Journal, 41*(3), 501-526.

Hall, S. (1999). Cultural composition: Stuart Hall on ethnicity and the discursive turn. In G. A. Olson & L. Worsham (Eds.) *Race, rhetoric, and the postcolonial* (pp. 171-196). Albany: State University of New York Press.

Harmon, D. A. (2012). Culturally responsive teaching through a historical lens: Will history repeat itself? *Interdisciplinary Journal of Teaching and Learning, 2*(1), 12-22.

Hidalgo, N.M., Siu, S., Bright, J.A., Swap, S.M., & Epstein, J.A. (1995). Research on families, schools, and communities: A multicultural perspective. In J. B. Banks & C. A. M. Banks (Eds.), *Handbook on research on multicultural education* (pp. 498-524). New York: MacMillan.

Hill, N.E., & Taylor, L.C.P. (2004). Parental school involvement and children's academic achievement: Pragmatics and issues. *Current Directions in Psychological Science, 13,* 161-164.

Holquist, M. (1990). Introduction. In M. H. V. Liapunov (Ed.), *Art and answerability: Early philosophical essays by M. M. Bakhtin* (pp. ix-xlix). Austin: University of Texas Press.

Irvine, J. J., & Armento, B. J. (2001). *Culturally responsive teaching: Lesson planning for elementary and middle grades*. New York: McGraw Hill.

Jeynes, W.H. (2003). A meta-analysis: The effects of parental involvement on minority children's academic achievement. *Education and Urban Society, 35,* 202-218.

Jeynes, W.H. (2005). A meta-analysis of the relation parent involvement to urban elementary school student academic achievement. *Urban Education, 40,* 237-269.

Johnstone, T.R. & Hiatt, D.B. (April, 1997). *Development of a school-based parent center for low income new immigrants*. Paper session presented at the Annual Meeting of the American Education Research Association. Chicago, IL.

Jones, T.G., and Valez, W. (April, 1997). *Effects of Latino parent involvement on academic achievement*. Paper session presented at the annual meeting of the American Educational Research Association, Chicago, IL.

Kincaid, J. (1998). *A small place*. New York: Farrar, Straus and Giroux.

Ladson-Billings, G.K. (1999). Preparing teachers for diverse student populations: A critical race theory perspective. *Review of Research in Education, 24,* 211-247.

Ladner, J. (1971). *Tomorrow's tomorrow*. Garden City, NY: Doubleday.

Lareau, A., & Horvat, E.M. (1999). Moments of social inclusion and exclusion race, class, and cultural capital in family-school relationships. *Sociology of Education, 72*(1), 37-53.

Lareau, A., & Shumar, W. (1996). The problems of individualism in family-school policies. *Sociology of Education (special issue),* 24-39.

Lopez, G.R. (2001). The value of hard work: Lessons on parent involvement from an (im)migrant household. *Harvard Educational Review, 71*(3), 416-437.

Lorde, A. (1984). *Sister outsider*. Freedom, CA: The Crossing Press.

McLeod, J. (2000). *Beginning postcolonialism*. Manchester, England: Manchester University Press.

Okagaki, L., & Frensch, P.A. (1998). Parenting and children's school achievement: A multiethnic perspective. *American Educational Research Journal, 35*(1), 123-144.

Pomerantz, E.M., Grolnick, W.S., & Price, C.E. (2005). The role of parents in how children approach school: A dynamic process perspective. In A.J. Elliot & C.S. Dweck (Eds.), *The handbook of competence and motivation* (pp. 259-278). New York: Guilford.

Powell, D.R., & Peet, S.H. (April, 1996). *Educational/occupational expectations and aspirations: Mothers' views of their children's futures*. Paper session presented at the Annual Meeting of the American Educational Research Association. New York, NY.

Ramirez, A.Y. (October, 1996). *Parent involvement is like apple pie: A study of a midwestern school*. Paper session presented at Journal of Curriculum Theorizing Conference. Monteagle, TN.

Ramirez, A.Y. (April, 1997). *Teacher's attitudes toward parental involvement: Looking within a rural secondary school*. Paper session presented at the American Educational Research Association Conference, "Talking Together in Educational Research and Practice," Chicago, IL.

Ramirez, A.Y. (1999). Survey on teachers' attitudes regarding parents and parental involvement. *The School Community Journal, 9*(2), 21–39.

Ramirez, A.Y. (2003). Dismay and disappointed: Parental involvement of Latino immigrant parents. *The Urban Review, 35*(2), 93-110.

Reese, L., Balzano, S., Gallimore, R., & Goldenberg, C. (1995). The concept of educacíon: Latino family values and American schooling. *International Journal of Educational Research, 23*(1), 57-81.

Ryan, C. S., Casas, J. F., Kelly-Vance, L., Ryalls, B. O., & Nero, C. (2010). Parent involvement and views of school success: The role of parents' Latino and White American cultural orientations. *Psychology in the Schools, 47*(4), 391-405.

Sleeter, C.E. (2001). Epistemological diversity in research on preservice teacher preparation for historically underserved children. *Review of Research in Education, 25,* 209-250.

Stelmach, B.L. & Preston, J.P. (2007). Cake or curriculum? Principal and parent views on transforming the parental role in Saskatchewan schools. *International Studies in Educational Administration, 36*(3), 59-74.

Weedon, C. (2004). *Identity and culture: Narratives of difference and belonging.* New York: Open University Press.

Weiss, H., Kreider, H., Lopez, M., & Chatman, C. (Eds.). (2005). *Preparing educators to involve families: From theory to practice.* Thousand Oaks, CA: Sage.

Wentzel, K.R. (1998). Parents' aspirations for children's educational attainments: Relations to parental beliefs and social address variables. *Merrill Palmer Quarterly, 44,* 20-37.

Young, R. (2003). *Postcolonialism: A very short introduction.* Oxford: Oxford University Press.

Zarate, M. (2007). *Understanding Latino parental involvement in education: Perceptions, expectations, and recommendations.* Los Angeles, CA: Tomas Rivera Policy Institute.

Jason Alemán is a Doctoral Candidate in the College of Education at Texas State University-San Marcos. His research agenda focuses on Latino issues in education, educational leadership, and postcolonial theory. Over the past decade, Jason has worked in creating community change and educational equity at the local, state, and national level for major non-profit organizations and foundations. His wealth of experience working with parents, school leaders, district administration, and community partners is the driving force in his attempt to integrate best practices into his emerging research. He can be contacted at akajaysun@yahoo.com.

Chapter 3

The Tears of Tiers: A Leadership Response to Teachers' Challenges with RTI

John M. Palladino

During its February meeting, the school board approved shifting math curriculum, such that eighth graders in my building would now start taking Algebra I as a requirement, including students in our special education programs. I knew the time was ripe for engaging math teachers in professional development decision-making activities throughout the winter and spring months about how to accommodate for middle school special education students' math instruction, starting in grade 6, and monitoring and revising interventions accordingly. I was beyond baffled when teachers solely wanted to simply "drill" elementary level math facts over-and-over to these students, as if they were 2nd graders. They were not ready to embrace the idea of teaching these students grade-level math with simultaneous interventions to address deficit areas. They could not conceptualize the 'why' and 'how' of it all. I knew the essential task before me as their new principal was not to worry about buying the right textbook and other materials, but to lead them through this new view of teaching and inclusion of special education students, while also managing the minute details that frustrate teachers when not in place, like scheduling.

(Andrea, first year middle school principal)

The Response-to-Intervention (RTI) model can help educational leaders like Andrea—whether motivated by a social justice commitment to make schools more inclusive, democratic, and equitable for students with disabilities or by local, state, and national policies that hold educators accountable for the learning of all students—address the needs of struggling learners. The National Center on Response to Intervention (NCRTI) (2010) provides the following technical definition of RTI:

> [RTI] integrates assessment and intervention within a multi-level prevention system to maximize student achievement and to reduce behavioral problems. With RTI, schools use data to identify students at risk for poor learning outcomes, monitor student progress, provide evidence-based interventions and adjust the intensity and nature of those interventions depending on a student's responsiveness, and identify students with learning disabilities or other disabilities. (p. 2)

NCRTI further states that their offered definition "reflects what is current and known from research and evidence-based practice" (p. 2).

In theory, the RTI movement espouses a clear-cut tertiary interventions definition, a cookie-cutter prescription of placing special education and academically at-risk students into tiers or types of interventions based on their academic-behavioral needs. At the lower level of placement, students receive quick, remedial interventions bolstering their skills and knowledge necessary for immediate inclusion within grade-level education. The highest level of placement requires greater amounts and types of interventions, ones that may require the temporary removal of students from general education settings for long-term accommodations and modifications.

Discussions throughout the literature and technical guides depict and describe the degrees of interventions within a triangular model (see Figure 3.1). The illustration shows how educators should target more intense interventions for smaller populations of students as the triangle narrows, thereby creating the notion that certain percentages of students will approximate each intervention tier. Figure 3.1 further displays how the depiction also applies to behavioral interventions. Saeki et al. (2011) reported the possibilities RTI offers:

> Until recently, RTI has been primarily utilized in the academic domain to identify students with specific learning disabilities. However, RTI may also serve as an effective approach for preventing and addressing the social, emotional, and behavioral problems of students who respond to behavioral intervention and therefore do not need more intensive services in special education. (p. 43)

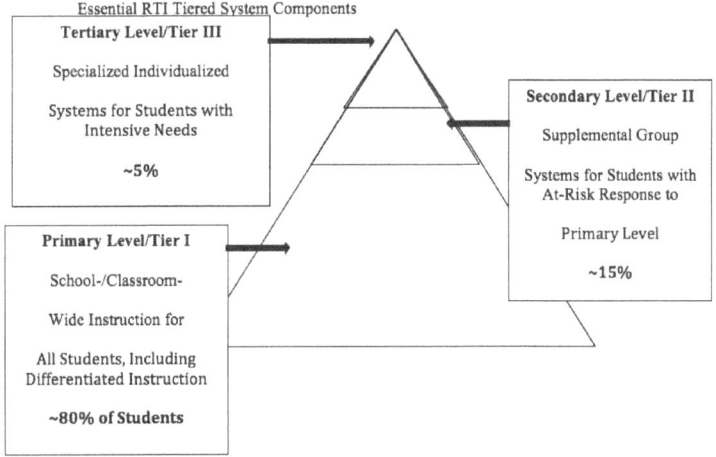

Figure 3.1. Model of the three tiers of interventions associated with Response to Intervention (RTI). Source: Bailey, T. (n.d.). *What is Response to Intervention (RTI?)* (National Center on Response to Intervention Powerpoint Presentation). Retrieved from http://www.rti4success.org/pdf/what_is_rti.pdf

While simplistic in appearance, the RTI triangle appears to have implementation challenges. Namely, the *Individuals with Disabilities Education Act* (IDEA) allows states and districts to adopt a RTI model for identifying and serving students with learning disabilities. In such an arrangement, a student's "disability" would be based on the extent to which she/he could succeed in general education curriculum based on tiered-level interventions, not historical practices of norm-reference testing the student's knowledge and skills. The paradigm shift accentuates students' abilities and strengths versus documenting deficits and shortcomings. However, special education has created a double-edge sword, one that wrangles RTI's intended proactive approach to special education interventions, a shortcoming the RTI Action Network (n.d.) recognized on its own website:

> The RTI movement is enabling public education in the United States to evolve from a reactive model in which students had to seriously deteriorate before being moved on to special education programs, to one that emphasizes early and high-quality research-based interventions in regular programs that generate useful data with which to make key decisions for each struggling student. This evolution, however, has taken place against a backdrop of legal requirements… [and] has many *scratching their heads* (emphasis added) over exactly how the rules fit into the modern intervention era. Both the misconceptions that have become commonplace, as well as the legal disputes created by this juncture, make one wonder whether we truly grasp the fundamental child-find obligation of IDEA in its present context. (para. 1)

Preservice and in-service administrators can find themselves caught in the quagmire of this "head scratching" confusion. Referencing the *A. P. v. Woodstock Board of Education, 2008,* school psychologists, Jacob, Decker, and Hartshorne (2011) pointed out trends developing within the courts that support RTI implementation prior to evaluating a student for special education eligibility. However, the expectation is that schools will monitor students' progress and proceed with an evaluation referral when RTI exposes the potential presence of a disability. Yet, at the same time, the courts have ruled that school districts may not mandate a predetermined number of weeks for their RTI interventions (e.g., 8 weeks) before proceeding with an evaluation referral. Districts must inform parents and legal guardians of their legal rights to challenge RTI timeline decisions. Thus, while the *Individuals with Disabilities Education Act* (IDEA) allows states and districts the option of adopting a RTI model, case law requires that schools choosing to do so must formally evaluate students when their RTI performance indicates a possible disability; further, case law suggests that there can be no hard and fast rules about how long educators should watch and wait for RTI interventions to ameliorate academic challenges. Complying with IDEA and case law can be complex and labyrinthine.

Christopher, a preservice administrator, predicted his struggle to comply with special education law while envisioning a future career as a change-agent principal committed to authentic academic and behavioral interventions for all students through such efforts as RTI, special education populations included:

> Prior to starting my graduate program, I taught 4th grade for 12 years. Every year I had special education students in my classroom. I was forced to make them my first priority. It was not that I wanted to overlook them, but that admins. were always paranoid about a special education student not having his or her IEP up and running. Although I think it's admirable that they adhere to the law and listen

to parents' requests, I resent the fact that we, the staff, never had down-to-Earth discussions about what we *really* should do for these kids. Sometimes we provided services just for the sake of checking-off a list. Rarely did we debate about the ins-and-outs of what we were doing, what we could do. Now, as a future principal, I see myself needing to dot my I's and cross my T's or I'll be out of compliance and in hot water. Why do I get the sense that I have to look at each special education case as a potential lawsuit?

Christopher and other aspirant school administrators must grapple with keeping one foot in the classroom door where RTI will be implemented and the other in the principal's office where it may be legally challenged, as they determine optimal leadership for special education students. The question remains: Where and how should they focus their special education leadership and with whom?

HISTORICAL TRENDS OF PREPARING SCHOOL ADMINISTRATORS FOR SPECIAL EDUCATION LEGAL COMPLIANCE: IMPLICATIONS FOR PRESENT-DAY RTI

For the past twenty years, discussions within the educational leadership literature have offered a skewed emphasis on legal compliance when identifying administrators' roles for special education populations. For example, Hirth and Valesky's (1990) quantitative analysis of school administration graduate programs exposed the philosophy that knowledge of special education law equates with adequate preservice administration preparation for serving special education populations:

> The universities [N=123] reveal that the most prevalent method for obtaining knowledge of special education law is through a general law course. It is disturbing, however, that over 74% of the universities devote 10% or less of class content to special education. (p. 171)

The law-only focus spurred criticism from Sirotnik and Kimball (1994) in a special address in *The Journal of School Leadership*: "Other than brief attention to legal requirements, the array of crucial and continuing issues in special education vis-à-vis general education receives no mention [in the literature]" (p. 600). Likewise, Pazey (1995) argued that the emphasis on special education law impedes ideal practice: "Failures and weaknesses of teachers and students [should be] viewed as opportunities for growth and improvement, not situations which must be highlighted, policed, or punished" (p. 307).

Towards the close of the 1990s and with the 1997 implementation of IDEA, discussions started appearing in the literature about inclusionary practices and ethical leadership responses for special education populations. For example, Quigney (1997) explained that inclusion would require principals "to examine their own belief systems and work toward altering or reinforcing certain core beliefs, such as accepting that children are capable of learning" (p. 62). Goor, Schwenn, and Boyer (1997) created a preservice training model, one that placed special education law as a backdrop for the more important work of identifying essential beliefs about special education populations through professional reflection.

Despite good efforts to change the culture of school leadership for special education, the turn of the century ushered in the reauthorization of IDEA and the *No Child left Behind* (NCLB) legislation and with them came greater emphasis on full inclusion practices and high-stakes testing accountability. Unfortunately, despite espoused intentions of moving away from "mainstreaming" toward broader "inclusion" of all students with disabilities in general education, IDEA and NCLB spurred a greater need for preservice administrators to effectively implement special education law. Davidson and Algozzine (2002) explained: "If a [preservice administrator] believes he or she has the knowledge and understanding of *special education law* (emphasis added) when he or she does not, then his or her rendering of decisions could vastly affect the outcome of services" (p. 47). Once again, the law was understood as the ultimate and necessary foundation for aspirant administrators' "success" with special education population, perhaps more so than actual best practices of special education intervention, teaching, and progress monitoring.

Present day preparation of school administrators must continue the challenge of determining the manner and extent to which special education law permeates throughout preservice curricula. DiPaola and Walther-Thomas's (2003) scholarship validated the need for such a determination: "In many schools, novice administrators are assigned special education as one of their primary responsibilities" (p. 11). Furthermore, if Marshall's (2004) predication has come true, then "educational administrators will [have] essentially [been] repopulated by 2010; tremendous turnover will [have occurred] among practitioners in educational administration in the next decades" (p. 8).

In conclusion, although RTI appears to be a unique and current practice within special education, it is but a new player within the historical debate about how to best prepare school administrators for optimal special education leadership. The years to come will offer hindsight that will expose if the best intentions of RTI had become entangled with and overshadowed by law and compliance. Such an outcome would be a shortcoming, given RTI's potential to encourage purposeful, evidence-based, and success-oriented outcomes for all students. Lashley's (2007) reflection about a tenured career in special education administration offers pertinent insight at the present-day juncture of RTI's implementation throughout the nation's schools:

> A new understanding of the school leader's accountability for the education of all students—an understanding that emerges from the knowledge traditions of special and general education, the provisions of IDEA and NCLB, and the wisdom of practice—is necessary to focus on leadership, not only for school improvement, but for social justice, equity, and democracy in schools. (p. 186)

Throughout the remainder of this chapter, I argue that the constructs of organizational theory provide school administrators the platform from which they could meet Lashley's calls for school improvement and equity on behalf of special education populations, all within the present-day RTI movement. Doing so could offset the default to a legal-only mindset that has historically prevailed with the introduction of new special education policies, mandates, and practices.

THE LENS OF ORGANIZATIONAL THEORY

I spotlight organizational theory as a way to help aspirant administrators delve into the core of "head scratching" that RTI and other related special education initiatives have historically created. Organizational theory focuses an examination of the values and norms that shape administrators' leadership and their ability to create a school culture capable of responding to changes in policies, mandates, and practices. After all, a vibrant and productive school culture is one that allows for survival and adaptation to new ways of functioning while concurrently executing day-to-day operations. Such a perspective of culture mirrors present day special education practice; day-to-day delivery of individualized programs must proceed while simultaneously building an infrastructure of personnel, services, and programs that more fully align with RTI and other evidence-based initiatives. Most important, taking stock of a school's culture forces administrators to seek out, reflect about, and respond to stakeholders' angst and support as change ensues. Schein (2004) articulated a definition of optimal culture applicable to special education leadership:

> The culture of a group is defined as a pattern of shared basic assumptions that was learned by a group as it solved its problems of external adaptation and internal integration, that has worked well enough to be considered valid and, therefore, to be taught to new members as the *correct way to perceive, think, and feel* (emphasis added). (p. 17)

Specifically, Schein's definition hones in on the way a stakeholder perceives, thinks, and feels. Although a continuum of stakeholders exist in all special education matters (e.g., students, teachers, administrators, parents/guardians), I argue that, at present, administrators need to more fully analyze and respond to preservice and in-service teachers' dispositions towards special education populations, a stakeholder group that could catalyze or thwart best intended leadership efforts. A recent graduate student of mine, Brenda, encountered this reality during her first year as a middle school principal:

> "Hatchet!" That is what they [teachers] called me behind my back and some said it to my face. Throughout my interview process, I knew that addressing the achievement gap among special education students was our superintendent's top priority and a major goal the school board had identified because of the state's monitoring of our district's standardized testing performance. I committed the summer prior to my first year to learn more about RTI and to set-up a yearlong professional development program for teachers to get tiered interventions in place. It blew-up in my face! They resisted my efforts, said I was out to fire special education teachers so I could "dump" kids into their classrooms who shouldn't be there. I was flabbergasted! I had to keep telling them that I, too, taught for 20 years and was making my decisions based on what I knew, what I thought was best practices. They called me, "The Hatchet."

The absence of an organizational lens to examine Brenda's experiences results in a depiction that portrays teachers as resistant to what they perceive as a top-down and out-of-touch mandate.

As illustrated in Figure 3.2, an administrator's responsibilities to enforce conformity and compliance with special education law and related district policies can challenge teachers' skewed beliefs regarding special education populations, thereby spurring an administrative response of further enforcement and compliance. Thus, a dysfunctional, vicious cycle plays out, and power struggles further perpetuate the likely outcome of viewing special education negatively.

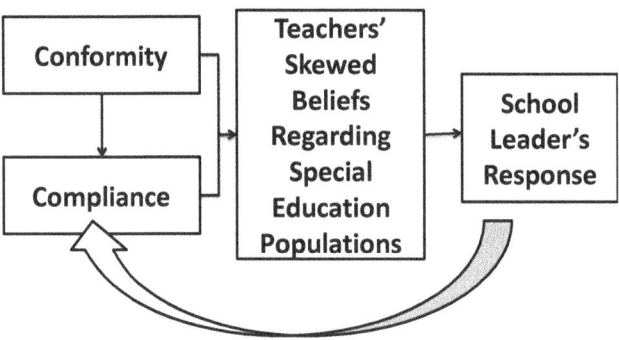

Figure 3.2. Model of how conformity and compliance are typically the starting point for special education programming, which can challenge teachers' beliefs about what should and should not constitute the programming, and thereby forcing an administrative response that usually defaults back to enforcing compliance.

An organizational theory mindset, however, forces a reflective administrator to better understand and honor the core of rifts between administrative requirements and teachers' skepticism. Applying Schein's (2004) organizational theory of culture to Brenda's situation above would outline that teachers must individually and collectively *perceive* Brenda's imposed model of special education/RTI as the correct and best method, *think* that it is their role to develop RTI and related interventions, and *feel* confident so doing. Their personal and professional dispositions are the strongest indicator of how the business of special education will proceed at Brenda's school.

Discussions in the literature articulate what should constitute an ideal teacher disposition for special education: The belief that all students can learn. For example, Reschly and Wood-Garnett (2009) identified three overarching and necessary skills teachers need for the development of such a belief system. First, they need instructional competencies that include in-depth knowledge of content and processes for matching high levels of student engagement with learners' needs. Second, they need classroom organization and behavior management skills necessary for creating positive and effective learning environments. Third, they require problem-solving skills that include the ability to collect and analyze data in order to develop and deliver evidence-based interventions with integrity. Brenda, the ever-cognizant and proactive administrator developed a yearlong professional development program for her teachers to develop such competencies. Yet, despite her purposeful design, teachers balked and confronted her. How did this breakdown occur?

Brenda, like Christopher, predicted that teachers would need "how to" training to best implement RTI. Fault was not in her professional development response. After all, she proposed training that matched best practices reported in the literature and her own classroom teaching experiences. The error resided in the often voiced and practiced assumption within present day administration and teaching that training *about and how to implement* RTI and similar interventions fully addresses teachers' needs. In reality, prior to such training, leaders need to determine teachers' *dispositions toward* the evidence-based intervention movement underway throughout the country and consider them worthy of a leadership response.

For example, on behalf of the National Center for Learning Disabilities (NCLD), Blanton, Pugach, and Florian (2011) co-authored and published a policy brief with the American Association of Colleges for Teacher Education (AACTE) about the preparation of general education teachers to improve the outcomes for students with disabilities. They summarized the problem at-hand that administrators encounter:

> Preparing teachers according to categories of learners such as bilingual, special education, or English language learners reinforces the idea that different groups of teachers are needed for different types of learners and that the normally wide range of students found in so many of today's general education classrooms in the United States cannot be met in the absence of such specialization. As a result, teachers may resist efforts to include students with disabilities—or students who are English language learners, or students who require bilingual education—in their classrooms on the grounds that they are not qualified or sufficiently prepared to teach them. (p. 9)

So whereas administrators endure legal pressures that might stymie and dominate their leadership for special education populations, preservice and in-service teachers typically distance themselves from special education populations altogether. Their cry, as the authors of the policy brief summarized, is, "It's not my job!" (p. 9). The experiences of legal pressure they do report is not so much about compliance, as it is about further justifying why they should not have to teach special education students:

> The pressures teachers feel to "get the job done" in the current accountability climate—in which the stakes keep getting higher for teachers, and international comparisons shape perceptions of how well the nation's schools are preparing students to participate in the global economy—are also factors that affect achievement. One unintended consequence of the pressure to show increased student performance on academic achievement measures has been an increase in the exclusion of students [with disabilities] who do not do well on these measures. (p. 10)

Thus, a need exists for administrative leadership for conformity and compliance with special education law and policy along with honoring and resolving common teacher rejection of responsibility for educating special education populations (see Figure 3.3). In this vain, administrators would not override and squelch teachers' negativity, but examine it, so as to know the best means for addressing it within a school culture perspective. It would force administrators to address what Goffee and Jones (1998) coined as the character of culture.

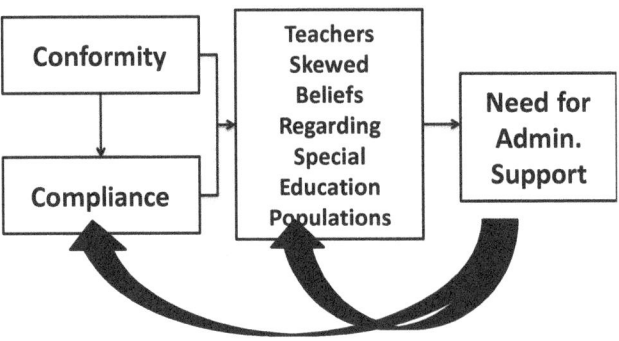

Figure 3.3. A new proposed model for administrative responses to teachers' beliefs about special education should concurrently address compliance while honoring and resolving teachers' dispositions.

THE CHARACTER OF THE CULTURE

Goffee and Jones (1998) explained that two constructs constitute a culture's character: (a) solidarity, the tendency to be like-minded and (b) sociability, the tendency to be friendly to each other. It is what I summarize as, "We are all in this together, and we are all watching each other's back." The character of a culture is a framework that encompasses perceptions, thoughts, and feelings (see Figure 3.4).

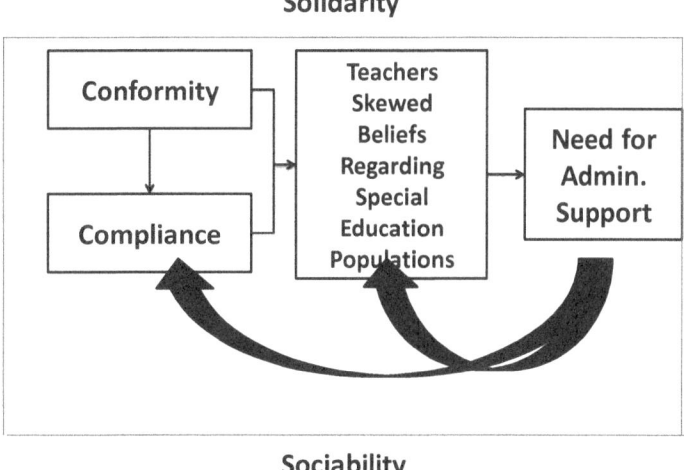

Figure 3.4. Solidarity and sociability are the overarching constructs of a culture's character and should influence all interpretations of teachers' dispositions and administrative responses. Source: Goffee, R., & Jones, G. (1998). *The character of a corporation: How your company's culture can make or break your business.* New York: Harper Business.

Applied to special education leadership, the following questions surface and require a leadership response:

1. In regards to solidarity, does a disconnect exist between administrators' beliefs and those of teachers? To what extent do the duties of an administrator require emphasis on special education compliance versus creating a culture of embracing special education populations?
2. In regards to sociability, does a breakdown in solidarity cause frustration among teachers who are more entrenched with day-to-day instructional delivery than with awareness of administrative compliance responsibilities?

An affirming "yes" to the questions would indicate that a fragmented typology of culture exists (Goffee & Jones, 1998).

Organizational theory teaches us the benefits and shortcomings of identifying typologies. Schein (2004) argued that they "simplify [our] thinking and provide useful categories for sorting out the complexities we must deal with when we confront organizational realities" (p. 175). The author also provided an alternative perspective: "They oversimplify these complexities and may provide us categories that are incorrect in terms of their relevance to what we are trying to understand" (p. 175).

Applied to Brenda's example above, typologies would be unhelpful if the only conclusion to be made pointed out that Brenda was concerned about compliance and the teachers were more entrenched in reality about the challenges a RTI paradigm imposes. In contrast, typographies would be helpful if more in-depth understanding of Brenda's and the teachers' beliefs were to surface. For example:

- Brenda: It appears as if the principal is fully aware (*perception*) of the special education agenda the school board and superintendent have set out for her to follow since day one on the job. It is therefore understandable that she would devote a significant amount of time during the summer preceding her first academic year at the school to plan a detailed professional development sequence for RTI. Her own investment of time to "brush-up" on her knowledge about RTI indicates her professional judgment that the district's movement towards full implementation of RTI is a correct direction (*perception*). The teachers' negative responses caught her off-guard because she sensed (*feeling*) that what she developed for the teachers would be a welcomed professional development sequence given her own, recent classroom teaching experiences.
- The Teachers: The teachers' labeling of the principal as, "Hatchet" most likely exposes the fear (*feeling*) they have about her RTI initiatives as reducing the number of teachers on staff. Their equally harsh comment about "dumping" special education students into their classrooms indicates their view (*perception*) that RTI is not about intervention, but placement. Their overall tone and immediate resistance to change might explain how overwhelmed (*feeling*) they are with day-to-day teaching, especially if the state is monitoring the district's standardized testing scores, which have been poor in recent years.

In Brenda's example, the character of culture that a typology reflection offers is one in which there appears to be a breakdown in both (a) solidarity between the principal and the teachers and (b) sociability from the teachers toward the principal. It does not appear as if the sociability fissure is reciprocal, as indicated by the principal's shock when teachers rejected her efforts and her personal outlook about the district's direction.

The above typographical analysis may or may not be correct. It illustrates one of several ways to ground a special education leadership issue in organizational theory. It is not the sole way to respond, either. For example, an argument could be made that Brenda should reflect about her potential shortcomings in designing a professional development program for teachers she had yet to meet or include in the design; her approach was a top-down one.

Regardless of any shortcoming and alternative perspectives that may exist, a cultural analysis appears to be a paramount quest for today's administrators given the known aforementioned resistance among some teachers towards special education populations. This crisis in education requires a response from multiple stakeholders, including those of us who prepare teachers and design preservice programs for them. Preservice and in-service administrators who only have had special education preparation in the area of law and compliance are not dismissed from playing a vital role, too. Their strengths in understanding the constructs of organizational theory and school culture are most applicable to the decision-making process required for optimal special education service delivery. Schein (2004) succinctly defined the overarching definition of a school culture as "a shared set of assumptions taken for granted" (p. 29). It may not be as necessary for school administrators to know all of the ins-and-outs of special education, as it is for them to account for a school's culture and those within it who may not consciously recognize the strengths and shortcomings of their perceptions, thoughts, and feelings towards teaching special education populations.

CONCLUSION

This chapter's title, "The Tears of Tiers" is based on the RTI Action Network's (n.d.) statement about "scratching heads," as quoted above, along with Blanton, Pugach, and Florian's (2011) co-authored policy brief with the American Association of Colleges for Teacher Education (AACTE). Policy makers and practitioners (teachers) are not in full agreement about current trends in special education service delivery; both sides have expressed, or at least acknowledged, some confusion. The commentary about leadership for special education populations that Andrea, Christopher, Brenda shared and as reported in this chapter mirror the strife discussed in the literature among practitioners.

As a former general education and special education teacher and administrator, I understand the hurt feelings and worries that graduate students share as they launch their administrative careers. I understand the pressure to take immediate action in response to school board and superintendent directives; sometimes, school leaders simply have to "act" for the sake of acting. At the same time, I had to encounter endless questions with negative tones from teachers whom I charged with the task of creating RTI interventions.

The most daunting challenge I encountered was during a five-year tenure as an elementary school principal of a building that had an unforeseen spike in Sudanese refugee student enrollments. The school was located in a community the federal Immigration and Naturalization Services (INS) had not designated for the Sudanese refugees who were welcomed into the United States during the 1990s; thus, we were not prepared for the enrollments. Sudanese refugees self-initiated their relocations throughout the country in pursuit of more stable housing and job opportunities (see Palladino, 2008 for further discussion). The newly enrolled Sudanese students (N=25) had no educational records, lacked confirmed birthdates that could identify grade-level placements, and could not speak or write fluent English. At best, each student had basic conversational English language skills. An apparent need existed for a RTI intervention system that could determine what each student needed to succeed in an American-based educational model. Furthermore, we needed to determine if tier-II RTI was needed to address special education and/or English language intervention needs.

Teachers struggled with the vagueness of the RTI approach I mandated and their uncertainty of knowing *exactly* how to implement tiered interventions for Sudanese refugee students. They wanted a cookie-cutter recipe to follow for potential special education eligibility, which would be inappropriate if the needed intervention was for English language (not a disability) and improper if special education is truly about individualized programming. I knew it was a matter of time before their frustrations would evolve into confrontations similar to ones Brenda faced. I admit my temptation to respond with stern directives to complete the task, and on occasion, it was how I acted in order to curtail the resistance.

I acknowledge that my best leadership for the challenge was when I paused and engaged teachers in dialogue that helped them voice their perceptions, thoughts, and feelings about inheriting the overwhelming task of acclimating 25 refugee students, several of whom had legitimate special education eligibility, and responding with RTI interventions. It was not until then that I could start the process of myth-busting, not to appease me, but to empower teachers' navigation of the many unknowns that they regularly encounter when instructing at-risk populations. Namely, I learned throughout these conversations that teachers perceived the Sudanese youth as temporary citizens. They questioned not the RTI process itself, as I had wrongly interpreted, but rather investing time for an RTI approach with a group of students they considered transient. In turn, I still required adherence to an RTI model, as transient status is not a reason for excluding students from interventions. At the same time, I involved teachers in designing an ongoing professional development program through which we invited government officials and leaders within the Sudanese community to dialogue with us about the long-term plans for the refugee families. Creating opportunities for teachers to voice, confront, and reflect about their perceptions of the refugee process garnered their buy-in for sustained RTI and other interventions for this particular population. Honoring their concerns, insights, and recommendations empowered them to work through the particulars of scheduling and other managerial RTI tasks, and ultimately the teachers cultivated a culture of embracing additional refugee families.

My experience with the Sudanese refugees underscores the importance of leveraging organizational theory and the character of culture for special education leadership because they provide a more accurate way to analyze and understand the rift among teachers and special education (see for example, Earle & Clark, 2001). Equally important, administrators are typically most versed in organizational theory and can use it as a platform of success for their special education leadership despite any shortcomings in their professional experiences and training relative to special education. Organization theory is an essential companion to the current RTI trend of special education, as success for it will depend on a culture of teachers capable of responding to change.

This chapter does not describe the "how to" of organizational leadership. That is, although it provides some insights that administrators might have otherwise not considered, it lacks specific protocol for implementation. How does a school administrator gauge teachers' perceptions, thoughts, and feelings? How do you use and discuss typography language in a faculty meeting? These questions reflect the open-endedness of theories.

I recommend that administrators revisit Figure 3.4 and engage in periodical assessments about teachers' perceptions, thoughts, and feelings regarding special education. It is important to remember that asking teachers to disclose any negative dispositions is often a challenge, especially if they anticipate retribution for their honesty. An administrator might have to arrange alternative and anonymous ways of sharing insights. Examples of how to establish an ongoing culture audit include the following:

1. Begin each faculty meeting with a 10-minute roundtable discussion about the academic and behavioral intervention needs of all at risk-students. Ask volunteers to share comments from the collective discussions. Summarize the responses into categories (e.g., perceptions, thoughts, feelings, solidarity, and sociability). Add administrative reflections, too. Lead a brief discussion about where commonalities do and do not exist among and between teachers and administrators. Identify a short-term and long-term goal to address based on the discussion.
2. Meet with teachers before an upcoming Individualized Education Program (IEP) meeting. Engage in dialogue with them about their beliefs and insights regarding the particular student for whom the team will meet. Help the educators

understand where and how their insights augment or challenge the school's current culture of special education service delivery. Follow-up by debriefing after the IEP and ascertain any changes in perceptions based on the team's discussion of services with parents/guardians and the student.
3. Designate specific times throughout the year to administer an anonymous survey to teachers with questions about their insights and feelings regarding the academic and behavioral intervention needs of all at-risk students.
4. When evaluating a teacher's classroom discussion and engaging in a follow-up meeting to provide constructive feedback, inquire about the thought process in which the teacher engaged as she/he accounted for the academic and behavior intervention needs of any at- risk students in the instruction.
5. Share a monthly report with teachers that summarizes dates and times you devoted to specific special education tasks. Categorize your tasks according to compliance or culture. Help teachers understand that you target your leadership for both compliance and culture matters, and that you are willing to adjust your commitment according to the needs of students, teachers, and other stakeholders.

I further recommend that the academy explore research projects in response to the activities and recommendations in this chapter. For example, a mixed-methods study could quantify the types of comments about special education that teachers report in monthly anonymous surveys and faculty meetings. Follow-up individual and focus group interviews could then discuss the quantitative data and allow the researcher to consider teacher and administrative awareness about the school's overall special education culture amidst day-to-day instruction. A second example would include a yearlong qualitative multiple case study whereby administrators engage in a series of interviews about their special education leadership from teacher in-services before the school year begins through to the end of the school year. The researcher could then note themes that best describe the formation, maintenance, and/or retooling of a school's culture towards special education. Overall, the academy would benefit from new scholarship about organization theory that could complement research about special education compliance.

References

Bailey, T. (n.d.). *What is Response to Intervention (RTI)?* (National Center on Response to Intervention Powerpoint Presentation). Retrieved from http://www.rti4success.org/pdf/what_is_rti.pdf

Blanton, L., Pugach, M., & Florian, L., (2011). *Preparing general education teachers to improve outcomes for students with disabilities.* Washington, DC: American Association of Colleges for Teacher Education (AACTE) & National Center for Learning Disabilities.

Davidson, D., & Algozzine, R. (2002). Administrators' perceptions of special education law. *Journal of Special Education Leadership, 15,* 43-48.

DiPaola, M., & Walther-Thomas, C. (2003). *Principals and special education: The critical role of school leaders.* Gainesville, FL: Center on Personnel Studies in Special Education, University of Florida. Retrieved from http://faculty.ksu.edu.sa/altamimi/Documents/reform%20sp%20ed%201.pdf

Earle, J., & Clark, S. (2001). Lessons learned from special education leadership development knowledge diffusion and schools as organization. *Electronic Journal for Inclusive Education, 1*(4), Article 3. Retrieved from http://corescholar.libraries.wright.edu/ejie/vol1/iss4/3/

Goffee, R., & Jones, G. (1998). *The character of a corporation: How your company's culture can make or break your business.* New York: Harper Business.

Goor, M., Schwenn, J., & Boyer, L. (1997). Preparing principals for leadership in special education. *Intervention in School and Clinic, 32,* 133-141.

Hirth, M., & Valesky, T. (1990). Survey of the states: Special education knowledge requirements for school administrators. *Planning and Changing, 21,* 165-172.

Jacob, S., Decker, D., & Hartshorne, T. (2011). *Ethics and the law for school psychologists.* Hoboken, NJ: Wiley & Sons, Inc.

Lashley, C. (2007). Principal leadership for special education: An ethic framework. *Exceptionality, 15,* 177-187.

Marshall, C. (2004). Social justice challenges to educational administration: Introduction to a special issue. *Educational Administration Quarterly, 40,* 3-13.

National Center on Response to Intervention (2010). *Essential Components of RTI: A close look at Response to Intervention.* United States Department of Education, Office of Special Education Programs: Author. Retrieved from http://www.cldinternational.org/articles/rtiessentialcomponents.pdf

Palladino, J. (2008). Identifying a theoretical perspective to meet the educational needs of twice-migrated Sudanese refugees. *Journal of Ethnographic and Qualitative Research, 2,* 197-204.

Pazey, B. (1995). An essential link for the administration of special education: The ethic of care. *Journal for a Just and Caring Education, 1,* 296-310.

Quigney, T. (1997). Special education and school administrator preparation programs: Finding the missing link. *British Columbia Journal of Special Education, 21,* 59-70.

Reschly, D., & Wood-Garnett, S. (2009). *Teacher preparation for Response to Intervention in middle and high schools.* Washington, DC: National Comprehensive Center for Teacher Quality.

RTI Action Network. (n.d.). *Legal implications of Response to Intervention and special education identification.* Retrieved from http://www.rtinetwork.org/learn/ld/legal-implications-of-response-to-intervention-and-special-education-identification

Saeki, E., Jimerson, S.R., Earhart, J., Hart, S.R., Renshaw, T., Singh, R., & Stewart, K. (2011). Response to Intervention (RtI) in the social, emotional, and behavioral domains: Current challenges and emerging possibilities. *Contemporary School Psychology, 15,* 43-52.

Schein, E. (2004). *Organizational culture and leadership.* San Francisco: Jossey-Bass.

Sirotnik, K., & Kimball, K. (1994). The unspecial place of special education in programs that prepare school administrators. *Journal of School Leadership, 4,* 598-630.

Dr. John M. Palladino is an associate professor in the Department of Special Education at Eastern Michigan University where he instructs in the emotional-behavior management and special education administration programs. He brings to the role experiences as a former teacher and principal. His scholarly passions include addressing the educational plight of youth in foster care, LGBT bullying in schools, and inter-collaborative special education decision-making among administrators, school social workers, and teachers. John can be contacted at john.palladino@emich.edu.

Chapter 4

21st Century Learning: Educating the Whole Brain

Daniel W. Eadens, Susan Ray, Danielle M. Eadens, and *Katherine Shirer*

Academie Da Vinci Charter School for the Arts (ADV), the first charter school in Pinellas County, Florida, uncovered a revelation about the lowest quartile of academic performers on standardized testing that has led to a commitment to training innovations designed to transform teaching methods and shift educational paradigms of stakeholders. Although ADV is currently a High Performing Charter School, the discovery occurred during tutoring of the lowest performers, part of ADV's continuous school improvement efforts. The Instructional Leadership Team (ILT) of practitioner scholars, including ADV's principal, two professors, and an ADV teacher, found that these lowest performing students, who continually struggled to make gains, exhibited characteristics common in visual-spatial learners (VSLs) (Silverman, 2002). Traditional instruction (sequential, detailed, rational, linear, and analytical) was synonymous with torture for these VSLs (simultaneous, big picture, non-linear, instinctive) who frequently disengaged from step-wise instruction (Pink, 2006). This chapter addresses scholarly treatment of the latest neuroscience research and best practice instructional methodology, while using ADV as an example of how student needs can be approached differently in an environment that respects their neurodiversity.

INTRODUCTION AND PROBLEM

Education and neuroscience seem light years apart as fields of study, and yet research in the past three decades has afforded neuroscientists and educators with both the challenge and opportunity to merge these seemingly disparate fields. According to Jensen (2005), "Understanding and applying relevant research about the brain is the single most powerful choice you can make to improve learning" (p. xi).

For many years, posthumous brains donated for research purposes have been anatomized for topography, and hemisections have been minutely dissected, textured, measured, and mapped. When researchers dissected Albert Einstein's brain, in the neocortex of glial cells, they found more possible usage and connections than in any other brain ever studied (Diamond, 1996). With the recent development and expanded usage of Functional Magnetic Resonance Imaging (*f*MRI), neuroscientists are now able to measure and map live neural brain chemical-electrical activity while the whole brain is actually functioning in different tasks such as thinking, feeling, and perceiving. The advent of Structural Magnetic Resonance Imaging (*s*MRI) has enabled neuroscientists to better document details from measuring and mapping exact amounts and topography of living grey matter of all parts of brains, while tracking their chronological development. The field of neuroscience has progressed rapidly. Less than two decades ago, it was widely assumed and accepted that major brain development occurred specifically during infancy; now we are beginning to realize that major brain cognitive and social development continues well into the thirties (Blakemore, 2012a). Additionally, it is now understood that brain cells can regenerate throughout a lifetime (Eriksson et al., 1998). Additionally, neuroscientists have studied the phenomenon of human brain cell "pruning" during primary and adolescent school years and have concluded that reduction in grey matter is visible in *s*MRIs, particularly tapering off during the end of adolescence in many parts of the brain (Blakemore, 2012a, para. 4).

Unfortunately, recent neuroscientific and behavioral research discoveries are not always fully realized, accepted, or actualized by educators. Subsequently, discoveries are not fully capitalized upon by many in education until the discoveries are dated. Cutting-edge brain research could begin to revolutionize the way educators think and use information about cognition, recall, and behavior in regards to teaching methods and classroom management. Neuroscience research is often perceived by educators as interesting and fascinating; however, due to lack of funding, lack of creativity for implementation, or a variety of other reasons, school leaders fail to act and enact lasting instructional reform at the district or school levels. In contrast, in the business sector, the embrace of new technologies, electronic devices, products, and discoveries is viewed as imperative to avoid becoming outdated and defunct. On the contrary, many educators tend to be leery and fail to act quickly with new developments in education, perhaps because they have seen countless "revolutionary" movements come and go. The educator's approach must involve carefully examining and choosing education innovations, beginning to trust neuroscience discoveries about the brain, and broadening knowledge about connections between education and brain research. The neuroscientist's obligation is to inform and package the latest discoveries in a more meaningful and timely way for educators to implement. Conversely, educators' involvement with diverse learners and their expertise at applying a variety of instructional strategies could inform the work of brain researchers. Informed educators, like those at ADV Charter, can greatly enhance and facilitate work with the lowest quartile of academic achievers. The following section highlights the past three decades of neuroscience discoveries that have motivated and influenced the field of education.

NEUROSCIENCE TIMELINE OF DEVELOPMENTS AFFECTING EDUCATORS

In the 1980s, educators and scientists started dialogues about learners and learning. It was during this period that the popular concept of visual-spatial learners emerged, particularly in engineering and gifted instruction. Steven Haas and Linda Silverman became leaders in the field in the 1990s, discussing visual-spatial learners both in the United States and abroad, and began the process of developing the VSL instrument to differentiate visual-spatial learners from auditory-sequential learners. Silverman (1989), a licensed psychologist and director of the Gifted Development Center in Denver,

Colorado, indicated that spatial abilities and visual abilities appear to be highly correlated, particularly in gifted students.

At that time, many other brain-in-education researchers played an integral role in shaping the way that educators and instructional leaders viewed learning differences. In 1997, Freed and Parsons compared some of the traditionally called *right-brain* characteristics in children who were also labeled with attention deficit disorder (ADD), now known as ADHD (Attention Deficit Hyperactivity Disorder). Although researchers continue to debate the actual locations of right/left brain traits and functions, the concept of understanding the unique needs of learners remains the same. Freed and Parsons (1997) focused on two primary types of learners, those who were very visual and seemingly random in intellectual processing of concepts versus those that were more auditory and sequential processors. The researchers also focused on the presence of learners with ADD who fit into this visual category, as also possessing hypersensitivity, powerful memories, perfectionism, competitiveness, self-deprecation, impulsivity, delayed motor skills, intuitiveness, and noted that students with this profile often felt like outcasts from same-age peers. Freed and Parsons (1997) offered prescriptions for teachers of these students that included increased positive reinforcement, high goals, tutoring, a quiet place to work, allowing movement for learning, including materials that are novel and relevant, offering the big picture by directly teaching students how to structure said big picture in their heads, utilizing humor in instruction, using color coding within spelling instruction, playing games to reinforce spelling, whole language reading instruction, oral reading, silent reading, and no timed tests.

At the end of the 20th Century, educational neuroscience continued to support the long-debated claim that development is part nature and part nurture (Sousa, 2005). Kotulak (1997) honed in on this concept, noting that early learning experiences not only influence development of personality and behavior, but also can actually affect intelligence. Kotulak and others (Blake & Gardner, 2007; Donovan, Bransford, & Pellegrino, 2000; Fischer, 2008; Sousa, 2005) pointed out that early language experiences are essential for learning. Studies conducted by Hart and Risley (1995) revealed students growing up in poverty have been exposed to about 30 million less words by age three than children in what researchers term a "professional family." Similarly, Kotulak (1997) went beyond vocabulary in examining the early childhood learning experiences in the home and noted that through the process of pruning, children with fewer experiences and learning stimuli lose up to 25% of the brain's ability to learn and retain information. Furthermore, he concluded that the physical anatomy of the brain is unique in that the process by which cells are pruned or reinforced and connected or nourished is important to one's ability to learn.

Marilee Springer's (1999) *Learning and Memory: The Brain in Action*, offered a refreshingly new perspective on the relationship between neuroscience and education and was one of the first to very effectively and logically combine the latest brain anatomy and neuroscience with memory retrieval, and actual instructional assessment strategies. Springer (1999) agreed that there were as many as a quadrillion neural connections, and furthered that the over 100 billion neurons and glial cells, (i.e., brain cells stored in columns in the upper quadrant of the neocortex, and mostly involved with learning), would lose their connections if not stimulated and nurtured. Impoverished neurons die and are eliminated during neural pruning. More specifically, she described that neurons, consisting of dendrites, a cell body, and the axon do not touch one another, but the messages are sent across a space between neurons called synapses. Chemical neurotransmitters are used in the process of neurons talking to each other through electrical-chemical processes, and Springer elaborated that even though neuron activity is initially electrical, as it travels between neurons, it becomes chemical. Springer (1999) mentioned that the glial cells, the cells that nurture the neurons, are as important as the myelin, which is the fatty substance that continually coats and insulates the axon part of the neuron. The more neurons are reinforced, the more they aid in speeding messaging. The last area to be myelinated is the frontal lobe where the short term memory is housed.

Springer (1999) postulated that students may have difficulty with higher order thinking skills and abstract thinking until they reach a certain age and stage of development. Additionally, she noted that what students eat either facilitates or inhibits a variety of neurotransmitters, including amino acid (Glutamate), monoamines (Catecholamines, Epinephrine, Norepinephrine, Dopamine, Indoleamines, Serotonin, Melatonin) and peptides (Endorphin), in firing and traveling to the correct destination in the brain, all of which can play a role in affecting the intelligence quotient (IQ), emotional quotient (EQ), and behavior. Springer's book identified the three main physical areas of the brain as neocortex (fore), limbic (mid), and stem (hind), and detailed aspects of each section along with the associated lobes of the brain. Most important to education and teaching, Springer (1999) devoted the largest part of her work to describing implicit memory systems including procedural, automatic, and emotional memory lanes, making memories last, memory retrieval, and matching assessments to memory lanes.

Linda Silverman (2002), in modifying her terminology from what had previously been called right-brained thinkers to visual-spatial learners as a more accurate representation of their strengths, contributed to the lay understanding of brain research and its application to education, noting that different learners see the world through their lens-preferred learning strategies. She described visual-spatial learners as *oddballs*, late bloomers, and usually at-risk in school because they operate non-sequentially in a school world designed in a sequential pattern. She claimed visual-spatial students are context-oriented, learn harder tasks while simultaneously struggling with what would appear to be simple tasks, and may stumble to find the right words to communicate what they are trying to say or write. Silverman (1989) further purported that "underachievers appear to be high on visual-spatial tasks and low on auditory sequential items" (p. 1).

Lipman (2003) championed student-centered decision making, believing that every aspect and decision of school must be in the best interest of students' individual and collective successes. For this success to take place, Lipman believed that all instruction must be constructivist. In doing so, a school should develop a community of inquiry, remain sensitive to the problematic, possess reasonableness, maintain and develop relationships, use rational judgments, and encourage critical thinking in the disciplines. These qualities enable both students and teachers to become independent, critical, creative, caring, and reflective thinkers.

Spelke (2008) explored the link between mathematics cognition and music instruction. Building on prior research that established that three core systems reside at the center of mathematical reasoning, researchers tested their hypothesis that learning and/or practicing music triggered these same systems, thus enhancing cognitive capacities. Three experiments were conducted on students, ages 5-17. Each experiment compared students with musical training to children with no specific training or training in other art forms. The first experiment tested against those who had mild to moderate training; the second tested for moderate to intense training in children; and the final tested those with musical training against a group with highly intense training. Each participant was administered six behavioral tests of mathematical and spatial abilities. Findings indicated that "music training is associated with one particular mathematical system: the core system for representing abstract geometry" (Spelke, 2008, p. 46). When musically-trained students' experiment results were compared to students in other forms of the arts (theater, writing, and visual arts), the music students had greater geometrical abilities. Conversely, the results can be linked to studies showing that students with impairments in music cognition likewise have spatial cognition impairments. It was noted that the greatest geometrical association was prevalent only for those students who were engaged in prolonged, intense musical training. Compared to students with little to no musical training, these students improved in "detecting geometric properties of physical forms, relating Euclidean distance to numerical magnitude, and using geometric relationships between forms on a map to locate objects in a larger spatial layout" (p. 18). The findings are important in framing questions about arts instruction. Rather than asking, "Is arts instruction good for children?" the question becomes, "In what ways do arts instruction enhance children's academic abilities, and what brain/cognitive systems are enhanced by training in the arts?" (p. 47).

Similar to Silverman's (2002) notions, Eric Jensen (2005) declared there to be no right or left brain-ness, just preferences towards what was termed learning perspectives. He believed that brain wiring and dominant behaviors are determined by those experiences that were first, occurred most frequently, and those that were the most coherent to the young child. Jensen's conclusion, along with Silverman's, that there is no left or right brain, lingered and has been expanded upon by others (Goleman, 2006; Paget, 2006; Pink, 2006).

In Daniel Pink's (2006), *A Whole New Mind: Why Right-Brainers Will Rule the Future*, he envisioned mind and thought with the future in mind. He compared the skills of what was traditionally termed *left-* versus *right-*brained thinking and noted that much of the East has dominated the work-world and left-brained thinking, with particular focus on the concepts of abundance and automation. According to Pink, there are over a quadrillion guiding connections in a human brain. He concluded:

> With more than three decades of research on the brain's hemispheres, it's possible to distill the findings to four key areas: (1) The left hemisphere controls the right side of the body; the right hemisphere controls the left side of the body. (2) The left hemisphere is sequential; the right hemisphere is simultaneous. (3) The left hemisphere specializes in text; the right hemisphere specializes in context. (4) The left hemisphere analyzes the details; the right hemisphere synthesizes the big picture. (p. 17-22)

Pink (2006) declared that the world needs more right-brained thinkers, i.e., more sensitive, creative, feeling individuals. This position is not unlike Daniel Goleman's (2006) that Emotional Intelligence (EQ) is just as important as Intellectual Quotient (IQ).

In Daniel Goleman's *New York Times* and *Wall Street Journal* bestseller book, *Working with Emotional Intelligence* (1998/2006) he claimed that education and corporate America have valued the teaching and training of cognitive academic skills. The wiring for these skills is primarily housed in the neocortex, a region that is proportionally much larger in the human species than in others. The neocortex typically is accepted as the area of the brain that aids with social interaction, planning, forethought, and inhibitions. Goleman (2006) claims this area has been increasing while EQ has decreased. He went on to say that neuroscientists have determined that this area of the brain in particular undergoes tremendous change in grey matter. According to Blakemore (2012a), this area of the brain contains cell bodies and connections that foster synapses and seem to peak around puberty during early adolescence. In addition to decreases in EQ among many children, Goleman (2006) further asserts that there has been a consistent prolonged ignoring of the mental states and emotional part of the brain, which requires a new model of learning. The EQ part of the brain is an area that builds one's self confidence, empathy, persuasion, self-awareness, motivation, conflict management skills, collaboration, initiative, and adaptation skills, many of which are the top traits companies look for in new hires because these traits foster abilities to synergize others and lead change. Goleman postulated that although EQ skills can be learned at any point in an individual's lifetime, because EQ development requires sustained repetition and practice until it is second nature, there must be a very clear goal and model, and the individual must vehemently want the skills. When IQ increases without EQ increasing, Goleman warned of spikes in violence, dropouts, teen pregnancies, suicides, eating disorders, impulse control issues, anger management issues, and depression—all traceable to a major defect or deficit of EQ. Because EQ is the ability to understand our own emotions and those of people around us, social and emotional intelligence is often times even a better indicator for future success than IQ (Goleman, 2006).

Roy Paget (2006), a neuro-psychologist and leading authority on brain based learning and educational and academic achievements of children, added to the concept of enhancing learning in his work entitled, *The Role of Music in Learning*. He made a bold claim that listening to selected works by Mozart, hence the "Mozart Effect," while actively or passively trying to learn, could measurably increase spatial learning, memory, and reasoning. As part of the reason for the original charter, ADV realized long ago that there are many ways music could increase learning, reasoning, and memory. Paget claimed (2006) that both hemispheres of the brain are utilized to process music and that music "stimulates the limbic system, which . . . is involved in engaging musical and emotional responses. More importantly, research has proven that the limbic part of the brain is responsible for long-term memory" (p. 5). This suggests that when music coincides with information, there is an increased likelihood that the new learning will be translated into long-term memory. A study at the Center for the Neurobiology of Learning and Memory at California's UC Irvine Campus found a nine-point average gain in intelligence test scores after subjects listened to Mozart for ten minutes prior to taking the test (Paget, 2006). Additionally, Paget found that studying while listening to music decreases blood pressure, relaxes muscles, and slows pulse—potentially increasing students' physiological readiness to learn.

In another perspective on learning, Tom Wujec (2009) asserted that instructional leadership should engage teachers in educational professional development that considers neuroscience discoveries. His *TEDTalks: 3 Ways the Brain Creates Meaning*, stated that initially the eyes send information as a series of mental moments and directly fires them to the primary visual cortex, located in the back of the brain that detects shapes and redirects information to other brain areas that are better served to create specific meaning. Wujec (2009) says from there, some information is sent to the left side of the brain and to the ventral stream to determine what something is; this can be thought of as the *what* detector, matching item and word. Another area where information travels, according to Wujec, is known as the dorsal stream, which locates the object in physical body space for a mental mapping. He describes the limbic system, another area where information is activated, as the part of the brain that is associated with feeling and connects strong associations to new material. The many ways individuals process information in these areas affects perception. Based on these findings, he concluded with three recommendations: create connecting and clarifying visuals, make visuals interactive to create engagement, and assist memory with persistent and consistent views. Understanding how students process information may help with better identifying and working with the lowest quartile of academic achievers at many schools, including ADV.

Sarah-Jayne Blakemore (2012b) in her TEDTalk presentation entitled, *The Mysterious Workings of the Adolescent Brain,* agreed with early theorists in regards to synaptic pruning, which is said to occur rapidly around adolescence and involves eliminating and discarding unused and unneeded synapses, thereby offering more strength and reinforcement to relevant in-use synapses. She claimed that the medial prefrontal cortex, which is located in the middle of the cortex and deals with social cognitive activity, as viewed on *f*MRI, is decreasing. This is true particularly during adolescence, perhaps reflecting the notion that adults use different mental strategies than teenagers for behavioral decisions. By mid-adolescence, the potential seems to be there, but the ability to take into account others' perspectives and to inhibit behaviors is still developing, which may explain teenagers' mood swings, risk-taking, impulse control, and self-consciousness. Blakemore (2012b) added that during adolescence, the limbic system, located deep in the middle of the brain, appears to be very sensitive and is still developing with regards to processing the rewards from any motivating activity. This is not so much the case when compared to the brain activity of adults. She also contends the limbic system is associated with long-term memory.

There are many areas and functions of the brain about which we know little. However, most theorists agree that the human brain is malleable during the developmental years and learning, creativity, and social development should be fostered and maximized, not stigmatized (Blakemore, 2012b).

The literature and research on cognition and cognitive practices are now becoming more commonplace as educators and scientists begin to join forces to discover and create best practices for the classroom and to better identify and work with the lowest quartile of academic achievers. Meanwhile, teachers like those at ADV need interpretation, training, and time to assimilate and implement the latest techniques and strategies that will best serve all types of learners. The gaps between neuroscience and education must narrow. This study is one such attempt to connect information and application by unpacking decades of research and creating new methods to serve students, parents, teachers, administrators, and pedagogues.

THE DISCOVERY

ADV, the first charter school in Pinellas County, Florida, has high achievement scores and is capitalizing on current neuroscience research to directly and uniquely benefit students. A group of educators at ADV has pieced together data that may inform neuroscientists and pique the interest of other educators regarding characteristics of students in the lowest quartile on standardized assessments. The discovery has led to a commitment to innovative professional development that has the potential to transform teaching methods.

Academie Da Vinci Charter School for the Arts emphasizes the visual and performing arts while teaching the locally mandated curriculum. One of the fundamental philosophies of the school is the theory of constructivism, and teachers are encouraged to build their standards-based lessons according to this educational philosophy. ADV proudly holds the title of *High Performing Charter School*. The Florida Department of Education recognizes charter schools with this distinction for maintaining high state test scores and having at least three years of financial stability, and authorizes them to replicate at the rate of one school per year. High-performing schools also have greater flexibility to expand grade levels, enrollment capacity, and charter terms, and to consolidate with other high-performing charter schools (Florida Department of Education, 2011). Annually, ADV pre- and post-assesses all students using the national Metropolitan-8 Achievement Test, and each spring administers the Florida Comprehensive Achievement Test (FCAT) to all third, fourth, and fifth grade students. Three years of data for various cohorts were disaggregated by the school's principal for her doctoral dissertation, with particular interest in identifying the lowest quartile of students and their performance over time.

The data revealed that those students situated in the lowest quartile started in that position early in their academic career, some identified as early as kindergarten, and while some remained in the lowest quartile each subsequent year, many of these students had scores all over the map. Immediately after identifying each student, the staff and principal rallied to offer interventions, including extra individual and small group assistance in the classroom and after-school tutoring with a variety of teachers, in an effort to counteract any biases. All students were evaluated and provided with Tier II Response to Intervention (RtI).

During the tutoring and RtI sessions, it was discovered that nearly all of these students were very much visual-spatial learners (VSLs). Traditionally, classroom instruction is taught in a method that focuses on sequential, detail-oriented, rational, linear, analytical learning—techniques synonymous with torture for these VSLs who are more simultaneous, big picture, non-linear, instinctive, and emotional, and who frequently disengaged from step-wise instruction (Pink, 2006). The ADV Instructional Leadership Team (ILT) explored the possibility that these low performing students, whom they knew through various activities and discussions to be bright and uniquely talented, were learners of a different kind. The problem, therefore, was how to get these different kinds of learners to draw upon and apply their skills in standardized assessments, as well as how to train teachers to help these unique learners succeed in the classroom.

CONNECTING THE DOTS

In the winter of 2011, the ADV principal pulled together data from the past three years of Metropolitan-8 Achievement Tests and disaggregated the data by cohorts in order to better identify and work with the lowest quartile of academic achievers. The Metropolitan-8 is administered each fall in mid-September as a pre-test of skills and knowledge in reading/sound and print, mathematics, and language arts. The post-test is administered in mid-May and assesses the same categories.

In reviewing the data as a whole, the scores of students in the top 75% were fairly consistent over time, only varying slightly from year to year. For example, children who scored in the 99th percentile tended to continue to score in that range. At ADV, the top three quartile scores do not reveal the same variability as the scores of the lowest quartile of students. Students in the lowest quartile tended to remain in the lowest quartile over time, but their scores within that quartile tended to bounce considerably from year to year. Additionally, the disaggregated data revealed that the same students who were in the lowest quartile in reading were also in the lowest quartile for mathematics. Even when students made significant gains in reading comprehension through third grade, they continued to struggle with classroom assignments and acceptable performance on measures of reading comprehension. In mathematics, the group showed inconsistent gains and losses, despite intense individual assistance and RtI interventions.

The ADV Instructional Leadership Team (ILT) reviewed these test results in order to better identify and work with the lowest quartile of academic achievers. These students all exhibited unique and special talents in other areas. Some had high emotional quotients and were leaders among their peers, another memorized pages and pages of dialogue for her starring role in a school play, and yet another was an amazing artist. Their problems involved standardized tests and standardized school work. These characteristics are consistent with what Robinson (2011) identified as education's inability to assess the entire range of a student's intellectual abilities. The timed, conventional assessment depends on good short-term memory and tests for strength in memorizing factual knowledge. Robinson asks, "What about the others, whose real interests or abilities lie elsewhere? For them education has always been an alienating experience" (p. 102-103). His question best describes the students in ADV's lowest quartile—students who, by their own admission, feel alienated and at odds with the educational system designed to help them. In fact, our experience indicates that many parents of students who are VSL gravitate towards the arts charter school as they identify it as a good fit for their child.

Identifying and Working with the Lowest Quartile

In January 2012, ADV's Principal, Susan Ray, recruited Katherine Shirer, a Harvard-trained educator and school parent, to meet in small groups and individually with those students exhibiting the greatest problems in school achievement, as part of the school's ongoing efforts to implement effective interventions, especially for the lowest quartile of academic achievers. Later, Shirer and Ray joined with Assistant Professor Daniel Eadens, member of the ILT and ADV parent, along with Professor Danielle Eadens, PTA president, director on the ADV board, and ADV parent, to review all their findings and begin conversations about how the school might use their findings to research and explore grants in order to provide educationally-based assistance to students in the bottom quartile, as well as learn more about students' cognitive strengths and weaknesses. Initially, Shirer focused on several students with reading, writing, and spelling issues that pointed to possible connections with dyslexia. She attended a seminar on dyslexia correction methods advocated by consultant Ronald Davis, in an attempt to learn about alternative options for helping these students, which led her to information about visual-spatial learners.

Ray and Shirer discussed data showing that students who initially score in the lowest quartile perform inconsistently over time but persist in the lowest quartile, regardless of traditional interventions by teachers. Shirer administered running records on a number of the low achieving students and noticed similarities in errors:

> The more I read about visual-spatial learners and meet one-on-one with kids, the more I think your bottom quartile are your strong visual-spatial learners. And maybe ADV attracts some unusually strong visuals because of our mission. I see the same pattern over and over when they read aloud: words, letters and punctuation omitted, altered or substituted; words transposed; slow pace; sometimes poor spelling; distraction, etc. From what I'm reading, these can be associated with strong visual learners and their perception of letters/symbols on a 2-D page. (personal communication, April 10, 2012)

Ray and Shirer began to notice other similarities among low performers. Ray and Shirer compiled a list of the outstanding characteristics of many of these students in the lowest quartile and those students near the boundary of the lowest quartile who struggle academically. Among these characteristics, the most outstanding were as follows:

- Each student missed or mixed up short words in their reading (e.g., the, them, that, those, at, with, or, and) but correctly pronounced and understood longer, more complex words with no trouble or hesitation (e.g., diabolical, congratulations, and salutations).
- Many of the students exhibited a great deal of intensity and sensitivity about how their teachers treated and spoke with them. A single negatively-interpreted remark from a teacher could derail one of these students for the entire day, demotivating him or her to complete any work or focus on instruction. If the music teacher said something the student perceived as negative or critical, the classroom teacher often dealt with the fallout of the student's despondency for the remainder of the day. These intense feelings were often verbally vented in tandem with expressions of low self-esteem.
- Many of the students in the lowest quartile were outwardly-appearing disorganized. Their desks and book bags often were in disarray, causing them to fail to turn in homework and other important paperwork. They often lost pencils, notebooks, assignments, and articles of clothing. Most were self-deprecating about their appearance and their losses, describing themselves as *scatterbrained* or *forgetful*.

- Another commonality of the students in the lowest quartile was each one's ability to excel in another particular area. Student W was an excellent dancer; Student E could write jokes and funny scripts and would perform them during lunch to entertain the entire school; Student R could memorize and recite all the dialogue in a play but could not correctly answer questions about what she had read an hour earlier in her Language Arts textbook. With all their similarities, each student in the lowest quartile was a unique individual. Student H consistently made four errors per paragraph in her reading until she read the book upside down. With the book inverted, she made no reading errors. Student T described how she tucked tidbits of information into various pockets she pictured located all over her body. She had pockets in the back of her hand, in her shoulder, in her knee, and other locations. She worried that when a teacher called on her for information retrieval that she would not be able to find the correct pocket and get the information out quickly. Also, Student M struggled with math but would pen copious pages of stories created on the spot.

Academie Da Vinci Charter School for the Arts classroom teachers were asked in late spring 2012 to complete the Visual Spatial Identifier (Observer Report) on each of their students to identify where students fell on the visual-spatial spectrum. These reports were developed by the Gifted Development Center at the Institute for the Study of Advanced Development in Westminster, Colorado, and the results were tabulated by Shirer. The instrument looked at characteristics including abilities to memorize math facts, spelling, budgeting time, oral expression versus written expression, organization, problem-solving strategies, and others identified by Silverman (1989; 2002). Additionally, students completed self-reports, and parents completed observer reports, which included, amongst other things, items regarding children's experience with homework. The results confirmed speculation that those struggling with the standardized tests administered in reading and math were some of ADV's strongest visual-spatial learners. The overlap between the bottom quartile of test scorers and the top visual-spatial scorers was remarkable—at ADV, 90% of those scoring in the lowest quartile had strong VSL characteristics. These findings warrant further study with larger sample sizes.

  Once the lower quartile were identified and it was noted that they had inconsistent performance over time, the ILT examined possible risk factors the group might have in common. Traditionally, administrators often look at home situations, prior schooling, disability or English Language Learner status, but the ILT also examined learning styles and classroom approaches.

  Following the discovery of these unique learners, and after additional training with the consultant, Shirer began to experiment with instructional strategies, including the use of clay during student tutoring sessions in an attempt to help students create visual representations of the letters and words with which they struggled in their reading and writing. The principal of ADV started targeted professional development with her teachers, providing teachers with resources regarding auditory-sequential versus visual-spatial learning needs, conducting training on how best to serve VSL students, increasing awareness of learning style impact on standardized test performance, and arranging small group discussions on teaching strategies for VSL students. Additionally, she offered information about VSL to interested parents and provided strategies at parent conferences for identified struggling students.

Over the course of this research, the charter school moved into a new building, doubled in size, and hired seven new teachers. The professional development process is an ongoing one, especially with a staff that is more than 50% new to the school. In hiring the new teachers, the principal ensured that they were a good fit with the school philosophy and that they were open to ongoing professional development.

Studying the needs and learning styles of the lowest quartile is beginning to pay dividends in academic achievement. Instead of eliminating the Arts, doubling academic engagement time, or adding more of the same ineffective methods, it will take creative thinking, professional development regarding VSL, support, and examining what actually motivates and demotivates students to learn to help each student to be successful in the school environment.

PRACTITIONER SCHOLARS

The school's ILT, consisting of practitioner scholars including the school's principal, two professors, and an ADV teacher, realized the value of utilizing the latest brain research in regards to VS learning in order to better facilitate and equip the school's administration, teachers, parents, and students to help VS learners excel. Based upon brain research and actualized instructional methods, the ILT plans to further develop a think tank called Da Vinci Center for Integrated Learning, consisting primarily of these same ILT members. The mission of the Center will be to unpack the latest discoveries of neuroscience and related teaching best practices in order to provide strategies for classroom teachers, parents, and administrators to use with visual-spatial and other types of learners. Initially, the Center will focus on training locally, but with grants, hopes to spread its vision, mission, and resources for educators more broadly. The school's principal described related challenges in her unpublished dissertation:

> The school's stakeholders recognize the dichotomy between the uniform requirements of the state and federal accountability systems and the mission of the school (Elmore, 2000), with student success defined contextually (Sergiovanni, 1999). Even fifteen years ago when the school started, of particular concern for the stakeholders was sustaining student engagement in constructivist learning, participation in the arts, and continuous development of creativity, compassion, and critical thinking (Ray, 2012). The stakeholders sought continuous improvement in not only what the students learned, but in how they learned, and who they were becoming in the process (Henderson & Gornick, 2007; Meier, 2004; Noddings, 2003). Achieving that mission means the school's staff must continually explore and apply the best teaching practices for students who, as in most public elementary schools, enter with a variety of experiences, backgrounds, home support, and learning and working preferences. (Ray, 2012, p. 3)

Recognizing these preferences can be the key to unlocking how a student assimilates, processes, and/or retrieves information. Educators have for years touted the benefit of identifying the "learning styles" of their students or determining strengths within "multiple intelligences." However, the recent advances in educational neuroscience within this work reveal the importance of every teacher understanding the nuances of how the brain works in order to tailor instruction for all students. Instructional leaders must remain committed to engaging teachers in ongoing and effective professional development, especially for the lowest quartile of visual-spatial students who may not learn in the traditional ways students are expected to learn. Ray (2012) also pointed out that student achievement is generally defined by standardized test scores:

> The district's general strategy to centralize educational policy has placed the burden of student test achievement on the shoulders of each school. "If policies fail to meet aspirations, the fault can then be attributed not to the policy makers, but to the schools, the teachers, and local authorities" (Hopkins, 2001, p. 3). The county in which Da Vinci is located has inaugurated a plan that started in the 2011 school year: 50% of the teacher summative evaluation is based on students' performance on standardized tests. Those teaching subjects without a year-end state exam are evaluated on how well students score on the FCAT reading tests (Matus, 2010). Schools and their staff are left then with a tension created by opposing paradigms: the standardized management paradigm which asks how do we get the students to pass the tests, and the constructivist best practices paradigm which challenges schools to help students demonstrate knowledge of subject matter and demonstrate understanding that is integrated in personally meaningful democratic self and social understanding (Henderson & Gornik, 2007). Elmore's research (2004) on school change came to the same conclusion: "the fate of educational reform lies largely in the tension between uniform requirements of external accountability systems and the particularities of real schools" (p. 135). Furthermore, Rothstein (2004) concluded standardized tests can indicate, though not with accuracy, if students have mastered basic skills. But, standardized tests "are of little use in assessing other important academic skills like creativity, insight, reasoning, and the application of knowledge to unrehearsed situations – each a part of what a high-quality school should teach" (p. 86). (Ray, 2012, p. 18-19)

Whether teachers are motivated by external or internal accountability systems, it benefits everyone to focus on the learning needs of the students and to be particularly attuned to the learning demands of those students in the lowest quartile, who in the case of Academie Da Vinci, are strong visual-spatial learners. According to Ray (2012), the annual tests administered by each state require students to show evidence of factual knowledge, based on uniformed and systemized goals (Henderson & Gornick, 2007). Elmore's research (2004) revealed that two decades of standardized testing show "students do relatively well on lower-level tests of achievement and cognitive skills, but relatively poorly on tests that require complex reasoning, inference, judgment, and knowledge transfer" (p. 13-14). The type of learning required for standardization is based in direct instruction and rote memorization; those advocating this style are called instructionists (Tobias & Duffy, 2009) and traditionalists (Ravitch, 2000). Conversely, some educators have promoted problem-solving, hands-on learning, and the construction of knowledge from experiential learning that is contextual in nature (i.e., assists learning for that student, in that situation, and applies to his world) (Henderson & Gornick, 2007; Zmuda, Kuklis, & Kline, 2004). Those advocating these types of learning have been termed constructivists (Tobias & Duffy, 2009) and progressives (Ravitch, 2000), and much of what Academie Da Vinci encourages its teachers to do is based on this latter philosophical ideal. The dissonance between these two paradigms creates a constant tension between what federal and state policy dictates through testing, and how many teachers believe students best learn and demonstrate their learning (Good & McCaslin, 2008; Henderson & Gornick, 2007; Ravitch, 2004; Windschitl, 2002). Moving to Common Core standards and the testing that will be affiliated with them will likely result in a continuation of opposing paradigms, depending on the level to which they are implemented as a replacement of current state standards and systems or another paradigm in and of itself.

TIPS FOR PRACTITIONERS

Ideas and strategies that instructional leaders and administrators might consider to proactively enhance academic achievement in their schools include becoming more informed about relevant discoveries in educational neuroscience, learning what motivates visual-spatial learners, and identifying how students learn best. Designating teacher leaders at each school and providing resources and time for individuals to become resident experts with visual-spatial and other unique learning styles, as well as giving opportunities for colleague trainings are also advisable strategies. Additionally, instructional leadership should engage teachers in educational professional development and professional learning networks that consider implementing neuroscience discoveries. Teachers should be provided with numerous opportunities for professional development in instruction of VSLs. Brief vignettes on how brains learn, function, recall, and what facilitates or inhibits learning can be incorporated into faculty meetings. Furthermore, a few, short designated minutes each week for teachers to practice, discuss, and create new techniques for classroom implementation can have positive results. Finally, promoting *what works for our kids* sessions among staff can be very helpful. This strategy provides time to share methods and insights gained about what works best for each unique population.

With initial guidance, a possible goal could be encouraging VSLs to learn about themselves and eventually self-advocate. There are many adaptive teaching techniques for VSLs, such as learning integrated concepts rather than individual disciplines. Implementing differentiated instruction and differentiated assessment are important. For example, when assigning spelling homework, simply offering students a *menu* of options allows specific opportunities for visual-spatial students to study in a manner that is meaningful and supportive. Some examples of this may include color coding segments of words, creating words in clay, and even offering a *free choice* where students themselves can show others exactly how they studied.

Parents of visual spatial students should receive strategies from teachers and administrators. As straightforward as this seems, parents can help their VSLs by encouraging a full understanding of the concept of time, perhaps utilizing various timers in a task analysis approach or helping their child create a mental picture of what will occur if they do not appear on time (Golon, 2004). Simplifying directions, especially in rushed or time-sensitive situations, may be helpful for visual-spatial learners. Likewise, another strategy is to implement a positive behavior support system with child-specific goals (e.g. gets dressed without assistance, studies spelling for 30 minutes, etc.) within a home to strengthen and reinforce needed sequential skills. Of course, being patient, allowing and encouraging the child's creative and visual talents, and celebrating special strengths they bring to the family with their unique vision of the world are useful strategies. Collaboration between students, teachers, parents, guidance counselors, and administration is highly encouraged and usually warmly welcomed.

CONCLUSION

Although those at the forefront of education have historically been sluggish to implement brain research, researchers and scientists in neuroscience could contribute more to the field of education. Conversely, with their plethora of strategies and expertise, teachers have much they could offer to the field of neuroscience. As both fields open themselves to sharing findings, attempting to implement change, and exploring information about students, new and unique discoveries would benefit all stakeholders. With recent developments and expanded use of *f*MRIs and *s*MRIs, neuroscientists are now uniquely positioned to work in tandem with educators to affect pedagogy. Unfortunately, neuroscientific discoveries, and their corresponding behavioral theories, are not always embraced by higher education pedagogues and methodologists. As a result, most classroom teachers are delayed in receiving the newest research translated into related in-service trainings that could be useful in instructional practice. Educators should forge more collaborative relationships with neuroscientists to capitalize on important discoveries and offer unique perspectives to policy makers that could foster beneficial and lasting educational reform.

More study is needed to explore the unique learning styles of visual-spatial learners, particularly to explore the link between underachieving students, visual-spatial learning, and neuroscience research. Due to the fact that many of these students are very uniquely intelligent and should not be overtly compared to a normed group, educators need to join forces and resources to highlight students' powerful talents and strengths. Many of tomorrow's jobs have not been created or even contemplated yet. Pink (2006) describes the needs of our future workforce, proposing that future professions will center upon designing stories, symphonies, and engaging in empathy, playing, finding and creating meaning. Visual-spatial learners are uniquely equipped to do just that. Temple Grandin (2010) beautifully states, "The world needs all kinds of minds." Jensen (2005) points out that "thousands of neuroscience studies are being produced every year, and some of them do apply in the classroom. In the classrooms are millions of teachers who need real-world solutions today, not 50 years from now" (p. 5). It is going to take more efficient and effective communication between both neuroscientists and educational leaders to build the necessary bridges that will synergize their knowledge and experiences to create better learning environments. This will eventually enable VSLs and other unique learners, not unlike the lowest quartile of students at Academie Da Vinci Charter School for the Arts, to understand and process information more effectively, to achieve academically and emotionally, and to become lifelong learners.

References

Blake, P.R. & Gardner, H. (2007). *A first course in mind, brain, and education.* Mind, brain and education, 1:61-65. doi:1111/j. 1751-228X. 2007.000007

Blakemore, S.J. (2012a, June). TEDTalks: A close-up look at the adolescent brain. Retrieved from: http://blog.ted.com/2012/06/27/a-close-up-look-at-the-adolescent-brain-sarah-jayne-blakemore-at-tedglobal2012/

Blakemore, S.J. (2012b, September). TEDTalks: The mysterious workings of the adolescent brain. Retrieved from: http://www.ted.com/talks/sarah_jayne_blakemore_the_mysterious_workings_of_the_adolescent_brain.html

Diamond, M. (1996). *The brain, the mind, and the classroom* (Cassette Recording). Alexandria VA: Association for Supervision and Curriculum.

Donovan, M.S., Bransford, J.D., & Pellegrino, J.W. (Eds.). (2000). *How people learn: mind, brain, experience, and school.* Washington, DC: National Academy Press.

Elmore, R. F. (2004). *School reform from the inside out.* Cambridge, MA: Harvard Education Press.

Eriksson, P. S., Perfilieva, E., Björk-Eriksson, T., Alborn, A., Nordborg, C., Peterson, D., & Gage, F. (1998). Neurogenesis in the adult human hippocampus. *Nature Medicine*, 4(11), 1313 - 1317. doi: 10.1038/3305

Fischer, K.W. (2008). Dynamic cycles of cognitive and brain development: Measuring growth in mind, brain, and education. In A.M. Bratto, K.W. Fischer, & Lena (Eds.) *The educated brain* (pp. 127-150). Cambridge, U.K.: Cambridge University Press

Florida Department of Education (2011*). Florida schools' accountability reports*, 2008-2011. Retrieved January 3, 2012 from: http/:school grades.floe.org/default.asp

Fraenkel, J.R. & Wallen, N.E. (2003). *How to design and evaluate research in education* (5th ed.). New York: McGraw-Hill Higher Education.

Freed, J. & Parsons, L. (1997). *Right-brained children in a left-brained world: Unlocking the potential of your ADD child.* NY: Simon & Schuster.

Goleman, D. (2006). *Emotional intelligence: Why it matters more than IQ.* NY: Bantam Books. Original work published (1998).

Golon, A. S. (2004). *Raising topsy-turvy kids: Successfully parenting your visual-spatial child*, Denver (2004): DeLeon Publishing.

Good, T. L. & McCaslin, M. (2008). What we learned about research on school reform: considerations for practice and policy. *Teachers College Record, 110*(11), 2475-2495.

Grandin, T. (2010, Feb.) TEDTalks: The world needs all kinds of minds. Retrieved from: http://www.ted.com/talks/temple_grandin_the_world_needs_all_kinds_of_minds.html

Hart, B., & Risely, T. (1995). *Meaningful Differences in the Everyday Experiences of Young American Children.* MD: Brookes.

Henderson, J. G. & Gornick, R. (2007). *Transformative curriculum leadership* (3rd ed.). Upper Saddle River, NJ: Pearson Education

Jensen, E. (2005). *Teaching with the brain in mind* (2nd ed.). Alexandria, VA: Association for Supervision and Curriculum Development.
Kotulak, R. (1997). *Inside the brain: Revolutionary discoveries of how the mind works.* MO: Andrews & McMeel.
Lipman, M. (2003). *Thinking in education.* (2nd ed.). NY: Cambridge. University Press
Paget, R. (2006). *The role of music in learning.* UK: BAAT.
Pink, D. (2006). *A whole new mind: Why right-brainers will rule the future.* NY: Riverhead Books.
Ravitch, D. (2000). *Left back: A century of battles over school reform.* New York: Simon & Schuster.
Ravitch, D. (Ed.). (2004). *Brookings papers on education policy: 2005.* Washington, D.C.: Brookings Institution Press.
Ray, S. (2012). *Action research using the advocacy design center process to assess an elementary school.* Unpublished doctoral dissertation. St. John's University, N.Y.
Robinson, K. (2011). *Out of our minds: Learning to be creative.* West Sussex, UK: Capstone.
Silverman, L.K. (1989). *The visual-spatial learner.* Available from Gifted Child Development Center. Denver: The Institute for the Study of Advanced Development.
Silverman, L. K. (2002). *Upside down brilliance: The visual-spatial learner.* Denver: DeLeon Publishing.
Sousa, D. A. (2005). *How the brain learns to read.* Thousand Oaks, CA: Corwin Press.
Spelke, E.S. (2008). Effects of music instruction on developing cognitive systems at the foundations of mathematics and science. *The Dana Consortium report on arts and cognition.*
Springer, M. (1999). *Learning and memory: The brain in action.* Alexandria: ASCD.
Tobias, S., & Duffy, T. M. (2009). *Constructivist instruction: Success or failure?* NY: Routledge.
Windschitl, M. (2002, Summer). Framing constructivism in practice as the negotiation of dilemmas: An analysis of the conceptual, pedagogical, cultural, and political challenges facing teachers. *Review of Educational Research, 72*(2), 131-175.
Wujec, T. (2009, July). TEDTalks: *3 ways the brain creates meaning.* Retrieved from: http://www.ted.com/talks/lang/en/tom_wujec_on_3_ways_the_brain_creates_mea ning.html
Zmuda, A., Kuklis, R. & Kline, E. (2004). *Transforming schools: Creating a culture of continuous improvement.* Alexandria, Virginia: ASCD.

Daniel W. Eadens, Ed.D., is currently an Assistant Professor of Educational Leadership and School Counseling at the University of Southern Mississippi. He was named 'Runner-Up Teacher of the Year' his first year of public school teaching, was one of five public school Florida teachers to win a 1997 Japan Fulbright, was a secondary Special Education teacher, and has served as an administrator at different locations. He graduated Magna Cum Laude with a BSME, M.Ed., and Ed.D. from the University of South Florida and is a retired Army Major with foreign service in Japan and a combat tour teaching the New Iraqi Army. In 2011, he was named the ELSC's recipient of the Hampton E.

Williams 'Research Award' and the Jack Mulcahy Award for 'Best Doctoral Dissertation', presented by The Association for the Advancement of Educational. Dr. Eadens passionately researches Special Education, Visual-Spatial Learning, Brain Research, Graduate Reform, and Shared Leadership and continues scholarly publications and research presentations in the region, nationally, and inter-nationally. He can be contacted at Daniel.Eadens@usm.edu,

Susan E. Ray, Ed.D., is the principal at Academie Da Vinci Charter School for the Arts in Dunedin, Florida. Prior to that, Dr. Ray worked in high-needs districts in Long Island, N.Y. and Durham, N.C. as a teacher and school administrator. In 2000, she received a fellowship and taught at Kamuzu College, in Lilongwe, Malawi, Africa. She is devoted to helping students who learn differently, particularly those exhibiting visual-spatial preferences. Dr. Ray holds a doctorate from St. John's University, Queens, N.Y. in Educational Administration and Supervision, a Master's in Educational Administration from The College of New Rochelle, N.Y, and Master's and Bachelor's in Education from Florida State University. She can be contacted at
c.rays@pcsb.org.

Danielle M. Eadens, Ph.D., is a Professor of Exceptional Student Education at St. Petersburg College. She has worked grant-funded course development projects in Autism and Exceptional Student Education, volunteers and serves on the board of directors of Academie Da Vinci, and serves on Pinellas County School's Exceptional Student Education Advisory Board. Dr. Eadens holds an Interdisciplinary Education doctorate, Special Education masters, and Mass Communications bachelor degree from the University of South Florida. She served in a high needs public school as a Special Educator in inclusive and self-contained settings and was involved in Special Olympics, Technology and Journalism training and instruction, and was Multiple-Year Grant winner. Dr. Eadens specializes in Interdisciplinary education, Social Justice education, Visual-Spatial learning, and Sensory Processing disorders. She can be contacted at eadens.danielle@spcollege.edu.

Katherine Hubbard Shirer's passion is reaching struggling students with Visual-Spatial learning methods. She holds an Ed.M. in Administration, Planning and Social Policy from Harvard University and a B.A. in Foreign Affairs from the University of Virginia. She has served on admissions committees at Harvard University and Wellesley College, worked at Academie Da Vinci Charter School for the Arts as an Interventionist and a Classroom Teacher, founded a non-profit organization dedicated to the welfare of mothers and their young children, managed International Education programs, handled education issues for a member of Congress, and has volunteered countless hours in schools, including being a board member of an independent school. She can be contacted at katherine.shirer@gmail.com.

Part 2

Rethinking Teacher Work

Chapter 5

When Teachers Find their Voice

Barbara A. Klocko and *Caryn M. Wells*

Some of the most profound experiences in our professional careers have been as teacher leaders, first in the classroom, then rising through the leadership ranks of public schools, and lastly, teaching teacher leaders at the university level. By means of introduction, we are professors in educational leadership programs who have enjoyed educational career transitions that have ranged from classroom teachers, to administrators, to college professors.

Barbara has experience as an art teacher, assistant high school principal, and building principal in an elementary school, as well as central office positions including director of early childhood programs, director of special programs, and director of administrative services. Caryn was a teacher of English, counselor, assistant principal and principal, all at the high school level. We teach courses in educational leadership and teacher leadership and conduct research studies of teacher leadership, exploring how principals and superintendents feel about teachers as leaders. The research affords us an interesting look at teacher leadership—how leaders view the contributions of teachers and how they may be working to cultivate teachers as leaders. Our work as professors affords us an ongoing and rich observation of the growth of teachers as leaders, and some privileged insights about their feelings during this growth.

As principals encourage their teachers to lead and develop their own professional voice, teacher leadership grows. Ayers and Sommers (2009) noted, "It is leadership that an organization must have, not a single leader. In the most robust and resilient organizations, anyone can step forward to provide leadership when that individual is best positioned and best equipped" (p. xxi).

In this chapter we share our reflections as practitioner scholars who are leading the efforts to develop the leadership skills of teachers. We share our insights and observations of teacher leaders and highlight their insights and observations as teacher leaders. They tell the important story of the transformational changes in their lives as they sought to find their voice as a teacher leader. In this chapter we relate personal narratives as we have watched teacher growth and development while teaching in the teacher leadership program; some of the stories are from our notes and recollections and others are a result of the written narratives that teachers have shared with us. We are fortunate to witness what actually occurs during the transformation of teachers to teacher leaders. As practitioners we understand the value of the study of practice; as professors we understand Lewin's (1945, 1951) cogent argument that there is nothing quite as practical as good theory.

In understanding the transformation to teacher leadership, we discovered five distinct platforms inherent in actual practice that inform our work as professors and researchers. The first platform is one of *reflection*, with teachers inquiring about who they are as teachers and what it means to be a teacher leader. The second platform highlights *culture*, the inherent way of doing business in the entrenched history of the school. Third, we consider *power and authority*, new designations of either formal roles or the informal or organic leadership teachers experienced while in the teacher leadership programs. The fourth platform is *instructional leadership* where we integrate and compare the concepts of instruction that are central to preservice education with instructional leadership skills that are foundational to educational leadership preparation. And finally, we reflect upon *influence*, how teachers get influence and how they can use this influence constructively to improve instruction and student achievement, by collaborating with colleagues in their building or district.

We share the stories of those teachers who stepped forward to provide leadership. It is a script told through the eyes of teacher leaders who have a strong commitment to teacher quality and a determination to extend the power of teacher reflection and collaboration throughout their schools.

REFLECTION: WHAT IS TEACHER LEADERSHIP? AM I A TEACHER LEADER?

As we reflect about what happens with the growth of teachers as leaders, teacher leaders' candor and emotions consistently strike us. Essentially, they reflect about themselves as teachers and leaders—how they relate their feelings, concerns, worries, and tensions in attempting new roles. Initially, teachers enter teacher leadership programs with one compelling question: *What is teacher leadership?* Teachers are not always sure whether they have advanced to the level of teacher leader, since it is not a formal category in most schools. In general there is a lack of understanding as to what teacher leadership even means, and more specifically, teachers wonder, "Am I a teacher leader?" "And Who are the teacher leaders?" For many reasons, the teachers who enter our teacher leadership programs come with myriad questions as to what exactly is meant by the term *teacher leader*. For one, the term, teacher leader is not typically used within the school to describe the various roles that teacher leaders enact—roles such as department chair, lead teacher, technology specialist, or literary coach. This often creates ambiguity and confusion. Teachers in our programs ask,

> Do I need to have a particular job title, such as literary coach, to be a teacher leader? Am I a teacher leader if I have no other formal title but I do some of the things that are beyond being in my classroom as a teacher? For example, I am helping a new teacher learn the curriculum even though I have no job title that acknowledges it. Is this what teacher leaders do?

Additionally, there is confusion regarding the distinction between leaders who are teachers and leaders who are administrators, often prompting the question whether teacher leaders are quasi-administrators. Consequently, some of the questions or confusion relates to the dichotomy of formal versus informal roles that teachers enact; other issues relate to the blending of shared responsibilities that can occur when authority is shared within a school. Finally, teachers seek clarification as to what leadership is all about, particularly since many teachers have not had formal leadership training.

The concept of teacher leadership continues to evolve as external pressures for schools to perform with greater success and accountability grow. While the interest in teacher leadership continues to grow, the definition of just what constitutes *teacher leadership* remains somewhat elusive. York-Barr and Duke (2004) reported their findings from two decades of research about teacher leadership and concluded:

> After reflecting on the literature as a whole, we suggest that teacher leadership is the process by which teachers, individually or collectively, influence their colleagues, principals, and other members of school communities to improve teaching and learning practices with the aim of increased student learning and achievement. (p. 287-288)

This definition of teacher leadership clearly characterizes the scope of teacher performances, with an emphasis on the power of influence to create the capacities to effect changes that result in improved student achievement. Influence has several connotations; it refers to the power that exists within the system to provide for interrelatedness of structures and people. While traditional authority will outrank some influence in certain specific administrative functions, it is true that the informal influence that teachers may exhibit can be deeper and more consequential to change the culture of a school. Ultimately, there is a need for a collaborative voice from teacher leaders and administrators to influence school culture, policies, and practices, as opposed to a dichotomy of formal vs. formal roles and traditions. Ultimately, it is a systems approach to change that allows us to review how people within districts function together to share leadership, develop professional voice, and increase their motivation and capacity to lead in order to support student learning.

The majority of the teachers in teacher leadership programs shared that they did not feel as though they were actually teacher leaders, describing instead, a hierarchical system that honors seniority with job placements and important decision-making in their schools. However, as teachers advanced within teacher leadership degree programs, the tone and tenor of their reflections began to change. The teachers shared their victories with trying new teaching strategies, learning how to more effectively teach and measure student learning, and how to more effectively navigate the political terrain of their school with all its complexity. *They were finding their voice.*

Teachers also reflected about the connection between their confidence level and their practice, noting that once their confidence increased, they felt compelled to try new methods and came to view their classrooms as places for deep inquiry and analysis. Teachers revealed that the safe environment of the teacher leadership program provided an ideal format for sharing questions and concerns about instructional practices, resolving issues together, and most importantly, learning from each other. In this sense, the teacher leadership classroom became a safe place for teachers to raise concerns and discuss personnel issues that they might not feel safe to discuss in their home school environment. Our teacher leadership curriculum is deliberately constructed to be teacher focused, rather than instructor led.

The issue of teacher leadership is not a new concept. The roots for empowering teachers in leadership roles were grounded in the reform movement of the 1980s (York-Barr & Duke, 2004). Teachers have long been involved as department chairs, grade level leaders, union representatives, literacy coaches, and various other appointed positions. We share the personal journey that we made as we experienced the various roles and opportunities as referred by York-Barr and Duke:

Barbara: I loved being "The Art Teacher." I loved my students, I loved the culture and climate of my classroom, and I loved the creative energy that I was able to experience every day. I loved watching students swell with pride when they completed a project that exceeded the boundaries of their expectations. So, why did I get the notion that I belonged in the office? After about five years of teaching, I started thinking and acting in a more collaborative, global way, long before terms like professional learning communities or teacher leadership were in vogue. I served as the school improvement steering committee chair when school improvement teams were first required by state law. I was a department chair (of the non-departments). I edited the school district newsletter, which incidentally means that you do very little editing and lots of writing and taking photos yourself. I assisted the superintendent in successful bond campaigns. All this while still loving life as "The Art Teacher."

One day the assistant superintendent came to my door between classes and asked if I'd be interested in an administrative position in the high school for the upcoming year. Had he recognized the collaborative contributions I had made to the school? That was unlikely, as I was convinced that somewhere along the line I would save the school district money, or it might be a chance to cut back the art department, or there was some other hidden agenda. I didn't know for sure, but without hesitation, in those life-changing four minutes of passing time, I said, "Sure," never interviewed, and set off on my administrative career, always placing teachers and student achievement at the center of my focus. I often wonder now whether I was a teacher leader in those days by York-Barr and Duke's definition, or was I simply preparing myself to climb the rungs of the established hierarchy? In the 1980s, the question wasn't firmly placed on anyone's radar yet.

Caryn: I loved being a teacher, which was probably what inspired me to return to teaching at the university level. I began my career as a teacher of high school English, enjoying every class with the excitement of hopefully building a bridge for students to love English language and literature. In my first year of teaching I was asked to be the chair of the English department, really by default because others had decided not to serve in that capacity. While I found the expectation overwhelming as a new teacher, it gave me the chance to organize at another level, and I found a group of committed teachers who were interested in teaching in their own rooms as opposed to leading or collaborating. Was I a teacher leader? At the time I did not consider the term 'teacher leader,' but I was excited to be making an important contribution to the department. It was in my second assignment of being a counselor that I thought more about being a leader in the school. As a counselor I was able to work on behalf of several teachers and to advocate for students. Suddenly I was involved with problem resolution, disputes between teachers and students, scheduling, and contact with myriad social agencies. I was definitely a teacher leader, and it was in the role of counselor that I knew I wanted to continue with the training that would allow me to work in an official capacity as an administrator. One day the principal of my school asked me to lead a group of teachers in professional development and then report back to the larger audience of teachers. I recall this opportunity as a distinct time where I felt recognized and appreciated as a leader within the school, something I vowed that I would offer to others should I ever be in the position of school leadership.

It is clear that our growth in developing leadership skills mirrored what we were hearing from our students. We found opportunities to lead, sometimes through default, and other times by being tapped on the shoulder and asked to serve, with or without formal title.

CULTURE: TEACHER LEADERS AS THE CATALYST FOR CHANGE

The work of teacher leaders is examined not only for the contributions that they bring to the benefit of student achievement, but for the possibilities of how teacher leaders might provide a new sense of balance to the often chaotic schoolhouse and how they can moderate perceptions and attitudes about teachers. "Within every school there is a sleeping giant of teacher leadership, which can be a strong catalyst for making change" (Katzenmeyer & Moller, 2001, p. 2). In order to create this change, the culture of the school must accept teachers as leaders, and the old practice of teachers working in isolation must be replaced with new norms of collaboration and teamwork.

Teacher leaders learn early to objectively assess the culture of their schools and their classrooms through the curriculum of the teacher leadership program. The observations they revealed in class were shared within the context of their new understanding of the political culture and history of their schools. Most teachers expressed that they were aware of the undercurrent of their schools but did not have the level of analysis to fully understand the culture of the school. Many teachers discussed the level of frustration they felt in trying to impact a strongly entrenched school culture. Teacher leaders generally concluded that their school's culture was not collaborative, where teachers share information that would help them with instruction or learning. Teachers also indicated that their school culture was not tightly focused on student learning and that their colleagues felt the responsibility for learning belonged to the students, rather than a shared enterprise with the teacher. Some teacher leaders revealed that their school cultures were more harmonious than others, but there was widespread agreement that the school was not tightly focused on issues of instruction and learning.

The majority of teachers in our classrooms also believed strongly that they work in schools where the older or more experienced teachers are not as interested in new teaching techniques. In fact, many of the teachers discussed how they deliberately avoided veteran teachers who might not share their interests or tendency to try new teaching or technological techniques. Some of the teachers indicated that they had been 'forced' to work with teachers in their school and that they were carefully broaching subjects with their colleagues. One optimistic teacher leader expressed concern for the way in which she would approach her colleagues, "I hope I can work with my colleagues to create a culture we want at our school." Another teacher remarked, "I intend to continue to grow in stepping up in my school and becoming more of a teacher leader... Since I started in this program, my principal has begun to offer me many leadership opportunities in my school."

The teachers in the teacher leadership program have assignments that required them to confer with their principals. This deliberate act of consultation allows teachers to have a different relationship with the principal and also allows for the principal to see the potential that the teacher had to offer the school. This deliberate act of consulting is one of the main methods that works to change the perceived status of the teacher and the culture of the school. As teachers in the program are asked to present information to their colleagues, they discover a new source of acknowledgment, and while these acts may not always be met with approval from other teachers, they served to be productive training in learning how to navigate the complex political terrain of the school.

The teachers learned how to present information fairly and objectively, and also to engage in conversations that might be potentially conflicting or controversial. This skill development for teacher leaders underscores the context of understanding educational change, as opposed to maintaining the status quo of the school. We are deliberate in choosing assignments that are field-based where the teachers can practice the skills of learning how to improve their craft of teaching, to lead, to influence, and to orchestrate change in the schools. We are dedicated to teacher involvement in educational change, as opposed to being bystanders who watch as change happens.

In practice, educational reforms are often top-down mandates that fail to generate the desired results and are a hindrance to increased teacher performance and an obstacle to sustained teacher leadership. While the notion that educational reform can be created by the acceptance of the teacher as leader seems credible, only recently has there been research conducted to examine this relationship (Lambert, 1998; Murphy, 2005).

Some teachers are searching for validation of teaching as a career choice. The momentum created by teacher leaders not only improves their practice, but also the performance of their peers. Additionally, teacher expertise can bring about improvements in student achievement (Mullen & Hutinger, 2008; Ogawa & Bossert, 1995; Smylie & Denny, 1990; Spillane, 2006).

Negative peer pressure continues to be a major barrier to the emergence of teacher leadership. One principal observed that teachers who assumed leadership roles often experienced a "sense of separation from teaching colleagues" and "perception by peers as being arrogant or seeming superior." A teacher leader agreed, noting, "Peers will put you down – almost sabotage your efforts." Additionally, the leader noted disparagingly, "You are a suck-up if you take a leadership role. You become one of *them*."

Teachers experience an incredible sense of freedom to exercise authority within the teacher leadership programs. These teachers expressed repeatedly how they felt they could truly be themselves -- honestly and openly expressing what they felt. As such, they developed their own sense of authority and power within their teacher leadership program. Some of the sense of power gained from a learning community developed in the classroom can be understood by this quote from a teacher leadership student, "I would have to say that my biggest gain is learning from my classmates. I truly appreciate their thoughts and the knowledge they shared with the cohort."

We observed an entire range of emotions as the teachers in the teacher leadership program began to be more reflective about their school cultures, their place in the context of the school, and their interest in trying new roles of greater authority. We observed situations where some teachers decided to hold back from "putting their necks out there" as they described, after experiencing pushback from teachers or principals. We also witnessed a gradual growth in teacher experimentation, fostered by the encouragement they felt from the teachers who were in the teacher leadership program with them.

POWER AND AUTHORITY: EXPANDING THE ROLE OF OF SCHOOL LEADERSHIP

As teachers expand their leadership in the schools, the balance of leadership with the principal may undergo change. There can and must be a relationship between teacher leaders and those traditionally responsible for providing leadership. Teacher leadership initiatives are correlated with improved quality (Katzenmeyer & Moller, 2001), with new and expanded formal and informal roles that may impact the balance of power with the principal (Smylie & Denny, 1990). Teachers in the teacher leadership program often described their tenuous relationship with their principals, especially considering that these principals were responsible for evaluating their teaching performance. Many of the teachers in the program were in the process of earning tenure and the issue of principal evaluation was a critical one. Many of the less experienced teachers were concerned with the power and authority of the principals in the building, aware of the balance of these roles and their 'place' with more senior teachers.

Traditionally, power and authority in schools were established and endorsed in many of the roles and tasks of teachers. The distribution of tasks and roles of the teachers with whom we worked, were typically assigned to delegated roles such as department chairs, grade level leaders, literacy coaches, or technology specialists. The power designation was made evident by the principal, with tasks and roles that have been in place as past practice and those negotiated and guaranteed by the contract.

Schools have historically embraced the traditional stratified view of leadership, which assumes a fundamental divide between the service delivery role of teachers and the leadership role of administrators. Following the *Nation at Risk* report of 1983, the emphasis on student achievement took a dominant role in conversations about improving schools. Despite national headlines, analysts have pointed to the resistance that often followed efforts to reform schools (Elmore, 2004). Sarason (1971) analyzed the relationship between the culture of the school and the change process stressed the need to share leadership and address pervasive barriers to change. The culture of the school proved to be an impediment to the changes the teachers in the program wanted to embrace, with varying concepts that ranged from technology to teaching practices.

The majority of teacher leaders expressed concern that they not go against the system that was firmly in place, so they described activities that were "under the radar" and not openly discussed. For example, many of the teacher leaders described working together with other younger or less experienced teachers where they felt they could be more authentic and less cautious about confronting the status quo. These teachers expressed concerns that they not alienate themselves from the more experienced faculty. In general, teacher leaders carefully volunteered to assist in the various school improvement activities that would not put themselves in a position of vulnerability. For example, teacher leaders rightly asserted that it was critical to not be put into a position where they would openly oppose the various traditions or philosophies of the school. One instance involved a teacher's decision not to openly oppose an idea that she personally did not support. She contended that it was not worth the pushback that she perceived was imminent because of her opposition. Another teacher revealed how he was asked by his principal to teach veteran teachers in his grade level to use the technology that he was using. When he shared that this was not a comfortable situation for him, the principal agreed and assigned him to instructional coaching responsibilities with the teachers in the grade level below.

In the words of a teacher who was asserting herself as a teacher leader, "I am no longer going to sit back and just listen to what other teachers in our building say. I now stand up and ask my questions and show what I am doing because I can back [it] up." Another teacher concurred, "Next year I would like to get on a couple of committees and give myself a new perspective and a bigger voice." The teachers talked in class about the strategies they tried to offer—the changes that could make a difference in the school, ones that would not alienate them from other teachers—while trying to be true to their convictions about changes that needed to occur in the school.

The teachers in our programs referred to the balance of power in their schools and their plans for participating in new and expanded positions of authority and decision-making. According to aspiring leaders, they need more opportunities to develop strategies for creating collaborative cultures, inclusive decision-making, effective teams, and focused school improvement plans. Moreover, aspiring leaders need to acquire the tools necessary to confront colleagues who are trapped in the *us vs. them* paradigm. Teachers must receive the support necessary to become the kind of school-based leader that Barth (2001) appropriately described:

> When teachers lock their cars in the parking lot each morning, too many of them also lock up astonishing skills, interest, abilities and potential. They then go inside and teach five classes of beginning algebra and monitor the lunchroom. To be sure teaching algebra is critical to the school, and so is the fulfillment of supervisory duties. Yet an opportunity resides within each of those 2.2 million new teachers, and within the veterans as well, to become far more than "just a teacher" at a school whose only leader resides down the hall in the principal's office. Each of these teachers can become—and must become—a school-based leader and thereby a school-based reformer. For only when we transform and re-create the teaching profession in this way will we be able to transform and recreate the nation's schools. (p. 116)

It's all about leadership and lifting the voice of the teacher. One important lesson that we have learned was that you cannot send a changed teacher back into an unchanged school as one teacher leader noted:

I went to this teacher leadership seminar, and I was all pumped up. I thought that finally somebody understood how important the things are that I do and think about every day. When I came back to my school, however, I couldn't find the energy and enthusiasm that I had just the day before. As a preschool teacher, I was still the outcast of the school and especially the kindergarten wing. I didn't have the opportunity to engage in school improvement or even to join in the casual conversations in the hallway. One of the teachers even asked me to remember to keep my door closed so that my babies wouldn't disturb the real learning that was happening in her classroom. I felt frustrated and alone, and collaboration seemed like an impossible dream.

Educating in a democracy requires not only building the capacity of the teacher to lead; it requires systemic change that transforms schools from hierarchies to communities (Murphy, 2005). This transformation is neither easy nor immediate. As principals consider new possibilities for teacher leadership, the tensions and ambiguities that exist will need to be evaluated and negotiated (Smylie & Denny, 1990).

At one small urban district, stakeholders found their voice through a two-year collaborative leadership initiative that involved monthly Saturday meetings intended to help this small, struggling school district grow its leadership from its ranks (Maxfield & Klocko, 2010). From this initiative emerged three values upon which to reframe school culture:

- *Cherish your history;* don't be controlled by it. Create stronger networks; be willing to abandon previous grievances; and involve community members, senior citizens and retirees as full stakeholders.
- Understand and embrace the notion that *People Matter.* Build Relationships; support leaders as they attempt to integrate new ideas into their schools and classrooms; and share best practices.
- *Honor differences.* Develop and encourage ongoing diversity projects to gain valuable understanding to address institutional lack of preparedness to meet the challenges posed by changing demographics and the socio-economic make-up of students; conduct a culture audit to recognize specific diversity issues that contribute to school climate; and most importantly, be willing to change. "We definitely have students that are high need—high need as far as they don't need a lot, but they need it often and different." (p. 21)

INSTRUCTIONAL LEADERSHIP: THE ESSENTIAL CORE OF TEACHER LEADERSHIP

Teacher leadership offers possibilities for growth and change in schools and may impact teacher effectiveness and student achievement in meaningful ways (Cochran-Smith & Lytle, 1999; Lambert, 2003; Silva, Gimbert, & Nolan, 2000; Smylie & Denny, 1990; York-Barr & Duke, 2004). As director of the Harvard Principals Center, Barth (2001) stressed the importance of shared leadership to systematically improve schools from within. Fullan (2001), Lieberman and Miller (2004), DuFour and Eaker (1998), and others have argued that the complex process of school improvement will be successful only if it involves the major stakeholders throughout the organization. Lieberman and Miller (2004) recognized the importance of shared leadership in improving student achievement:

> Teacher leaders are in a unique position to make change happen. They are close to the ground and have the knowledge and ability to control the conditions for teaching and learning in schools and classrooms. We believe that they are critical partners in transforming schooling. (p. 12)

Elmore (2006) reaffirmed the vital role of teachers in the school improvement process when he cautioned:

> ...one does not "control" school improvement processes so much as one guides them and provides direction for them, since most of the knowledge required for improvement must inevitably reside in the people who deliver instruction not in the people who manage them. (p.58)

When one particular teacher started teaching, she always wanted to collaborate with her colleagues about lessons, strategies, how to use new technology, ideas for centers, and bulletin board ideas. Many evenings she would be in her classroom sharing her expertise, sometimes even with parents. When she moved from her classroom and informal teacher leadership role, she assumed an instructional coaching position for literacy and math for grades kindergarten through eighth grade within the district. Although she maintains her teacher status, she is now in the powerful position of mentoring, providing professional development, and offering instructional feedback for teachers.

Because of her outstanding instructional repertoire, the transition from the classroom wasn't difficult, yet she found that acceptance of her new role by her peers was not automatic.. In her first year as an instructional coach, she wasn't readily welcomed into classrooms to observe, despite the fact that she had set out to help teachers in the same supportive manner that she provided when she was in the classroom. While she openly accepted specific suggestions for instructional improvement as a teacher, as a teacher leader, she needed to get into the classrooms before she could be the guide on the side for her colleagues. She chuckled, "It took a lot of chocolate for me to get into the classrooms where I needed to be." She coupled chocolate, often referred to as *Vitamin C* for teacher leaders, with her persuasive nature to build the trust that is essential for teachers to work collaboratively to make steady gains in student achievement. It may have taken chocolate to get this teacher leader into her colleagues' classrooms, however it was specific targeted strategies, honest assessment, and teacher ownership that ultimately created an environment of success for students in those classrooms.

Teachers in teacher leadership programs spend a considerable amount of time reviewing research about quality teaching. In traditional teacher preparation courses, instruction might be centered on content or a particular grade level, while the emphasis in teacher leadership programs is on instructional leadership with the learning that is centered on *process,* or the *how* of improving instruction. Teacher leaders appreciate the opportunity to improve their teaching practice through teacher leadership programs, as one teacher leader explains:

> *The second big gain that I have made is the confidence to try some new techniques in my own classroom and approach my principal about these ideas. I have always been hesitant to talk to my principal about the things in my classroom because I did not want her to think that I was incompetent. We all want to be highly effective teachers but sometimes we do not know about the method we are using, so I am happy that we are learning about the practice of teaching.*

Instructional leadership for the teachers in the teacher leadership program includes the process of sharing the influence more broadly with other teachers. Instructional expertise, if not shared, is not likely to improve teaching methods or increase student achievement.

PROFESSIONAL PREPARATION FOR TEACHER LEADERSHIP

Realizing the potential of teacher leadership requires a fundamental change in the culture and structure of schools, the preparation and continuing professional development of teachers and administrators, and the political, legal and fiscal context in which schools operate. From our research experience, we have noted that principals believe in teachers as leaders, yet there is confusion as to how those roles and responsibilities may be enacted (Wells, Maxfield, Klocko, & Feun, 2010). We also reviewed the high levels of stress that principals feel in their workplace and learned from principals that they believed strongly that teachers could alleviate some stressors if they could enact roles that include instructional leadership (Wells, Maxfield, & Klocko, 2011). Our research into the world of teacher leaders and principals has shown us how these changes—some subtle, and some more dramatic—begin to alter the culture of the school to be more focused on teaching and learning.

In our experience as university professors we noticed that teachers began to lead from their classrooms, working quietly with colleagues to make inroads and build relationships. Partly motivated by fear, the teachers were concerned not to make 'waves' with the status quo in the schools. One teacher commented, "I know after our class I try the approaches we learn in class. I struggle with conflict because I want to be liked by my colleagues." Another teacher added, "I have learned to be more flexible and collaborative to avoid conflict." Another teacher added, "I see conflict on almost a daily basis." To teach teachers to lead is to help them understand the culture of the school and ways to increase collaboration. In the most effective school settings, teacher leaders are not being given *permission* to lead and share a voice; they are being given a *voice* to lead from where they stand.

Teacher leadership programs at the university level are designed to help aspiring teacher leaders become reflective practitioners, collaborative professionals, educational change agents and leaders in the teaching profession. Participants in our programs conduct on-going action research projects that show the potential and power of teacher leadership. Our programs are offered in traditional, hybrid, and online formats to serve the needs of teacher leaders. This newly acknowledged teacher leader truly appreciates the professional preparation she has received in an online teacher leadership program:

I'm excited about the journey I have started toward becoming a teacher leader. When starting my journey to become a teacher I was unaware of all the possible leadership roles I could take on. I thought leadership roles were only for teachers who wanted to be part of the administration. I have had some time to reflect and think about the leadership roles I would like to take on in the future. I see myself leading staff meetings and leading a committee. At some point in my career, I would like to be known as an in-house expert. I know this all comes with time and good leadership skills.

This teacher goes on to explain:

This course has helped me to discover all of the leadership roles I am already taking on, and to help me hone in on the skills that I need to work on to be an exemplary teacher leader...I feel this course has not only aided me with my leadership skills, but it has assisted me in becoming a better teacher.

Our goals, as professors, are to encourage teachers who are reflective, creative and committed to working collaboratively to improve student achievement and assume important responsibilities as role models, innovators and project leaders. We have developed programs where the classroom is the learning laboratory and practice is coached and supported with the close working partnership of the professors. From our perspective, influence must be developed, supported, and coached in a teacher leadership program.

INFLUENCE: THE POLITICS OF TEACHER LEADERSHIP

Teacher leadership programs emphasize strategies for the teacher to gain credibility as a teacher leader in order to influence instructional programs and practices within their schools. Teachers develop skills in understanding the political terrain of the schools. Without political insights, teachers are left to struggle with competing forces within the school culture; political implications are essential to understanding school reform efforts (Elmore, 2006).

The most recent and arguably the most successful school leadership models are based upon collaborative initiatives. Marzano, Waters, and McNulty (2005) researched high performing schools and found that those that developed a culture of collaboration and professional inquiry enjoyed higher degrees of student achievement than their traditional counterparts.

However, many barriers to the redistribution of leadership in school systems still remain, which include traditions, policies and procedures, union contracts, peer pressure and simply the force of habit. Urbanski (2001) responded to these concerns in his leadership role as president of the American Federation of Teachers affiliate in Rochester, New York. Working closely with the administration and community, Rochester teachers negotiated a contract that institutionalized procedures and practices for identifying, training and supporting teacher leaders. Smylie and Denny (1990) reported, "What is new are increased recognition of teacher leadership, visions of expanded teacher leadership roles, and new hope for the contributions these expanded roles might make in improving schools" (p. 237).

The concept of distributed leadership extends beyond the traditional K-12 setting but is rarely discussed as an issue for higher education. According to Bolden, Petrov, and Gosling (2008) distributed leadership is largely used to shape perceptions of shared leadership and shroud the underlying dynamics of power within universities. A student leadership programs director at a New England college claimed that her dean is directly responsible for her expanded leadership role and responsibility. "She has created a culture of discovery. If you have an idea, then you are encouraged to do your homework and present it for approval." This savvy dean knows how to work with others and will defend the decisions that staff members make as long as they are well developed and ultimately will benefit students. Early on in her tenure, she claimed the division: "These are my people, and they are doing good work." However, she expects results both quickly and consistently in exchange for this empowerment.

Few people consider teacher leadership in the higher education setting, the bastion of ritualized hierarchies and institutionalized leadership roles (Bolden et al., 2008; Mayrowetz, 2008). Leaders in higher education classically hone their leadership strategies from the traditional industry playbook, with little regard for the importance of growing leaders through an expanded culture of collaborative leadership. This student leadership programs director has been given freedom to both create and jettison institutional practices, policies, and procedures as she develops her leadership mettle. Whether eliminating a flagship leadership program, or instituting dynamic new programs, "I have moved from acting in ways that I simply thought were what I wanted…to a richer perspective that focuses on the needs and desires of others." We assert that distributive leadership can help shape organizational culture at the university level as well as in K-12 schools.

According to Harris and Spillane (2008), "Distributed leadership is not a panacea or a blueprint or a recipe. It is a way of getting under the skin of leadership practice, of seeing leadership practice differently and illuminating the possibilities for organizational transformation" (p. 32). We argue that distributed leadership not only transforms the organization, it also provides intentional transformation for the teacher leader, as well as the professional regard for the teaching profession.

The professional standing of teachers has been negatively affected by the lack of opportunities to grow and to play a leadership role within their school or school district. Many educational reforms have been touted to respond to the crises in our classrooms. By far, teacher leadership holds great promise of all the proposed initiatives because it seeks to make the structural changes necessary to improve student achievement, address school improvement goals, and enlarge the professional standing of teachers. Teacher leadership is not a bandage; it addresses issues much larger than "quick fix" solutions— issues such as collaborative inquiry and change in the culture of the school where student achievement and teacher improvement are essential habits.

A loss of respect for teachers in this country is seemingly isolated to a group of antagonists and has not extended to parents or even to average Americans. Bushaw and Lopez (2011) shared the results of the 2010 PDK/Gallup Report, in which 71% of all Americans indicated they have trust and confidence in the men and women who are teaching children in the public schools. Public school parents showed a 78% confidence level. College graduates (76%) and Americans under 40 (76%) ascribed higher levels of confidence in teachers as contrasted with high school graduates (67%) and older Americans (68%). Clearly, all politicians and policy makers do not embrace these attitudes, leaving one to wonder exactly whose voice these pundits are representing.

We have found that teaching concepts of political understanding demand careful orchestration of classroom discussions, readings, case simulations, and assignments. The teachers in our programs have had little to no training in studying political elements of their schools, yet they feel the results of political life deeply, and can articulate how the politics of behavior impact them in their daily life. Teachers analyze formal and informal hierarchies within their buildings, and review pathways that could lead to collaborative problem solving, advocacy for improved teaching and student learning, and ways to engage with other positive teachers. The lessons are never linear; they are complete with frustrations, false starts, and some retrenching. Elmore (2006) defined the challenge for producing quality schools if the political side of schooling does not change how leadership is distributed:

> Rather than focusing on the character traits and actions of individual leaders- in the heroic American tradition of charismatic leadership- we will increasingly have to focus on the distribution of leadership, dispersing responsibilities for guidance and direction along the same contours as the distribution of competence and expertise in improving the quality of instructional practice and the level of student learning. (p.42)

It is our belief that understanding the political nature of schools is essential for teachers as they learn how to lead and use their influence.

"IF YOU WANT TO IMPROVE SCHOOLS, YOU NEED TEACHER LEADERSHIP"

In a recent *Washington Post* blog posting, David M. Cohen (2010, October 6) boldly proclaimed, "Apparently, I'm clinging to a strange notion about education: If you want to improve schools, you need teacher leadership; and if you try to improve schools while alienating teachers, you will fail" (para. 4).

We concur with Cohen because we believe that teacher leadership is associated with the hope for the continuously evolving professionalism of teachers, and hence student achievement. Teacher leadership can change the culture of the school, especially if principals recognize and respect teachers as partners in important, instructional decision making in the school (Cochran-Smith & Lytle, 1999; Crowther, Kaagan, Ferguson, & Hann, 2008; Katzenmeyer & Moller, 2001; Mujis & Harris, 2003; Rogus, 1988; York-Barr & Duke, 2004).

Teachers have a profound need to feel consequential. As university professors, we have the opportunity to teach teachers from a wide array of public and private schools, in this state and others. We have seen teacher leaders weep openly in Atlanta because their voice was not heard above the clamor for accountability and standardized test scores. We have listened to teachers who talk about finding their voice as a teacher leader and who have transformed their practice and their lives both personally and professionally. One teacher remarked about the changes: "My growth in my own classroom has given me confidence beyond the classroom." Another added, "It's because of this program that I feel fully competent to take on any challenge that comes my way."

The purpose of carefully crafted teacher leadership is to improve student learning, elevate the education profession, and fulfill the vital role of public education in achieving democratic ideals. Supporting and disseminating research on teacher leadership remain our primary goals at our respective institutions as we seek to develop *leaderful* organizations—those where teacher leaders become real agents of meaningful transformation. The best teachers that we have known are intellectually curious, create a love of learning in their students, and have a creativity that inspires their colleagues to join in advancing and improving their professional practice.

The teachers in our programs were proud of the growth they had relative to teaching and learning. We heard repeatedly about their new sense of confidence and pride with their new skills and influence. One teacher remarked, "It's amazing to me the lens that I now look though whether it be my own teaching methods and how to decide what to teach or how to teach or set up meetings." Teachers told us that using action research to review classroom teaching strategies makes considerable difference in their teaching. One teacher remarked, "When I began this class I did not know exactly what to think. I now have new confidence to try new teaching techniques and approach my principal about new ideas." Another added, "I learned to actually use data to improve my instructional methods."

In teaching these programs and listening to the voices of the teachers in the program, we have learned that the transition to teacher as leader is one that involves a personal journey, one without a roadmap, and one that is unique to each person making the journey. The common denominators are ones of deep reflection, where the teacher examines the culture of the school, develops and shares instructional skill, and in doing so, actively influences the power and authority that are established in the school—all platforms shared by the teachers in our programs. We are indebted to these teachers for illuminating the paths that may lead to organic and expanded roles and relationships for teachers as leaders. Their histories, their stories, and their reflections teach others how to include their leadership in the schools where they and other teachers work. The work that one teacher leader shared sums up our personal feelings, "I have a renewed excitement about teaching again."

Our excitement never wanes for teaching, and the enthusiasm we have witnessed with teachers in our programs continues to inspire us. As we watched and listened to the teachers in our teacher leadership programs, we learned that teacher voice develops over time and is fraught with ups and downs, and many emotions. The development of teacher voice continues to be about practice and patience; the patience helps to develop the skills and the power of influence. The practice contains many concepts: instructional practice, conversational practice, the practice of observation, analysis, and listening.

There are many paradoxes that we observed as we listened to the teachers tell their stories. The teachers in our programs indicated that they are bolstered by other teachers, and also that they are threatened by other teachers. The teachers in our programs learned how to navigate the complex and challenging world of the schoolhouse by trial and error, by taking risks, and by being compassionate with themselves and others.

We learned how strong and how fragile the teachers are with regard to their feelings. Some teachers explained the crushing blows they felt from other teachers' comments, and yet they began to develop a sense of resolve as they felt they now had new tools with which to handle difficulty and conflict. Our teachers also reflected about their principals; some teachers had incredible support from the beginning, and others walked carefully in the presence of their principal.

All of these lessons affirm the importance of developing teacher leadership programs that blend the content and practice of both instructional and leadership principles. The story of our teachers is far from over. New chapters will be written as they continue to practice leadership and influence in their schools. We hope to remain part of their journeys. We have learned that the voice of teachers can be cultivated, supported, encouraged, and even given a platform. We are indebted to the teachers who taught us so much as we watched them develop their voice. It was a privilege.

References

Ayers, M. B., & Sommers, W. A. (2009). *The principal's field manual.* Thousand Oaks, CA: Corwin.

Barth, R. (2001). *Learning by heart.* San Francisco, CA: Jossey-Bass.

Bolden, R., Petrov, G., & Gosling, J. (2008). Distributed leadership in higher education: Rhetoric and reality. *Educational Management, Administration and Leadership, 37*(2), 257-277.

Bolden, R., Petrov, G., & Gosling, J. (2009). Distributed leadership in higher education: What does it accomplish? *Leadership, 5,* 299-311.

Bushaw, W. J., & Lopez, S. J. (2011). A time for change: The 42nd annual Phi Delta Kappa/Gallup Poll of the public's attitudes toward the public schools. *Phi Delta Kappan,* 3-20.

Cochran-Smith, M., & Lytle, S. L. (1999). The teacher research movement: A decade later. *Educational Researcher, 28*(7), 15-25.

Cohen, D. (2010, October 6). Education down the rabbit hole [Web log comment]. Retrieved from http://voices.washingtonpost.com/answer-sheet/guest-bloggers/down-the-education-rabbit-hole.html

Crowther, F., Kaagan, S. S., Ferguson, M., & Hann, L. (2008). *Developing teacher leaders: How teacher leadership enhances school success.* Thousand Oaks, CA: Corwin.

DuFour, R., & Eaker, R. (1998). *Professional learning communities at work.* Bloomington, IN: National Education Service.

Elmore, R. (2006). *School reform from the inside out: Policy, practice and performance.* Cambridge, MA: Harvard University Press.

Fullan, M. (2001). *Leading in a culture of change.* San Francisco, CA: Jossey-Bass.

Harris, A., & Spillane, J. (2008). Distributed leadership through the looking glass. *Management in Education, 22*(1), 31-34.

Lambert, L. (2003). Leadership redefined: An evocative context for teacher leadership. *School Leadership and Management, 23*(4), 421-430. Doi: 10.1080/1363243032000150953

Lambert, L. (1998). *Building leadership capacity in schools.* Alexandria, VA: ASCD.

Lewin, K. (1945). The research center for group dynamics at Massachusetts Institute of Technology. *Sociometry, 8*, 126-135.

Lewin, K. (1951). *Field theory in social sciences.* New York, NY: Harper Row.

Lieberman, A., & Miller, L. (2004). *Teacher leadership.* San Francisco, CA: Jossey-Bass.

Katzenmeyer, M., & Moller, G. (2001). *Awakening the sleeping giant: Helping teachers develop as leaders.* Thousand Oaks, CA: Corwin.

Marzano, R., Waters, T., & McNulty, B. (2005). *School leadership that works: From research to results.* Alexandria, VA: ASCD.

Maxfield, C. R., & Klocko, B. A. (2010). Everybody leads: A model for collaborative leadership. *ERS Spectrum. 28*(3), 13-24

Mayrowetz, D. (2008). Making sense of distributed leadership: Exploring the multiple usages of the concept in the field. *Educational Administration Quarterly, 44*(3), 424-435.

Mujis, D., & Harris, A. (2003). Teacher leadership- improvement through empowerment?: An overview of the literature. *Educational Management Administration and Leadership, 31*(4), 437-448. doi: 10.1177/0263211030314007

Murphy, J. (2005). *Connecting teacher leadership and school improvement.* Thousand Oaks, CA: Corwin.

Mullen, C. A., & Hutinger, J. L. (2008). The principal's role in fostering collaborative learning communities through faculty study group development. *Theory Into Practice, 47*, 276-285. doi: 10: 10800/0040580239136

Ogawa, R. T., & Bossert, S. T. (1995). Leadership as an organizational quality. *Educational Administration Quarterly, 31*, 221-243.

Rogus, J. F. (1988). Teacher leader programming: Theoretical underpinnings. *Journal of Teacher Education, 39*(1), 46- 51.

Sarason, S. (1971). *The culture of the school and the problem of change.* Boston, MA: Allyn and Bacon.

Silva, D. Y., Gimbert, B., & Nolan, J. (2000). Sliding the doors: Locking and unlocking possibilities for teacher leadership. *Teachers College Record, 102*(4), 779- 804.

Smylie, M. A., & Denny, J. W. (1990). Teacher leadership: Tensions and ambiguities in organizational perspective. *Educational Administration Quarterly, 26*(3), 235-259.

Spillane, J. (2006). *Distributed leadership.* San Francisco, CA: Jossey-Bass.

Urbanski, A. (2001). Reform or be reformed. *Education Next, 1*(3), 46-50.

Wells, C. M., Maxfield, C. R., & Klocko, B. A. (2011). Complexities inherent in the workload of principals: Implications for teacher leadership. In Alford, B. J. (Ed.) *Blazing new trails: Preparing leaders to improve access and equity in today's schools.* Lancaster, PA: ProActive Publications, (pp. 29-46.)

Wells, C. M., Maxfield, C.R., Klocko, B., & Feun, L. (2010). The role of superintendents in supporting teacher leadership: A study of principal perceptions. The *Journal of School Leadership, 20*(5), 669-693.

York-Barr, J., & Duke, K. (2004). What do we know about teacher leadership? Findings from two decades of scholarship. *Review of Educational Research, 74*(3), 255-316. doi: 10.3102/00346543074003255

Dr. Barbara A. Klocko is an Assistant Professor for the Department of Educational Leadership at Central Michigan University and Director of M.A. in Teacher Leadership and M.A. in School Principalship programs. Her research interests include resiliency of educational leaders; teacher leadership; and Charter School Leadership. She is a former public school administrator and classroom teacher. She can be contacted at klock1ba@cmich.edu.

Dr. Caryn M. Wells is an Associate Professor for the Department of Educational Leadership for Oakland University in Rochester, MI. She is the Coordinator for the Education Specialist program. Her research agenda includes the leadership of teachers, superintendents, and principals; the stress level of change efforts; and PLC implementation. She is a former high school principal, counselor, and teacher. In August our department will be merged with another department and the new name will be "Department of Organizational Leadership." She can be contacted at cmwells2@oakland.edu.

Chapter 6

A Journey Toward Distributed Teacher Leadership

Cherese Childers-McKee

During this era of increased public scrutiny of teachers and educational leaders, schools are being flooded with educational initiatives and programs intended to raise test scores, close the achievement gap, promote lifelong learning, prepare students for the 21st century, and successfully compete with educational systems around the world. Leadership has been explored from a variety of perspectives, frameworks, and ideologies as scholars have questioned the idea of one individual who possesses the sole authority and power as decision-maker in a school (Barth, 2001; Beachum & Dentith, 2004; Danielson, 2007; Dentith, Beachum, & Frattura, 2006; Horsford, 2012; Singh, 2011), and for years interrogated possibilities of distributed and teacher leadership. While my intention is not to discuss various styles of leadership, I suggest that perhaps the way leadership actually operates in many schools privileges particular leadership styles that deem certain individuals inadequate or lacking in leadership qualities.

Although we as educators tout the importance of site-based decision making, autonomy, collective collaboration, an awareness of cultural diversity, and a focus on community, public schools continue to be plagued by a top-down hierarchical model of enacting change in school (Hargreaves & Fink, 2008). Public perception too often characterizes teachers as quasi-professionals, most of whom are bereft of the knowledge to inform curriculum and policy in education (Gardner, 2011). Often missing from the discussion of educational policies are the voices of diverse populations of educators, parents, and students who are most affected by top-down educational initiatives that purport to fix what is broken in schools. Teacher leadership is often "cloaked in ambivalence" as "we look to teachers and their leadership to help solve today's educational problems, yet we consider teachers a primary cause of the problems that we call on their leadership to solve" (Smylie, Conley, & Marks, 2002, p. 162-163).

I suggest that in order to explore teacher leadership, first we must interrogate the way we conceptualize it and explore the power dynamics that exist in educational settings. Cultivating and empowering diverse populations of teachers as leaders in their schools and communities could unleash a wealth of innovation and creativity in confronting the challenges that schools face to promote education for a new generation of learners. In the pages that follow, I explore past and present scholarship in the area of teacher leadership in an effort to highlight benefits and strategies for reconceptualizing leadership practice and empowering teachers to perceive themselves as leaders for change.

CONCEPTUALIZING TEACHER LEADERSHIP

Over the past 30 years, the theory and practice of teacher leadership have been expressed in a variety of ways and for a multitude of purposes. Most reviews identify three distinct periods in how teacher leadership has been conceptualized (Dentith, Beachum, & Frattura, 2006; Silva, Gimbert, & Nolan, 2000; Smylie, Conley, & Marks, 2002; York-Barr & Duke, 2004). While scholars as early as the 1900's argued that school structures should reflect the democratic principles they sought to promote, increased bureaucratization and centralized control of schools minimized emphasis on teacher leadership (Smylie, Conley, & Marks, 2002). However, the 1980's brought an increased focus on viewing teachers as leaders and emphasized individual empowerment of teachers (Smylie, Conley, & Marks, 2002; York-Barr & Duke, 2004). During this time, the focus on teacher leadership sought to professionalize teaching, provide greater incentives for "master" and "lead" teachers, and involve teachers in district-level decisions through official positions usually outside of the classroom setting (Dentith, Beachum, & Frattura, 2006; Smylie, Conley, & Marks, 2002; York-Barr & Duke, 2004). Critics of teacher leadership practice during this time period asserted that simply delegating administrative duties to teachers failed to address the hierarchy present in schools and in many cases created undo tension and conflict among teachers and between teachers and administrators (Smylie, Conley, & Marks, 2002). In contrast, the third wave of teacher leadership, from the 1990's to present, has involved a shift from a focus on individual and managerial roles of the teacher to a more collaborative, mentoring, curriculum-oriented style of leadership (Smylie, Conley, & Marks, 2002). Despite the growing acceptance and popularity of teacher leadership, questions remain regarding how teacher leadership is cultivated, how teacher leaders are chosen, the effects of teacher leadership on student achievement and school reform, what challenges or barriers exist in how leadership is conceptualized, and how schools operate that may be hindering the development of teacher leaders.

Teacher leadership is closely related to a larger concept of distributed leadership, a "form of shared or collective leadership in which expertise is developed by working collaboratively" (Grenda, 2006, p. 567). Although the theoretical underpinnings and conceptualization of distributed leadership have been widely studied, interpretation and implementation of the concept varies significantly (Grenda, 2006; Harris & Spillane, 2008). While some define distributed leadership as a sharing or delegation of leadership tasks to other designated individuals in the school, others perceive that it shifts away from thinking in terms of roles and involves a total reconceptualization of leadership—one that taps into the talents of the entire school in a collective, collaborative effort to meet the increasingly complex challenges of schools. (Grenda, 2006; Smylie, Conley, & Marks, 2002). Interestingly, although it is difficult to explore teacher leadership without some mention of distributed leadership, proponents of distributed leadership caution against the cooptation of the term as a "'catch all' term to describe any form of devolved, shared, or dispersed leadership practice" (Harris & Spillane, 2008, p. 38; Spillane, 2005). Critics of connecting other types of shared leadership to distributed leadership also suggest that, "Flattening the hierarchy or delegation of leadership does not necessarily equate with distributed leadership, nor does it automatically improve performance. It is the nature and quality of *leadership practice* that matters" (Harris & Spillane, 2008, p.

33). Similarly, simply placing teachers in the roles of leaders or delegating managerial or instructional duties has not proven, historically, to be an effective means of effecting change in schools (Silva, Gimbert, & Nolan, 2000). However, distributed leadership and teacher leadership are intimately connected in that effectively transitioning to a distributed approach requires the innovation and cooperation of teachers (Harris, 2002). Therefore, in many places throughout this chapter, I put forth the idea of *distributed teacher leadership* as one that applies aspects of distributed leadership to the empowerment and collaboration of teachers as both formal and informal leaders within a web of interaction in a school community.

Literature on distributed leadership, as well as what I have termed *distributed teacher leadership,* both possess many similarities to what Blackmore (1989/2005) calls a "feminist reconstruction of the concept of leadership" (p. 64). She counters a style of leadership that emphasizes "individualism, hierarchical relationships," and "bureaucratic rationality" and instead proposes a reconceptualization of power that is "multi-dimensional" and "multi-directional," "seeks to empower others rather than have power over others," and is "communitarian and collective" (p. 64). In speaking of increasing the number of women in leadership, Blackmore (1989/2005) suggests,

> It is necessary to "go beyond the numbers game," in which gender equity is assumed to result purely from the better "representation" of women in positions of authority, and to question the very concept of leadership itself, how it is portrayed in the literature, and how it is perceived by women and the community in education. (64-65)

Likewise, while increasing the presence of teachers in leadership positions has been noteworthy, I suggest that these measures may be largely ineffective if a hierarchical structure of leadership that privileges certain voices and perspectives over others remains intact. Similarly, Dentith (2004) articulates a framework for viewing teacher leadership through a feminist lens focused on relationships involving care, empathy, fairness, and equity. In this relational, highly contextualized vision of teacher leadership, she focuses on connecting the private and political aspects of schooling in which there is a "commitment to caring immersed within principles of social justice" (p. 390). In her accounts of teachers who embody relational leadership, Dentith (2004) contends, "When leadership encompasses a strong ethical basis and is grounded in an ethics of justice and care, it will likely lead to transformed schools as sites of equity and excellence" (p. 397). Continuing to promote teacher leadership without changing hierarchical structures inherent in the ways many schools operate is reminiscent of Lorde's (1984/2007), assertion that "the master's tools will never dismantle the master's house" (p. 10). Therefore, striving to examine how we conceptualize leadership as well as intentionally cultivating relational, collaborative interaction that flows between and among teachers and administrators is essential in transforming and renewing school communities.

DEFINITIONS AND CHARACTERISTICS OF TEACHER LEADERS

Vignette 1:

Paradoxically, yet perhaps true to some research on the complexity of teacher leadership, I felt less effective in my position as a formal teacher leader than in my earlier more informal role. Previously a part of a strong school community, in which I spent 5 years building relationships, rapport, and mutual respect with colleagues and administrators, I now found myself alienated, floating between five high schools and seven middle schools. My official role was teacher leader, while unofficially I was "peace keeper" between administrators and English as a Second Language (ESL) teachers at each of the schools; ESL staff development coordinator; and contact for content area teachers in the schools who were struggling with students acquiring English as a new language. The position was fairly straightforward and typical of what many teachers leaders had been doing for years; however, throughout that school year, I was plagued by a nagging feeling that I was simply "marching in place"-- moving, but not moving forward. Rather than building leadership capacity amongst my ESL colleagues, my role as their "go-between" actually hindered their development as leaders, resulting in further alienating them in their schools. Instead of capitalizing on their unique personal knowledge of students and families, challenging and mentoring them to step forward as leaders and advocates in their schools, I bought into a vision of teacher leadership that placed me on a rung of the managerial ladder. Aspiring to improve my leadership qualities, I did my best to fit into the mold created for me as I attempted to ignore that nagging voice inside that insisted I was failing to tap into the greatest resources—my fellow teachers.

Scholars have endeavored to characterize teacher leadership in a variety of ways. In data collected on teacher leaders from 1983-1985, Lieberman, Saxl, and Miles (2007) describe widely-held views of teacher leaders as being "master teachers" with a "broad range of skills, abilities, and experience," "involved in curriculum development in the past, as well as having held positions that enabled them to teach new curriculum to others," possessing "academic pursuits and accomplishments," and "many academic degrees, as well as having attended a broad spectrum of courses, conferences, and workshops on topics as diverse as conflict resolution, teacher effectiveness, and adult development" (p. 405). Teacher leaders were described as "strong, yet caring and compassionate" individuals who were well versed in administrative skills enabling them to navigate the "complexity of school cultures" (p. 405).

Katzenmeyer and Moller (2001/2009) divide the roles of a teacher leader in three categories: 1) Leadership in relation to students or colleagues as "counselor, facilitator, provider of feedback" and "mentors, peer coaches, teacher trainers, curriculum specialists, or simply as willing listeners" (p. 12). 2) Formal roles outside of the school in research or task forces. 3) Decision making roles as "school improvement team member, school advisory council, PTO, community action groups, chairing committees, faculty chairpersons, elected officials in organizations" (p. 12). Although Katzenmeyer and Moller (2001/2009) articulate specific roles of teacher leaders, they emphasize the importance of teacher leadership that involves "all teachers versus selected teachers," "functions versus formal positions," and "classroom based versus administrative based" (p. 28-31).

While within distributed teacher leadership teachers may possess many of the characteristics and roles described in the previous paragraphs, the focus shifts from an individual, isolated, role-based view of leadership to one that is collaborative, empowering, and fluid. Distributed teacher leadership is complex, highly contextualized, and therefore multi-faceted in nature. Crowther, Kaagan, Ferguson, and Hann (2002) assert that "educational policy and leadership theory continue to operate, for the most part, on the flawed rationale that equates position with leadership" (p. 24) which perhaps explains why increases in formal teacher leadership positions have had little impact on student learning and engagement and school reform overall (Crowther et al., 2002; Leithwood & Jantzi, 1999). Crowther et al. (2002) suggest that, "Teacher leadership is powerful in its diversity, its sensitivity to situation and context, and its capacity to enhance and enrich communal meaning and quality of life (p. 32). Therefore, while teacher leadership may encompass a variety of roles, both formal and informal, at its crux, "it is about action that transforms teaching and learning in a school, that ties school and community together on behalf of learning, and that advances social sustainability and quality of life for a community" (Crowther et al., 2002, p. xvii). Teacher leadership is "principled action to achieve whole school success" (Crowther et al., 2002, p. 10) not through roles or intrinsic personal qualities but as "exercised through interactive processes that were centered on serious professional and communal dialogue and trust (p. 12). In their research on teacher leaders they found that "teacher leaders themselves derived strength and confidence from one another" and that "informal alliance of teachers and administrators working as equal partners proved to be the root of the school's success" (p. 13). Therefore, the innovative approach of distributed teacher leadership allows teachers and administrators to "share passion for their work, pursue a common vision, take advantage of expertise within the group, and optimize collaboration" (Singh, 2011, p. 8). Although teacher leaders may lead from their classrooms as instructional leaders, their concerns also go beyond their classroom in fighting for change or pursuing social justice issues that relate to the education and wellbeing of their schools and school communities (Danielson, 2007).

RELATIONSHIPS AND TEACHER LEADERSHIP

Just as distributed leadership flows back and forth between members of the school, distributed teacher leadership involves the cultivation of mentoring, empowering, and collaborative relationships. Rather than an image of a linear hierarchical flow of knowledge, distributed teacher leadership implies an intersecting web of relationships in which knowledge and information flow in multidirectional ways. In a study of three school districts, Firestone and Martinez (2007) evaluated teacher leaders' relationships with their colleagues in implementing new math and science initiatives. The teacher leaders interviewed had been selected by the district and placed in roles as math coaches, math specialists, and science specialists. Firestone and Martinez (2007) found that teacher leaders were instrumental in facilitating the district initiative, and that their effectiveness was influenced by their content knowledge and experience as teachers as well as how well they balanced monitoring and coaching. While teacher leaders lacked the formal authority to mandate that their colleagues embrace the district initiatives, some explicitly and deliberately used relationships and personal connections to share knowledge and resources. Therefore, in a school community focused on distributed teacher leadership, there must be an intentional focus on building and nurturing relationships based on respect, trust, and collegiality.

ADMINISTRATORS' ROLES IN TEACHER LEADERSHIP

Although transitioning to a more distributed form of teacher leadership is not without a host of challenges, which I will discuss in the section that follows, successful implementation of this approach involves the entire school community working to facilitate change through collaborative networks and teams. While "fellow teachers also hold the power to unlock one another's leadership potential and to foster its growth," (Barth, 2001, p. 446) principals play a critical role in empowering teachers and creating a culture that embraces collaboration (Barth, 2001; Gigante, 2006; Harris, 2009; Harris, 2012). Although some identify the need for administrative support as a "paradox of teacher leadership," (Harris, 2009; Smylie, Conley, & Marks, 2002; p. 182) perhaps rather than a paradox, this simply reaffirms the intense interconnectedness and relational nature of the school environment. For example, Hargreaves and Fink (2008) conceptualize the school environment as a complex, "living system" in which "an action in one part of the web affects all other parts" (p. 231). They go on to differentiate the "sick living system" (p. 232) that may be characterized by "technocratic structures of command and control where teachers, departments, and schools are separated from or even pitted against one another" (p. 232) from a healthier and more democratic living system in which,

> Leadership is distributed in an emergent and benevolent way—so the community engages in robust dialogue, in an evidence-informed and experience-grounded manner, about the best means to promote the goals of deep and broad student learning for all. (p. 232)

Therefore, the suggestion that administrative support may represent a key ingredient in promoting teacher leadership does not belittle the fight for teacher autonomy nor does it give credence to a hierarchical way of operating schools; rather, it simply confirms the idea that the power and effectiveness of distributed teacher leadership lies in mutually respectful, collaborative relationships established among members of the school community (Singh, 2011). Therefore, as the roles of those in formal leadership positions are reconfigured, they must "relinquish power and control to others" while working toward the critical objective of attempting to "create a common culture of expectations around the use of individual skills and abilities" and "maximizing the human capacity within the organization" (Harris, 2002, p. 11-12). A new vision of distributed teacher leadership requires present educational leaders to provide space and opportunities for teacher leaders to develop and thrive.

CHALLENGES TO CULTIVATING TEACHER LEADERSHIP

Vignette 2:

After years of mulling over the idea of pursuing a doctoral degree, I finally decided to leave teaching and become a full-time student. As I went to discuss my decision with my school administrator, I found him to be supportive. Our conversation proceeded something like this.
Me: This is such a big step for me, but it's something I've always wanted to do.
Him: That's great! What program are you considering?
Me: A PhD in Educational Studies
Him: Yeah, I thought you were going to say that. I didn't think you would be pursuing an Ed.D. I don't really see you as the leadership type.
We went on to discuss many other things about balancing school and family life, but as I left the meeting, I continued to ponder his assessment of me as not a "leadership type." Prior to coming to that particular school, I was an instructional leader in my school, later held a district leadership position in my field, and never felt that I lacked leadership skills. So, as I began my doctoral program and began to consider what type of career I would pursue in academia, I continued to ponder the conversation with my administrator and what it said about both how we conceptualize leadership as well as how we identify and choose leaders. Many would have us believe that there is an "it" factor that some people just possess. Can this be cultivated....or should we interrogate this "it" factor and what it says about maintaining patriarchal and race/ethnicity-based views of leadership?

Who Qualifies as a Leader?

Truly teasing out the nuances of teacher leadership necessitates a closer look at how we determine who possesses qualities to lead. In considering who "fits" in a leadership role, Tooms, Lugg, and Bogotch (2009) describe the use of the term "fit" as based on vague qualities not always associated with leadership and often used to maintain the status quo by excluding certain individuals based on "what is desirable along the lines of ethnicity, gender, sexual identity, and age" (p. 106). They assert that,

> Current organizational practices and the commonsense uses of the term fit have not only blurred the important distinctions among persons, roles, and communities but also hindered the capacity of public school officials to recruit, select, and support leaders who might better serve us in facilitating school reforms. (p. 101)

Therefore, the silent forces of hegemony and socially constructed notions of a leader shape and contour our notions of who "fits" in leadership often to the exclusion, detriment, and marginalization of certain voices. Therefore, a true reconceptualization of teacher leadership demands a closer look at larger systems of power and privilege that serve as obstacles to promoting a diverse population of educational leaders.

Most agree that the concept of the single, heroic leader has been replaced with more shared and collaborative forms of leadership, but a critical look at the nuances of leadership practice and educational policy suggest that we should continue to explore these concerns. Although the numbers of women and people of color in educational leadership have increased over the past several decades (Shakeshaft, Brown, Irby, Grogan, & Ballenger, 2007), Eurocentric, patriarchal views of leadership continue to pervade our consciousness and should be explored in a discussion of promoting diversity in teacher leaders. Shields (2004) urges educational leaders to interrogate how maintaining the status quo marginalizes and silences students and families. A critically important task of educational leaders is responding appropriately to an increasingly racially, ethnically, religiously, and socioeconomically diverse student population. In order to effectively address this monumental challenge with students and families, educational leaders must first challenge the structures, processes, beliefs, and perspectives within our schools and communities that marginalize and silence all of those lacking privilege and power. Shields (2004) urges educational leaders to challenge the status quo by engaging in "transformative leadership," "acknowledging the centrality of relationships," and "facilitating moral dialogue" (p. 113-115). Shields (2004) explains,

> [Because] educators are often uncomfortable with difference, we fail not only to develop strong relationships but even to hear or acknowledge some of the diverse voices that make up our schools and classrooms. Moreover, our discomfort often manifests itself in what I am calling pathologies of silence. (p. 117)

Although her description of leadership for social justice is intended for educational leaders and teachers to embrace more democratic schooling for all students, I posit that perhaps we have failed to achieve this beautiful vision of school because we must first challenge our discomfort with diversity within the ranks of educators and school leaders. Essentializing leadership ability as an "it" factor or some inherent personality trait possessed by the best and brightest masks and disguises harsh truths about the ways that racism, patriarchy, and false notions of meritocracy function in our society. If we operate with sex/colorblindness and a failure to acknowledge the voices of diversity amongst ourselves, we encourage a school culture that lacks the ability to achieve the vision of leadership that Shields describes.

Structural Challenges

Vignette 3:
I walked down the hall with a group of veteran teachers on my first day in a new high school. I thought happily to myself about how my anxiety about a new environment was quickly dissipating, replaced by the excitement of a new school year and new challenges. As I walked down the hall with the group, one of them remarked, "Did you see that new teacher, Amy, over there? Smiling and going on the whole time. What's she so happy about?" Conscious of the fact that I had a big dopey grin on my face as well, I wiped it off quickly and put on a more professional, serious face as I continued listening. "Too early in the morning for all that smiling," they continued. "Just wait until the kids get here. They're gonna eat her alive." One teacher says matter-of-factly. "Well, if she thinks

she's going to come in here and start changing things, well good luck--ain't gonna happen!"

Additional challenges that schools face in cultivating and encouraging teacher leadership often come from educators themselves. Whether resulting from logistical issues such as scheduling and time constraints or social issues such as resentment from peers or balancing instructional and administrative leadership roles, cultivating teacher leadership is loaded with challenges. I highlight three major challenges that school communities may face in promoting the distributed vision of teacher leadership discussed in this chapter. First, Harris (2003) suggests that a social exchange theory of leadership works in conjunction with the hierarchical structures of schools in which "leaders provide services to a group in exchange for the group's approval or compliance with the leader's demands" (p. 314). Thus, does the idea of encouraging all teachers to embrace their leadership potential threaten the very notion of leadership at its core? If everyone were considered a leader in an organization, who would be left to follow and who would hold the final authority and responsibility? In response, Harris (2003) argues that teacher leadership is situated within a more cultural or symbolic theory of leadership that challenges the dichotomy of a leader/follower and promotes a collaborative, locally constructed vision of leadership that involves mutual respect and a shared vision for change. Similarly, Reeves (2008) asserts, "we are creatures of networks, not hierarchies" (p. 64). Therefore, rather than creating additional positions or contrived networks, distributed teacher leadership implies a strengthening and cultivation of existing networks through intentional and sustained development of educators' abilities to collaborate and empower one another.

As an additional barrier, efforts at establishing more collaborative, collective leadership are still occurring in service to higher top-down agendas over which many teachers and administrators have no control. For instance, although distributed forms of leadership have gained popularity, Hargreaves & Fink (2008) assert there still exists a prevalence of "externally set performance targets that are still decreed non-democratically, and in a way that is politically arbitrary work and professionally exclusionary" (p. 238). As many teachers and administrators confront the daily reality of failing schools, initiative fatigue, and a desperate need for rapid reform, perhaps we must consider the extent to which we have tapped into the power of all human resources in the school and community. By operating as a collaborative team of individuals participating in a healthy "living system," (Hargreaves & Fink, 2008, p. 231) educators can maximize their power to effect change in hierarchical systems of governing schools.

A third barrier to distributed teacher leadership emanates from the structures and norms of the traditional school environment. In this linearly oriented, hierarchically structured, dichotomous environment, autonomy and isolation prevail. Teachers labor in the privacy of their classrooms, while administrators serve in managerial and supervisory roles. Therefore, with this type of environment as the reference point, some have, not surprisingly, deemed teacher leadership as both a paradox and a contradiction (Lord & Miller, 2000; Mangin & Stoelinga, 2011). For example, Mangin and Stoelinga (2011) found that, "The nonsupervisory nature of the teacher leader role creates a paradoxical challenge for the teacher leader" in that "to gain teachers' trust, teacher leaders deemphasize their status as experts and avoid delivering hard feedback about teaching practice" (p. 48). Although mentoring and relationships were critical in teacher leader effectiveness, Firestone (2007) identified role ambiguity about authority and purpose as a significant obstacle as teachers expressed a tension between instructional and mentoring duties and other managerial leadership duties assigned to them by school principals. In being forced into a managerial role, struggling to decide whether their role constitutes one of peer or expert, teacher leaders are "neutered" (Silva, Gimbert, & Nolan, 2000) and rendered largely ineffective. Lord & Miller (2000) assert, "The term teacher leader embodies a contradiction identified by many individuals in the role" in that teacher leaders reside in a "different professional space" elevated above other teachers, but not quite administrators, resulting in an uncomfortable state of ambiguity (p. 7). I concur with Barth (2001) that "something deep and powerful within school cultures seems to work against teacher leadership" (p. 444). In proposing a revolutionary view of teacher leadership, Barth (2001) suggests,

> "All teachers can lead." Indeed, if schools are going to become places in which all children are learning, all teachers must lead. Skeptics might amend this assertion to "some teachers," or "a few teachers," or even "many teachers." These low expectations are as destructive, limiting, and self-fulfilling as "some children can learn." The fact of the matter is that all teachers harbor leadership capabilities waiting to be unlocked and engaged for the good of the school. (p. 444)

Therefore, in reconceptualizing teacher leadership as distributed, collaborative, and relational, teachers and administrators must work to shift this culture away from one in which individuals must be coerced into effectiveness or only open to "hard feedback" (Mangin & Stoelinga, 2011) from someone in a position of power and authority, to a setting characterized by mutual respect, mutual accountability, intrinsic motivation, a shared vision for change, and an openness to critical feedback from peers.

MOVING TOWARD DISTRIBUTED TEACHER LEADERSHIP

Vignette 4:

In need of a new challenge, I accepted a position at Reddingsdale High School, a majority minority school characterized by a high-poverty, low-performing population, often in crisis-mode, and usually under threat of state takeover. Due to the fresh crop of novice teachers every August, mostly through either the Teach for America or Teaching Fellows programs, and the subsequent mass exodus of teachers every June, building relationships and establishing bonds within and across departments was challenging. However, despite the constant changes in personnel, there were core groups of teachers who always decided to stay and work hard for change. Because of the numerous reform initiatives that had been introduced and soon forgotten about, teachers were very suspicious and fairly resistant when the administrative staff and a team of teacher leaders they had chosen attempted to implement professional learning communities (PLCs). Rather than cultivating true professional learning communities, what actually occurred in many departments was more of an "everyone needs to be doing the same lesson at the same time every day"-

"teacher-proof" focus that further alienated those individuals already suspicious of the new initiative. After two years of coercion, monitoring, and threatening emails about documenting PLC meetings, scheduling common planning and creating common assessments, PLC faded into the background and was rarely mentioned again. While some departments breathed a sigh of relief and continued with "business as usual," others decided they liked the collaborative spirit cultivated by their PLC groups and in turn saw tremendous improvement in their instruction and students' achievement. While coercion and threats were ineffective in getting teachers to embrace the concept of PLC, teacher leadership and collegial relationships made the difference. The departments that had strong, well-established networks of teachers who believed in the benefit of PLCs continued to successfully maintain their PLC groups even after the school stopped mandating/enforcing participation. Other departments with teachers who were more isolated and had less interaction with one another, some of which had department chairs who had been drafted into the position unwillingly, were unable to encourage colleagues to fully embrace the model. Interestingly, those departments that did not experience success with PLCs were primarily in state-tested areas and experienced more pressure to conform to more standardized, routine, less creative lessons and assessments than some of their colleagues. Many teachers in these departments went through the motions of PLC so that when the school-wide focus on PLC diminished and school leadership moved on to the "next reform initiative" these departments promptly stopped implementing, using, and engaging in PLC activities.

Teacher leadership is intricately interwoven with virtually all issues that influence current educational practice, including increased emphasis placed on testing and accountability in schools. As the previous vignette described, many schools labor with student populations experiencing poverty, the pressure of federal mandates to increase test scores, and a complex and diverse set of challenges in reforming school culture. Some assert that distributed and teacher leadership are essential keys to success when faced with the complexity of school improvement, change, and reform (Harris, 2009; Katzenmeyer & Moller, 2001/2009). In a study of 81 schools in Clark County, Nevada, Reeves (2008) found that teachers significantly influenced not only the performance of students, but also the performance of fellow teachers and school leaders. In fact, the "professional practices and action research" (p. 2) of teachers' colleagues were reported to be more influential than journal readings or graduate school courses. The National Comprehensive Center for Teacher Quality (2007) contends, "In order to implement curricular and instructional reforms at the classroom level, a commitment from the teachers who lead at that level is essential" (p. 6). They also draw a strong link between teacher learning and student learning. As teacher leaders mentor and empower their colleagues to learn and grow, they "infuse this expertise across the faculty" (National Comprehensive Center for Teacher Quality, 2007, p. 6), and student achievement greatly improves as well.

Although many teachers routinely engage in formal and informal leadership, distributed teacher leadership continues to be a complex challenge for many school communities. Moving beyond a notion of leadership as intrinsic or a natural talent and

being intentional about promoting teacher leadership across an entire school involves effective, meaningful, and continual professional development opportunities for teachers to cultivate and practice leadership development focused on teaching and learning as well as building positive, empowering relationships. Katzenmeyer and Moller (2001/2009) assert that teachers should be engaged in "collaborative strategies such as action research and study groups," (p. 46) focused on "real-world curriculum, instructional, and assessment problems teachers face," (p. 48) and responsible for their own and their colleagues learning and development through mentoring and coaching. If school leaders fail to provide quality professional development that is results-driven and sustained, teacher leaders have an obligation to advocate for themselves (p. 47).

Both Katzenmeyer and Moller (2001/2009) and Crowther et al. (2002) assert that the teacher leadership "giant is rousing" but as we reflect upon the concept of teacher leadership and its development over the last 10 years, perhaps we need to revive this conversation. Why has teacher leadership yet to achieve its full potential? Perhaps, as Crowther et al. (2002) describe,

> The sleeping giant of teacher leadership is indeed rousing, its image discernible, its movement palpable. These developments we regard with enthusiasm but also with a degree of trepidation, because they could dramatically reshape the school workplace, the status of the teaching profession, and the place of schools within communities. (p. 10)

Although, a new vision of teacher leadership may be approached with considerable angst by some, the potential for better relationships, instruction, and student achievement make this journey worthy of the effort. In the following section, I endeavor to continue the conversation about distributed teacher leadership through concrete suggestions and recommendations gleaned from both my personal experiences as well as current scholarship in the area of educational leadership.

> *Vignette 5:*
>
> *My first glimpse into the world of teacher leadership came from my mentor, an individual who practically built the English as a Second Language program in her school district as the first wave of immigrant families began to flood into her rural county in the early '90s. At the time she became my mentor she had taught for close to 30 years, served as the district leader of the ESL and Migrant Education programs, and was highly respected and esteemed—the "go to" person for all things related to language acquisition, literacy, and schooling for second language learners. In addition to her vast pedagogical knowledge, she was extremely skilled in recognizing and cultivating strengths and talents in the teachers she mentored. While always supportive and a listener, she modeled and expected excellence from her colleagues. During the time I worked with her, she continually nudged, challenged, taught, and cultivated me to be an instructional leader within my school. She never led by exerting her power but always began from a place of relationship, care, and deep concern for her teachers, students, and families. While always placing emphasis on effective instruction, she also encouraged and expected teachers to advocate for their students, both within the*

school and surrounding community. Long before I could articulate that I esteemed a more participatory vision of leadership that highly values relationships and caring and seeks to empower individuals within the group, my mentor exemplified this, and I personally experienced the merit of this approach.

SUGGESTIONS AND RECOMMENDATIONS

Teachers

1) Resist the "I'm just a teacher" mentality, investigate diverse leadership styles, and embrace the leadership qualities that you possess with self-confidence and verve.
2) Advocate for a decreased emphasis on positional power that emphasizes "reward and coerciveness" in favor of personal power "grounded in mutual respect, collaboration, credibility, and acknowledgement of individuals' potential and expertise" (Katzenmeyer & Moller, 2001/2009, p. 25).
3) Cultivate your expertise in pedagogy, your content area, mentoring, and leadership through professional development, involvement in professional organizations, graduate courses, and engagement in school and community activities.
4) Resist the individualism and isolation so prevalent in teaching, and advocate for collaboration with colleagues and shared decision-making.
5) Embrace the fact that with leadership comes increased accountability and responsibility and be willing to follow through on projects and innovations (Katzenmeyer & Moller, 2001/2009, p. 11).
6) Be transgressive, take risks, and engage in innovation beyond your classroom.

Principals

1) Cultivate a school culture of respect, trust, and collegiality in which power and decision-making are shared, active listening is valued, honest dialogue is encouraged, and teachers and administrators share a common vision for school improvement and change. For additional reading on school culture see Beaudoin (2011) and Cohen, McCabe, Michelli, and Pickeral (2009).
2) Be mindful and intentional in promoting language that furthers the vision of distributed teacher leadership (e.g., avoid terms such as "my staff," "my teachers," and "boss," in favor of terms such as "our school," "our team," "professionals," and "colleagues").
3) Challenge the assumptions behind *who* we consider to be "good leaders," seek to cultivate ingenuity and innovativeness in *all* teachers at your school, and expect them to do the same for one another.
4) Resist actions that pit teachers against one another and further encourage isolation and individualism (e.g. routinely showering teachers with the highest test scores with praise in every teachers meeting, establishing hierarchies among teachers in which teachers in content and tested areas have higher status than instructional assistants or support personnel). Instead, promote shared responsibility and accountability.

5) Avoid the assumption or expectation that collaboration and distributed teacher leadership will spontaneously develop without investing a great deal of time and energy. Be explicit and intentional in promoting team building activities, developing relationships through collaborative projects and activities, frequently discussing your vision for shared leadership, expecting teachers to be confident and innovative in partnering with you for change, and addressing time constraints that hinder leadership development.
6) Encourage teachers to assume a variety of positions within the school community; encourage teachers to change roles and responsibilities to cultivate diverse talents.
7) Implement specific strategies for increasing instructional collaboration in your school: 1) Use faculty meetings solely for sharing of instructional ideas. 2) Encourage teachers to collaborate to form a "best practices book" (or wiki) that can be shared with current as well as new teachers. 3) Allow parents and students to offer suggestions for best practices that were especially meaningful or effective to them. (Reeves, 2008, p. 73-74).

References

Barth, R. (2001). Teacher leader. *Phi Delta Kappa, 82*(6), 442-449.

Beachum, F. & Dentith, A. (2004). Teacher leaders creating cultures of school renewal and transformation. *The Educational Forum, 68*, 276-286.

Beaudoin, M. (2011). Respect-Where do we start? *Educational Leadership, 69*(1), 40-44.

Blackmore, J. (2005). Educational leadership: A feminist critique and reconstruction. In J. Smyth (Ed.), *Critical perspectives on educational leadership* (pp. 63-87). Bristol: Taylor and Francis Inc.

Cohen, J., McCabe, E., Michelli, N. & Pickeral, T. (2009). School climate: Research, policy, practice, and teacher education. *Teachers College Record, 111*(1), 180-213.

Crowther, F., Kaagan, S., Ferguson, M. & Hann, L. (2002). *Developing teacher leaders: How teacher leadership enhances school success.* Thousand Oaks, CA: Corwin Press, Inc.

Danielson, C. (2007). The many faces of leadership. *Educational Leadership, 65*(1), 14–19.

Dentith, A. (2004). Toward a feminist ethics of teacher leadership: A portrait of one teacher. *Teacher Education and Practice, 17*(4), 386-399.

Dentith, A., Beachum, F., & Frattura, E. (2006). Leadership, teacher. In F. English (Ed.), *Encyclopedia of educational leadership and administration* (Vol. 2) (pp. 583-586). Thousand Oaks, CA: Sage.

Firestone, W.A., Martinez, C. M. (2007) Districts, teacher leaders, and distributed leadership: Changing instructional practice. *Leadership and Policy in Schools, 6*(1), 3-35. Reprinted in K. Leithwood, B. Mascall, & T. Strauss (Eds.). (2009) *Distributed leadership according to the evidence* (pp. 61-86). New York: Routledge.

Gardner, H. (2011, July 18). To improve U.S. education, it's time to treat teachers as professionals. *The Washington Post.* Retrieved from http://www.washingtonpost.com

Gigante, N. (2006). *Teacher leadership in context: Its relationship with social, material, and human resources in schools implementing reform.* (Doctoral dissertation), Rutgers University, New Brunswick, NJ.

Grenda, J. P. (2006). Leadership, distributed. In F. English (Ed.), *Encyclopedia of educational leadership and administration* (Vol. 2) (pp. 566-568). Thousand Oaks, CA: Sage.

Hargreaves, A. & Fink, D. (2008). Distributed leadership: Democracy or delivery. *Journal of Educational Administration, 46*(2), 229-240.

Harris, A. (2002). Distributed leadership in schools: Leading or misleading. *Management in Education, 16*(5), 10-13.

Harris, A. (2003). Teacher leadership as distributed leadership: Heresy, fantasy, or possibility? *School Leadership and Management, 23*(3), 313-324.

Harris, A. (2009). Coda. In A. Harris (Ed.), *Distributed leadership: Different perspectives* (pp. 241-243). London: Springer.

Harris, A. & Spillane, J. (2008). Distributed leadership through the looking glass. *Management in Education, 22*(1), 31-34.

Harris, A. (2012). Distributed leadership: Implications for the role of the principal. *Journal of Management Development, 31*(1), 7-17.

Horsford, S. (2012). This bridge called my leadership: An essay on black women as bridge leaders in education. *International Journal of Qualitative Studies in Education, 25*(1), 11-22.

Katzenmeyer, M. & Moller, G. (2001/2009). *Awakening the sleeping giant: Helping teachers develop as leaders* (2nd ed.). Thousand Oaks, CA: Corwin Press, Inc.

Lieberman, A., Saxl, E., & Miles, M. (2007). Teacher leadership: Ideology and practice. In *The Jossey-Bass reader on educational leadership* (pp. 403–420). San Francisco: Jossey-Bass.

Leithwood, K. & Jantzi, D. (1999). The relative effects of principal and teacher sources of leadership on student engagement with school. *Educational Administration Quarterly, 35,* 679-706.

Lorde, A. (1984, 2007). *Sister Outsider.* Berkeley, CA: Crossing Press.

Lord, B., & Miller, B. (2000). *Teacher leadership: An appealing and inescapable force in school reform?* Boston: Education Development Center.

Mangin, M. & Stoelinga, S. (2011). Peer? Expert? Teacher leaders struggle to gain trust while establishing their expertise. *Journal of Staff Development, 32*(3), 48-52.

National Comprehensive Center for Teacher Quality. (2007). *Enhancing teacher leadership* (Government Cooperative Agreement Number S283B050051). Washington DC: www.ncctq.org

Reeves, D. (2008). *Reframing teacher leadership to improve your school.* Alexandria, VA: ASCD.

Shakeshaft, C., Brown, G., Irby, B., Grogan, M., & Ballenger, J. (2007). Increasing equity in educational leadership. In S. Klein, C. Dwyer, L. Fox, D. Grayson, C. Kramarae, D. Pollard, & B. Richardson (Eds.), *Handbook for achieving gender equity through education* (pp. 103-129). Hillsdale, NJ: Erlbaum.

Shields, C. (2004). Dialogic leadership for social justice: Overcoming pathologies of silence, *Educational Administration Quarterly, 40*(1), 109-132.

Silva, D., Gimbert, B., & Nolan, J. (2000). Sliding the doors: Locking and unlocking possibilities for teacher leadership. *Teacher College Record, 102(*4), 779-804.

Singh, K. (2011). Teacher leadership: Making your voice count. *Kappa Delta Pi Record, 48*(1), 6-10.

Smylie, M., Conley, S., & Marks, H. (2002). Exploring new approaches to teacher leadership for school improvement. In J. Murphy (Ed.), *The educational leadership challenge: Redefining leadership for the 21st century* (pp. 162-188). Chicago: University of Chicago Press.

Spillane, J. (2005). Distributed leadership. *The Educational Forum, 69*(2), 143-150.

Tooms, A., Lugg, C., & Bogotch, I. (2009). Rethinking the politics of fit and educational leadership. *Educational Administration Quarterly, 46(*1), 96-131.

York-Barr, J. & Duke, K. (2004). What do we know about teacher leadership? Findings from two decades of scholarship. *Review of Educational Research, 74(*3), 255-316.

Cherese D. Childers-McKee is a Ph.D. student and Holmes Scholar at the University of North Carolina at Greensboro in the department of Educational Leadership and Cultural Foundations (ELC). She is also a member of the Urban Education Collaborative at UNC Charlotte. Cherese has a Master of Education in Teaching English as a Second Language (TESL) from UNC Charlotte and a bachelor's in Spanish from Wake Forest University. Cherese is National Board Certified with 13 years of experience as a middle and high school teacher of English as a Second Language and teacher leader. Her research interests include African-American and Latina/o relations in urban schools and communities; equity in schools experiencing poverty, and women's and gender studies. She can be contacted at cdchilde@uncg.edu.

Chapter 7

A Postcard from Members of a PLC

Linda K. Lemasters, Michael J. Cieslak, Marguerita DeSander, and *Jennifer Clayton*

Over the past several years, words such as collaboration, collaborative teams, data, data dialogues, data driven instruction, and intervention have become ubiquitous with Professional Learning Communities (PLCs). There is little argument that these words are important aspects of a successful PLC; however, the ultimate success of a PLC is a much more complex issue. Peterson, McCarthey, and Elmore (1996) argued, "While school structures can provide opportunities for learning new practices, the structures, by themselves, do not cause the learning to occur" (p. 119). A successful PLC goes far beyond building common assessments, analyzing data, and providing intervention. A mature PLC that truly impacts student achievement focuses on building organizational capacity.

While one "postcard" cannot provide a "how to" for PLCs, we will discuss the essential components of effective PLCs by sharing the voices of teachers from group interviews both from schools that successfully use learning communities to enhance achievement and from schools that are beginning the journey. We also will focus on specific guidelines to assist in developing mature and effective PLCs. In order to have successful learning communities, leaders must increase their awareness of research and literature about schools that have been successful in their implementation.

OVERVIEW OF THE LITERATURE

During the last two decades, professional learning communities (PLCs) have become popular among school systems across the United States as a means to improve teaching and student achievement. While some researchers have investigated the effectiveness of PLCs (Ireland, 2010; Long, 2008; Wells & Feun, 2007), others have written about how to implement ever-changing PLC models (DuFour & Eaker, 1998; DuFour, 2004; DuFour, DuFour, & Eaker, 2008; Hord, 2004; Hord & Sommers, 2008). Hord (1997a, 2004) articulates five key dimensions of mature PLCs. Of these, shared or distributed leadership that produces a less hierarchical staff structure is an important approach to a mature, functioning PLC. Whether considering effectiveness or implementation, the PLC is not a program, a prepackaged reading or mathematics series, a new technology, or a legislative initiative. Rather, it is a process that focuses on changing the culture of a school from an industrial-age, top-down model to a learning organization. Harris and Spillane (2008) argued, "There is a growing recognition that the old organizational structures of schooling simply do not fit the requirements of learning in the twenty-first century" (p. 31). Although practitioners closest to students are often mandated to lead and learn collaboratively in focusing on student achievement, the ambiguity amongst the current research and literature leads to uncertainty about PLC effectiveness. Harris and Spillane (2008) questioned, "Do we have evidence to show that lateral, less hierarchical staff structures result in notable gains in student performance?" (p. 32).

Drawing upon our own research and experience and those of others, this "postcard" illustrates that supportive and shared leadership, shared values and vision, collective learning and application of learning, shared personal practice, and supportive conditions (Hord, 1997, 2004) fundamentally affect PLCs and have positive implications for student achievement. Before we delve into a description of the perspectives of teachers currently a part of a PLC, we would like to explore significant literature about professional learning communities in an effort to demonstrate how our research parallels and extends that of others who have written and theorized about PLCs.

The Beginning of the Issue

To gain a clear understanding of the fundamental concept of the PLC, a brief review of the history of the movement is required. Although the term, "PLC" became commonplace in many school systems in the 1990s, the concept took on different connotations from state to state, from school system to school system, and even among schools within the same system. Although PLCs can be flexible, their burgeoning popularity is unfortunate in some ways because they are often implemented using standard conceptual frameworks forced to fit unique situations. For instance, many schools implemented a PLC for the first time and modeled their implementation procedures after a school that had very different environmental and physical conditions. Therefore, in making modifications designed for completely different circumstances, they may not have had all of the key elements specific to their school needs in place before beginning. DuFour, DuFour, and Eaker (2008) summarized this sentiment by stating,

> While the term *professional learning communities* has become commonplace, the actual practices of a PLC have yet to become the norm in education. Too many schools, districts, and organizations calling themselves PLCs do virtually none of the things that characterize PLCs. (p. 14)

Breaking Ground

Reflective of the ambiguity of PLCs in schools, research also has been uncertain. For example, the purpose of Long's (2008) work was to determine if there were differences in student achievement between participants and nonparticipants in PLCs. While Long did not find a statistically significant relationship between participation in PLCs and student achievement, he recognized that implementation was a key factor. Similar to other researchers such as DuFour (2004), and Wells and Feun (2007), Long suggested,

> There is no assurance, therefore, that the sites identified as PLC schools in this study demonstrated full adherence or implementation of PLC characteristics and

ideals. Nor is there evidence to contradict the possibility that the schools that were *not* members of the Missouri Professional Learning Community Project at the time of the study might have adhered to many of the precepts and philosophies of the PLC model. (p. 84)

Indeed, all schools that claim to implement PLCs do not actually function as true PLCs (DuFour et al., 2008). Hord (1997a, 2004) identified five dimensions of a PLC: supportive and shared leadership, shared values and vision, collective learning and application of learning, shared personal practice and supportive conditions.

In the latter part of the 2000s, evidence of PLC effectiveness began to change. Ireland (2010) conducted a quantitative study that measured the relationship between the results of a 6-point Likert-like survey based on Hord's (1997a, 2004) five dimensions of a PLC and 10th-grade student performance on the California Standards Tests. The study involved 172 math, language arts, science, and social studies teachers and their 3,811 students in 12 California high schools. Ireland (2010) found that "some relationship does exist between teacher perception of PLC attributes and student achievement results" (p. 123), but these relationships were mixed. Ireland (2010) discovered that the relationship between PLC attributes and student achievement were all positive for history, mostly positive for science, mostly negative for math, and all negative for English. She attributed these findings to not only departmentalization and isolation in high schools but also hypothesized that most teachers had been trained with PLC literature. They knew, therefore, the correct things to say, but may not have necessarily applied them in practice.

As the first decade closed, the ambiguity began to dissipate. Researchers and practitioners (Arroyo, 2011; Cieslak, 2011; Gallozzi, 2011; Wilson, 2011 & Wolford, 2011) found that when the fundamental principles of a PLC were followed, student achievement was enhanced. Ireland's (2010) study to that date was one of the most valuable studies that pointed to the effectiveness of PLCs, while others were indicative of (a) the varied implementation of PLCs and (b) the ability to identify PLCs.

Wolford (2011) conducted a phenomenological study on two principals and their leadership practices in the sustainability of PLCs in two elementary schools. Wolford used purposeful sampling to ensure that the schools under study were indeed behaving as a mature professional learning community. One of the criteria was sustained improved student achievement. Wolford used semi-structured interviews and the Professional Learning Communities Assessment–Revised (PLCA-R) to triangulate data. Both of the principals supported effective PLCs, with Wolford (2011) finding the following in both schools:

1. Staff members were involved in making decisions.
2. The principal incorporated advice from the staff members.
3. Power and authority were shared democratically with the principal.
4. Decision-making was through committees across grade levels.
5. Leadership was promoted and nurtured. (p. 72)

These leadership characteristics are congruent with the PLC principles articulated by Hord (1997a, 2004) and DuFour and Eaker (1998). Likewise, Wolford's conclusions also supported Cieslak's (2011) findings that mature PLCs have a strong sense of the

PLC principles (supportive and shared leadership, shared values and vision, collective learning and application of learning, shared personal practice and supportive conditions) as defined by Hord.

Arroyo (2011) conducted a study to identify the strategies used to maintain a successful PLC and to address the issue of adding new members. Framed once more in Hord's five dimensions of a PLC, Arroyo created five questions to reflect each dimension and one additional question to address the addition of new members to the PLC. The researcher identified 22 middle schools of interest, eight of which demonstrated strong evidence of a PLC. Of those eight schools, six "met state and federal learning targets" (p. 58). Of the six schools, five principals agreed to participate in the study. Arroyo's choice to interview the principals as opposed to actual teachers lends balance to Cieslak's (2011) research, which used teacher focus groups, in that findings from both studies were similar.

For each of Hord's five dimensions, Arroyo found the mean score for the five schools included in the interview portion of the study to be several points higher than those schools that did not participate in the interview portion of the study. Again, schools asked to participate in the study "met state and federal learning targets" (p. 58). These findings lent evidence to the positive relationship between PLCs and student achievement.

Another study that speaks to the relationship of PLC maturity and positive student achievement is Wilson's (2011) research on teacher leadership in PLCs. Wilson conducted a mixed methods study using Hord's School Professional Staff as a Learning Community Questionnaire (SPSLCQ) instrument and semi-structured interviews. Wilson's sample was identified by using schools that received funding for the Smaller Learning Communities (SLC) federal grant. In order for these schools to qualify for the grant, schools must have failed to make adequate yearly progress, consisted of sizeable low performing subgroups, and had "large student subgroups underrepresented in rigorous work" (p. 58).

While finding that a significant number of teachers did not grow as teacher leaders as a result of their participation in a PLC, Wilson indicated that "barriers to teacher leadership were time constraints, added responsibilities, a lack of teacher buy-in, and a lack of shared leadership" (p. 104). These findings indirectly support research done by Arroyo (2011), Cieslak (2011), and Wolford (2011). Their research found that Wilson's barriers to teacher leadership were also in conflict with successful PLCs, particularly shared leadership.

In some schools, teachers view the PLC as a vehicle to improve their teaching and the success of their students. In other schools, principals and teachers view the PLC as another responsibility heaped upon their already demanding schedules. Wilson (2011) substantiated this notion when he found that, among several other factors, an absence of shared leadership inhibited teacher leadership. This research explains why some PLCs are successful and others are not.

In the descriptions that follow, we identify the factors that influenced the teaching staff's level of maturity as a PLC. We found that a successful PLC goes far beyond building common assessments, analyzing data, and providing intervention. A mature PLC that truly impacts student achievement focuses on building organizational capacity. This begins with a principal who understands that building the culture of a PLC is equally important as teaching the processes of a PLC. By focusing on shared leadership, shared values and vision, collective learning and application of learning, and supportive conditions, a PLC will develop that truly impacts teaching, learning, and student achievement.

OUR RESEARCH

We conducted a study using the SPSLCQ to identify and measure the maturity level of PLCs in schools that were identified by their division's central office as *having* a PLC according to Hord's (1997a, 2004) five dimensions of a PLC (supportive and shared leadership, shared values and vision, collective learning and application of learning, shared personal practice, and supportive conditions). The SPSLCQ, chosen because it both measures the maturity level of a PLC and has been satisfactorily tested for validity and reliability, contains 17 items, with overall scores ranging from 17 to 85 points. After administering the SPSLCQ to 59 teachers at 21 schools, we conducted focus groups at the two schools that were identified as having the highest scores for maturity level as a PLC and the two that were identified as having the lowest scores for maturity level as a PLC. Due to the various sizes of the schools, participants who took the SPSLCQ varied between one and six teachers per school. Schools in which only one participant responded were not asked to participate in the study. In addition, several schools (Alantown, Leesburgh, Larry Lemon, and John Glenn) opted not to participate in the focus group portion of the study.

Of the schools that agreed to participate in the focus group portion, the two schools that scored highest on the SPSLCQ were Milton Brand ($n = 4$, $\bar{x} = 70$) and Duck Creek ($n = 5$, $\bar{x} = 68.60$). The two schools that scored the lowest were Petunia ($n = 3$, $\bar{x} = 58.00$) and Pebeland ($n = 2$, $\bar{x} = 57.00$). Figure 7.1 details the SPSLCQ scores of the 21 schools that participated. Scores from the four schools (Milton Brand, Duck Creek, Petunia, and Pebeland) were compared against data on standardized testing throughout the analysis of the data. Students at Milton Brand consistently scored the highest in reading, writing, and mathematics assessments overall and within subcategories.

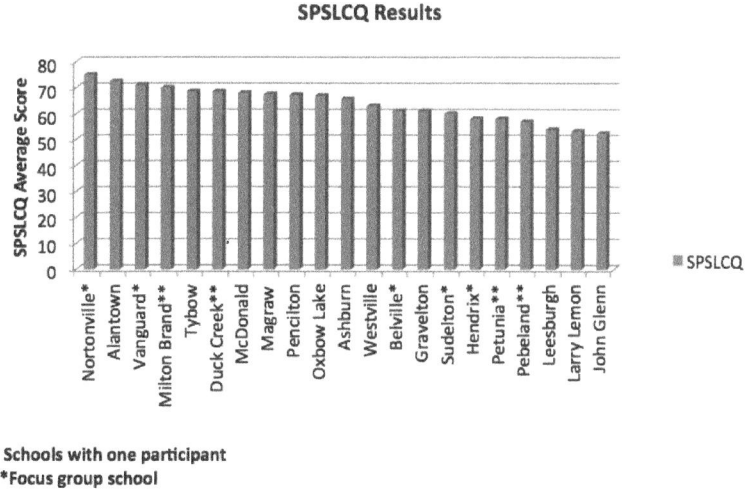

* Schools with one participant
**Focus group school

Figure 7.1. Coded Frequency SPSLCQ Responses from Participants

Through an analysis of the SPSLCQ data and perspectives shared in focus groups, we identify specific suggestions for both developing mature PLCs and assisting leadership in making PLCs more than a vogue stratagem. Leaders within contemporary schools cannot expect to nurture successful learning communities if they are unaware of research and literature from schools that have been successful in their implementation—information gleaned from real journeys of practitioners involved in PLCs.

Supportive and Shared Leadership

The literature around *supportive and shared leadership* points away from the industrial-age, top down model that emphasizes staff as the people charged with carrying out the principal's decisions (Covey, 2004; Northouse, 2013, Oshry, 1995, Spillane, 2006). Alternatively, leadership in a PLC focuses on governance spread across a horizontal plane. Mature PLCs have principals who involve the entire staff in discussing and making decisions about school issues. In contrast, less mature PLCs fail to share information with staff or provide them opportunities to be involved.

Milton Brand faculty expressed positive impressions of the supportive and shared leadership that their principal fostered, thereby indicating a mature dimension of the PLC (Wolford, 2011). Multiple times, one focus group participant spoke with high regard of the principal's sharing power, authority, and decision making with the staff, stating that the school administrator involved the entire staff and participated democratically when discussing and making decisions about school issues. When asked how frequently the staff was involved in making decisions about school issues, the participant replied, "I would say frequently. . . . Yeah. We are a major part of the decisions that are made in our school," (Participant 1). This teacher's comments support the notion of shared leadership between the principal and staff as a mechanism that contributes to student achievement.

In contrast, schools that demonstrated a lower level of maturity articulated the relationship between school leadership and the classroom teacher as asymmetric. Pebeland, Petunia, and Duck Creek all had higher frequencies of feelings of minimal power and decision sharing than Milton Brand. Participant 2 from Petunia stated,

> Everything we do as a teacher, as a staff, as a community—there is no other choice. There's not a whole lot of room for individual variation on that. This is where we have to go. This is our testing schedule. This is our pacing guide. This is how it relates to the SOL, and this is what we need to get done, so you check your test and teach.

Participant 2's comment supports the findings of researchers that point to autonomy as an important element of motivation (Pink, 2009). Because of the role of autonomy in the industrial-age model of education, the challenge of balancing autonomy and interdependence in the contemporary school setting is an issue confronted by many educators. Senge (1990) captured the idea of this balance by stating, "People continually expand their capacity to create the results they truly desire, where new and expansive patterns of thinking are nurtured, where collective aspiration is set free, and where people are continually learning how to learn together" (p. 3).

Teachers from Petunia held similar sentiments. When asked about staff involvement in the process of making decisions, Participant 2 responded,

> Most of—no. Most of the staff has been head down, so . . . I don't think they have a whole lot of decision on . . . . We have a decision as far as like what book we want to read and things of that nature. We're given kind of some leeway on how we want to present it or what parts we want to do, but . . . . Most of those decisions are county, head/face down. We're not site based as far as anything goes—those decisions are made.

These characteristics, described by Participant 2, show the limited flexibility of an industrial-age, top-down management model. On the other hand, PLCs that emphasize shared leadership are better able to meet the needs of teachers and students in a school.

Duck Creek, though in the middle of the spectrum of PLC maturity, still had minimal shared leadership. The coded transcript of the Duck Creek group interview revealed a low frequency of the highest positive remarks based on the SPSLCQ subcategories. For instance, Duck Creek had only one positive remark about principal leadership compared to Milton Brand's nine positive remarks. However, this finding could be a result of the temperament of self-reported data. A participant from Duck Creek indicated that the principal involved the staff by providing "journal articles and opportunities to talk back and forth—ideas that she would like to see" (Participant 1). In this case, the principal is initiating the direction and allowing the staff to form their own opinions.

Duck Creek, Pebeland, and Petunia frequently achieved at a lower rate than Milton Brand on the mathematics, English reading, and English writing Standards of Learning (SOL). Milton Brand's strong democratic leadership and student achievement success demonstrated that the maturity of their PLC was in contrast to Oshry's (1995) and Covey's (2004) belief that schools operate best in top-down systems, in which the school is driven entirely by the principal. The success of Milton Brand demonstrated that mature PLCs were moving away from the asymmetric relationships between school leadership and classroom teachers (Northouse, 2013; Spillane, 2006).

Specifically, what do these shared, collaborative relationships look like? According to Hord's (1997b) first dimension of supportive and shared leadership, the staff is a major part of the decision-making process, which should be democratic in nature. The principal relies on staffs' local expertise to guide instruction by engaging them holistically or tapping staff that have an expertise in a particular area. This was best measured by the staff's feeling of value in the process instead of an arbitrary number of times a staff voted on an issue. This evidence was consistent with Arroyo (2011), who found that principals who provide members with leadership opportunities and limited mandates met state and federal learning targets. Wolford (2011) also found that shared, collaborative relationships were essential to a successful PLC. Our research results indicated that schools that are less mature have little choice with little room for variation. The staff perceives leadership and teaching as hierarchical and dictated by state and district policy.

Shared Values and Vision

According to Hord (1997b), "Sharing vision is not just agreeing with a good idea; it is a particular mental image of what is important to an individual and to an organization" (p. 3). Mature PLCs share visions that are focused on student learning—visions consistently referenced in the staff's work (Hord, 1997b). In contrast, in less mature PLCs, the school vision is widely divergent among staff members (Hord, 1997a). Milton Brand had the most positive perspective of the staff vision. Six times a focus group participant spoke about how the staff's vision was embraced by the entire staff before the school year began and emphasized to students every day. The faculty could recite main facets of the school mission from memory, emphasizing the focus on student learning and improvement. A participant also indicated that the entire staff discussed the vision: "Yeah, we have a vision and mission and goal, and we go through our—you know, our vision and mission goals like being lifelong learners, critical and compassionate thinkers of the world" (Participant 1). This sentiment reinforces Senge's (1990) articulation of the importance of mental models or unconscious influences on a person's thought process and approach to solving problems.

Milton Brand Participant 1's statement was in contrast to the SPSLCQ shared vision subcategory results for Petunia and Pebeland. Petunia and Pebeland had the weakest perspective on school vision and indicated that visions for improvement held by staff members were widely divergent. Participant 3 from Pebeland said,

> What we talked about—the Baldrige Program that we do here—which relates to an effective way of controlling, I guess I can say controlling, discipline in our classroom. It's a program that we're using now. We started with the vision, mission, and goal already and I think that kind of relates back to the PLC. It's just under a different program. And we've actually had our staff meetings already. (Participant 3)

PLCs develop a vision and incorporate programs that fit within that vision, not the other way around. The vision also has to be meaningful. If the vision is not meaningful, the words become insignificant as noted by Participant 3:

> We actually have a vision statement somewhere.... If you want to brush everything aside and be honest about it, the entire focus is to pass the SOL. You can throw whatever adjectives you want on it, but that's why we're here. That's why I'm hired.

Another telling statement from Petunia was "Two years ago, we needed that vision...." (Participant 4), to which Participant 3 replied,

> He's basically saying that's window dressing. The reality of the situation is . . . it's passing the SOL and becoming a school of excellence is what it comes down to.

Participant 5 then replied, "And maybe there's nothing dishonest about that because that sort of translates that all children will succeed, right? So, maybe it's not all that phony anyway, even though it sure sounds phony" (Participant 5).

The teachers from Pebeland and Petunia understood that the goal of helping children succeed had not changed, but they had become exasperated with "window dressings" and the multitude of programs initiated at their school that focused on passing a standardized test. Dodd's (2006) research substantiated this, finding that teachers were skeptical of implementing a PLC because of the plethora of programs and reform initiatives that had come and gone. Likewise, Wilson (2011) found that a significant number of teachers who participated in a PLC did not grow as leaders because they lacked buy-in. Consistent with findings from Cieslak (2011), participants in our study from Pebeland and Petunia reiterated their feeling that the vision was more district-based than their own. These findings suggest that ownership, one of the most important aspects of the PLC, relies on the principal's ability to engage faculty in co-creating a genuine vision for the school.

Overall, these findings support Hord's (1997b, 2004) and DuFour and Eaker's (1998) notion that shared power is established by creating a vision, mission, values, and goals. This process can serve as a mental model for how teachers think and behave (Senge, 1990). In our research, we found that Milton Brand had a mature command of this PLC principle, which was reflected both in their focus group responses and in their student achievement scores.

Collective Learning and Application of Learning

In this dimension, a mature PLC staff learns collectively and applies their learning to create high cognitive demand tasks and solutions to address student needs (Hord, 1997a). The entire staff meets to discuss issues, share information, and learn with and from one another. In contrast, less mature PLCs meet infrequently or randomly with little emphasis on collaboration and student learning. One of the main themes that emerged during the group interview with Milton Brand was the importance of collaboration and collective learning. A participant indicated that the staff met weekly and described their meetings as instructionally focused. The participant said, "They're not staff meetings where they're just talking at us. We're really doing instructional—our focus is instruction" (Participant 1).

Exemplified in the case of Milton Brand, Coldren and Spillane (2007) found that instructional leadership and collective learning were key components of a mature learning community. According to Hord (1997a, 2004) and Senge (1990), collaborating and operating within a team framework promote collective creativity that will affect student learning and systems thinking—the practice of understanding how external and internal influences affect the entire organization—in this case, the school. Frequently, schools focus on assembling homogenous teams of teachers, referred to as collaborative learning teams. While these are aspects of a PLC, Milton Brand exemplified more mature dimensions of a PLC in that teachers had moved beyond simply acquiring information from a few colleagues in their departments to sharing best practices and learning from one another as an entire staff. Products generated from this collaboration included creative programs like gallery and graffiti walks.

The other focus group schools did not meet the level of maturity demonstrated by Milton Brand. The other three schools met primarily in subgroups. One teacher from Pebeland indicated they sometimes met with "vertical [teams], a specialist and look[ed] at the [math] scope and sequence across the entire building with data and curriculum" (Participant 4). On the other hand, the staff rarely met to discuss substantive student-centered educational issues:

> We're departmentalized, so therefore we all teach math but we—I teach writing, she teaches reading. She teaches science, and then Jack teaches geography. So we pretty much go back and, you know, if we have to reteach for mastery, we go back and probably make up our own assessments. (Participant 3)

Participant 2 substantiated Participant 3's comment by stating, "And it keeps—in our individual subjects, it keeps it very easy since with me being the reading teacher, I've created or chosen—all 90 students get the exact same assessment and the exact same format." The keyword from Participant 3 was "individual." The staff from Pebeland was not using its collective talents.

In regards to collective learning, the participants frequently referred to informal meetings between subgroups. Participant 2 from Petunia indicated that the grade-level team held a day-long meeting once a quarter to plan and discuss data. They also had daily common planning time. Beyond that time, collective learning was informal:

> Well, we certainly share products. We share the social studies study guides and assessments, and special projects. We share the science experiments that we're supposed to do, a weekly science experiment. So, it's like, 'Hey, what are you doing? What are you doing? Okay. Great—here,' passing out information about it—you just pull this up on the Web. It's almost to the point where you accept this, even though you've got a treasure trove that's stored. And you take, even though you've got a whole bunch more, and just simply to be polite, because there's so much sharing going on . . . so, there's been—this has been going on for years. I kind of have to chuckle about, 'Oh, gee, the PLCs and you guys have got to get out of your four-walled room and you got to talk to people and work together on . . .' We've been talking and working with each other for years. It's not some—it's not an epiphany that, oh my God! This has been going on for a long time, maybe not to the extent that it is now, but especially with data. (Participant 5)

Participant 3 indicated that he sometimes visited his friend who taught third grade to get ideas about students whom his friend may have had 2 years ago with the goal of learning strategies to help a student having difficulty. As shown by Participant 5's comments, while there is sharing at Petunia, the arbitrary nature of the practice, coupled with the disconnect between collaboration and a shared vision, limit its effectiveness and potential.

There is little doubt about Participant 5's assertion that teachers have been working together for years, but Participant 3, who "visited his *friend*," captures the limitations of collaboration in the industrial-age school model in which collaboration is limited to closest colleagues. Limiting oneself to a *circle of friends* restricts the potential of the entire teaching staff. It inhibits the exposure of collective talent to the rest of the staff. Similarly, while important to work in homogenous teams, it is essential for the entire staff, together, to share its collective creativity.

Milton Brand had the highest frequency of remarks concerning the entire staff's collective learning and application of what they learned. This finding substantiated the importance of the relationship between a staff's collective learning and application thereof and their high student achievement. In contrast, Pebeland and Petunia, whose achievement scores were not as high as Milton Brand's, had a multitude of midlevel frequency remarks showing limited collaboration. This evidence supported the argument that the PLC dimension of collective learning and application functions as a mechanism that contributes to student achievement.

One term that was mentioned in all four focus group interviews was data. Many researchers indicated that the term PLC had become ubiquitous; in this case, so had the term data. Wells and Feun (2007) found that teachers seldom examined and compared student learning results, thus indicating a low level of maturity as a PLC. The use of data by the schools has been a vehicle for increasing the maturity level of Hord's *collective learning and application of learning* dimension. Participant 5 from Petunia captured this sentiment when he spoke (as previously quoted) of sharing data: "So, there's been [sharing]—this has been going on for years. . . . maybe not to the extent that it is now . . . especially with data." The staff at least occasionally assesses, acts on their findings, and implements plans to improve teaching and learning. Therefore, the responses from the four schools suggests that although the most mature PLCs frequently implemented plans that addressed student needs and assessed the impact of those actions, other less mature PLCs also showed budding potential and promise in this area.

Shared Personal Practice

According to the literature, staff within mature PLCs frequently review and give feedback on one another's teaching (Hord, 1997a). The PLC dimension of peer review and feedback was the lowest area of PLC maturity among all focus groups. Several of the focus group schools indicated that although they were interested in observing colleagues, they rarely had an opportunity to do so. Many of the interviewed teachers perceived that the inability to find coverage for their classrooms during observation periods was due to school budget constraints brought on by a depressed economy. Participant 2 from Pebeland captured this sentiment: "Within the budget, no. [Laugh] Yeah. I mean our budget is extremely tight this year across the county and so—no." There simply were not enough funds in the budget to allow substitutes to cover classes and enable teachers to observe their peers. Moreover, this idea was in contrast to the industrial-age model, in which peer observation was the least innate behavior, teachers taught behind closed doors, and accountability was limited to attendance, compliance, and tenure. For example, Participant 2 from Pebeland stated,

> We have a lot of ladies in the building that have been teaching for multiple decades, and they have their groove and have, with our past principal, we've been

a school of excellence for 8, 9 years. And everybody was just let, walk their own pace, their own route.

Even at Milton Brand, peer observation and feedback were not practiced regularly. When asked about how often teachers were able to observe other classrooms, Participant 1 responded, "Not very often, which is unfortunate. It's one of the things that we're working towards as a school." She explained that as they added a new dimension to their PLC every year, peer observation was something they desired to do more of in the near future. Referencing the economic crisis as well as the tradition of teachers' acting independently in their classrooms, schools in the implementation process indicated that peer observation and review were the most difficult mechanism of the PLC process.

When asked about how often teachers were able to observe other classrooms, Participant 2 from Petunia responded, "If we wanted . . . I've gone to other schools to observe different things, especially last year when we did not make AYP. We were given time—team leaders were given time to go observe and bring something back to hopefully change." Beyond last year's experience, however, teachers were not given formal time to observe and receive feedback from other teachers. Participant 3 concurred:

> Yeah, on an individual basis, we're not really given a ton of time to go and see—like if, from time to time during my planning time, I will go and watch someone else's classroom just for something else, and I like to see how different people interact.

It was clear in all cases that formal observation of peers was limited and unstructured. Several participants attributed the limitations to budget concerns, while others did informal drop-ins with peers. Despite these difficulties, the participants' reactions toward this dimension demonstrated enthusiasm for change; however, a great deal of effort will be needed to implement this element of mature PLCs.

Supportive Conditions

Supportive conditions that promote positive use of time, physical conditions, and emotional health characterize mature PLCs. Supportive conditions are critical in the maturation of the other four dimensions discussed in the previous sections. Less mature PLCs meet infrequently, the facility is not favorable for staff interaction, and trust and openness are limited. For example, a school that has overcrowding may displace teachers to obscure places inside or outside of the building. This isolation inhibits the communication and collaboration among teachers.

In terms of time committed to whole-staff interactions, Milton Brand reported that they met as an entire staff every Thursday before school, even if school was delayed for weather. Participant 1 from Milton Brand expressed the importance of meeting regularly: "We're having staff meetings, and if school's delayed, we have it an hour before the school—the kids show up. That's every week." This situation was quite different for Petunia, which met twice a month as a staff. A staff's commitment to meet is driven from the mental model they created through their vision of commitment to one another and student achievement. However, as mentioned previously, equally important to the frequency of staff interactions, is the nature and quality of those interactions.

The size, structure, and arrangement of the school are essential components of a successful PLC (Hord 1997a, 2004). This PLC dimension reflected varying levels of maturity among the focus group schools. Three of the focus groups indicated that the natural size and structure of the school facilitated interaction. For example, Participant 2 from Pebeland described:

> The physical condition of the school, we're actually one of the smallest elementaries in the county. And I have to state for faculty and for the students—I love it. Some of our schools from the county elementary have 900 to 1,200 students. And here at Pebeland we're only at about 500, to 600.

The Duck Creek participant thought the lack of a large meeting space hindered entire staff interaction but that the arrangement of fifth-grade teachers on one team was favorable. School size can certainly impact the intimacy of a school, yet we have seen success at larger schools when there are processes in place that facilitate communication within the scope of the school's vision.

Supportive conditions reach beyond design of the building and arrangement of staff. Supportive conditions include trust and caring relationships. Hord (1997a, 2004) and Eaker, Dufour, and Dufour (2002) stress the importance of trust and collaborative relationships in a mature, full-functioning PLC. Maturity in this area is essential for schools wishing to encompass all of the dimensions of a PLC and make progress toward student achievement. Participant 4 from Milton Brand said, "I think we are on our way. I think we still have some work to do." According to the participant, the grade-level team was new, and they were still working toward their common goal. "On my grade level, we're a new team, so we're still working on building that trust and that communication piece" (Participant 1).

An emphasis on trust and caring relationships was evident in other focus group schools as well. Participant 4 from Pebeland captured this sentiment:

> We don't get to see everybody in the building. But I think for the majority, even if we don't get to see them on a day-to-day basis or you see them for 1 week, I think that anybody would be willing to sit down and talk to you and you know. I don't think there's any one person in the building that I wouldn't be able to trust to go to and say, "Hey, I have this issue. Can you help me out?"

The participants also indicated that trust and openness characterized the school and created a camaraderie that maintained enthusiasm for open communication:

> I'm excited about being here because I do feel that when I need to go to someone, you know, I can talk to them, you know. They're open to listen, they respect my opinion and so forth and it's just been wonderful, you know, knowing that you do have those people that you can go to here. It's not everybody because I don't see everybody, but for those that I have come in contact with, you know, trustworthiness, I think is a plus. (Participant 3)

Despite the positive emphasis on trust and caring relationships and overall supportive conditions at Pebeland, structured, collaborative meetings were infrequent, and the school was weak in many of the other four dimensions, perhaps explaining the school's designation as a less mature, still developing PLC.

Hord (1997a, 2004) stressed that a mature PLC possesses a variety of strategies and structures that promote communication. The SPSLCQ and focus group results revealed that while many of the school buildings' designs facilitated communication, schools often lacked necessary processes and procedures to encourage staff communication. With the exception of unstructured, common planning time, all focus group schools indicated much more informal communication than formal strategies. Teachers at Petunia had a "Data Day" once a quarter to talk about data and planning, but were left to their own devices for the remainder of the term. Milton Brand was the only school, with the exception of "Data Day" at Petunia, in which a communication strategy was facilitated by the principal. The principal at Milton Brand frequently placed teachers in small groups to facilitate interaction and communication. Facility design and facilitated collaboration are essential to developing a mature PLC. Without strong maturity in both of these categories, formal, directed communication becomes ineffective.

CONCLUSIONS

We discovered supportive and shared leadership, shared values and vision, collective learning and application of learning, shared personal practice, and supportive conditions affect the maturity of a PLC and have positive implications for student achievement.

It is important to recognize that none of the schools we surveyed approached full maturity as a PLC according to Hord's (1997a, 2004) five dimensions. Even Milton Brand ($\bar{x} = 70.00$), which had been implementing PLCs for 5 years, was 15 points below the highest possible score on the SPSLCQ. One of their teachers noted,

> And at every year it [PLC], it's another dimension added to it . . . . It functions different every year because every year we get a little more experience. Every year, we learn to collaborate a little bit more. (Participant 1)

Participant 2 from Pebeland ($\bar{x} = 57.00$) stated, "We're just now starting to learn about it [PLC] and just to begin dabbling and just understanding what truly is a PLC." The expressed sentiment and scores on the SPSLCQ from Milton Brand and Pebeland indicate that maturing as a PLC is a growth process that occurs over time. Implementing a PLC involves time to sow, nurture, and cultivate a vision, as well as collaborate and create trust among staff. Supportive conditions make these processes easier.

Value and vision are essential tenants of the PLC as articulated by Hord (1997a, 2004). Schools that have mature values and vision go beyond arbitrary recitation of the school vision. Mature schools *live* their values and vision. Staff demonstrates enthusiasm in these tenets because they truly believe in them, and the tenets are a central principle of everything they do. In addition, the vision is focused on teaching and learning, as in Milton Brand. This finding is supported by Arroyo (2011), who found that mature schools that met federal learning targets collectively create and regularly revisit their vision and values. Less mature PLCs, as demonstrated thorough conversations with participants from Pebeland and Petunia, often demonstrate cynicism when it comes to values and vision. They may or may not be aware of them and treat values and vision as superficial. In less mature PLCs (e.g., with the Baldridge program at Pebeland) visions may be emphasized at the beginning of the year, fade in the subsequent days, and not be focused on student learning.

Mature PLCs exemplify the collective learning and application of learning dimension. Mature PLCs meet frequently with an emphasis on sharing and learning, as well as on the analysis of data (Wolford, 2011). In mature PLCs, the entire staff meets in both vertical and horizontal teams, while less mature PLCs primarily meet as subgroups or in whole staff meetings that are infrequent and primarily information-based. In a mature PLC the administrator behaves as an instructional leader as opposed to simply being a disseminator of information as in less mature PLCs. Mature PLCs value data and meet frequently to discuss evidence of results in the forms of both qualitative and quantitative data. Less mature PLCs look at data with cynicism or reserve the analysis of data for a specific day (Data Day).

As mentioned earlier, peer review and feedback was the least developed dimension of the four schools' PLCs. Arroyo (2011) found that PLCs that "openly promote teacher observations of instructional methods, lesson plans, and student engagement" (p. 165) met federal learning targets. This finding also was corroborated by Wolford (2011). However, participants' weakness in this dimension was not due to lack of enthusiasm; rather, all four focus groups felt there was either inadequate funding or time for peers to observe one another. The school that demonstrated the most mature PLC, Milton Brand, indicated that peer observation was to be the focus of their development as a PLC for the next school year.

In terms of Hord's fifth dimension—supportive conditions—a mature PLC such as Milton Brand commits time for whole staff *interaction*. For example, they met every Thursday regardless of weather delay. This is supported by Arroyo (2011), who found that mature PLCs need "formal blocks of time in the schedule for collaboration" (p. 165). On the other hand, less mature PLCs meet less frequently, and may have either routine or unstructured meeting times. In a less mature PLC, a whole staff meeting might take the form of staff sitting in rows of chairs receiving information. In contrast, in a mature learning community, structured meetings are organized with a focus on promoting interaction amongst peers. Finally, more mature staffs have emphasized trusting and caring relationships, another essential characteristic of a mature PLC (Arroyo, 2011).

Where Long's (2008) study found that *true* identification of a PLC was near impossible to gauge, in the research presented in this postcard, we were able to identify varying maturity levels of a PLC and suggest important connections to student achievement. These findings also elucidated the statistically significant relationship that Ireland (2010) found between student achievement and teacher perception of PLC attributes. The findings from our research further help to explain the specific PLC mechanisms that affect student achievement. Several other studies (Arroyo, 2011; Gallozzi, 2011; Wilson, 2011, & Wolford, 2011) had similar research questions and found similar conclusions.

This study, however, highlights the characteristics of mature PLCs. Through focus group interviews, the critical dimensions of a mature PLC are explained through the voices of actual teachers. A mature PLC that truly impacts student achievement must focus on building organizational capacity. By nurturing and focusing on shared leadership, shared values and vision, collective learning and application of learning, shared personal practice, and supportive conditions, a PLC will impact teaching, learning, and student achievement.

References

Arroyo, H. (2011). *Strategies used by successful professional learning communities to maintain Hord's dimensions of PLCs and include new members.* (University of La Verne). ProQuest Dissertations and Theses, Retrieved from http://search.proquest.com/docview/896956740?accountid=11243

Cieslak, M. J. (2011). *The impact on student achievement of an elementary school teaching staff's maturity level as a professional learning community, according to Hord's five-dimensional conceptual framework: A mixed-methods study.* The George Washington University). ProQuest Dissertations and Theses, 262. Retrieved from http://search.proquest.com/docview/861744488?accountid=11243. (861744488).

Coldren, A., & Spillane, J. (2007). Making connections to teaching practice: The role of boundary practices in instructional leadership. *Education Policy, 2*(21), 369-396.

Covey, S. R. (2004). *The 8th habit: From effectiveness to greatness.* New York, NY: Free Press.

Dodd, K. T. (2006). *It is the process, not the test: A mixed method study of a professional learning community at one elementary school in Oklahoma* (Doctoral dissertation). Retrieved from Dissertation Abstracts International-A, 67(03). (UMI No. 3211366)

DuFour, R. (2004). What is a "professional learning community"? *Educational Leadership, 61*(8), 6-11.

DuFour, R., DuFour, R., & Eaker, R. (2008). *Revisiting professional learning communities at work: New insights for improving schools.* Bloomington, IN: National Education Services.

DuFour, R., & Eaker, R. (1998). *Professional Learning Communities at work: Best practices for enhancing student achievement.* Bloomington, IN: National Education Service.

Eaker, R., DuFour, R., & DuFour, R. (2002). *Getting started: Reculturing schools to become PLCs.* Bloomington, IN: Solution Tree.

Gallozzi, J. (2011). *The correlation between professional learning communities & collective efficacy & the resulting impact on student growth data.* (University of Denver). ProQuest Dissertations and Theses, Retrieved from http://search.proquest.com/docview/902174765?accountid=11243

Harris, A., & Spillane, J. (2008). Distributive leadership through the looking glass. *Management in Education, 22*(1), 31-34.

Hord, S. M. (1997a). *Professional Learning Communities: Communities of continuous inquiry and improvement*. Austin, TX: Southwest Educational Development Laboratory.

Hord, S. (1997b). Professional Learning Communities: What Are They and Why Are They Important? *Issues About Change, 6*(1), 1-8.

Hord, S. M. (Ed.). (2004). *Learning together, leading together: Changing schools through Professional Learning Communities*. New York, NY: Teachers College Press.

Hord, S. M., & Sommers, W. A. (2008). *Leading professional learning communities*. Thousand Oaks, CA: Corwin Press.

Ireland, M. W. (2010). *An examination of the relationship between teachers' perceptions of the presence of professional learning community attributes and student achievement* (Doctoral dissertation). Retrieved from Dissertation Abstracts International, 71(10). (UMI No. 3424356)

Long, C. N. (2008). *A comparison of student achievement between Missouri professional learning community participants and non-participants* (Doctoral dissertation). Retrieved from Dissertation Abstracts International, 69(10). (UMI No. 3330538)

Northouse, P. G. (2013). *Leadership theory and practice* (6th Ed.) Thousand Oaks, CA: Sage Publications.

Oshry, B. (1995). *Seeing systems: Unlocking the mysteries of organizational life*. San Francisco, CA: Berrett-Koehler.

Peterson, P., McCarthy, S., & Elmore, R. (1996). Learning from school restructuring. *American Educational Research Journal, 33*(1), 119–153.

Senge, P. M. (1990). *The fifth discipline: The art & practice of the learning organization*. New York: Doubleday.

Spillane, J. P. (2006). *Distributed Leadership*. San Francisco, CA: Jossey-Bass.

Wells, C., & Feun, L. (2007). Implementation of learning community principles: A study of six high schools. *NASSP Bulletin, 91*(2), 141-160.

Wilson, A. G. (2011). *Understanding the cultivation of teacher leadership in professional learning communities*. (University of South Florida). ProQuest Dissertations and Theses, Retrieved from http://search.proquest.com/docview/884221864?accountid=11243

Wolford, D. W. (2011). *Effective leadership practices in the sustainability of professional learning communities in two elementary schools*. (East Tennessee State University). ProQuest Dissertations and Theses, Retrieved from http://search.proquest.com/docview/918227220?accountid=11243

Dr. Linda K. Lemasters completed her EdD at Virginia Polytechnic Institute and State University and was a former assistant superintendent of administrative services, director of human resources, instructional supervisor, as well as teacher. Linda currently is an associate professor of educational administration and policy studies in the Graduate School of Education and Human Development with The George Washington University. Her areas of expertise and research interests include strategic planning, facilities management, and women in leadership. She is president of the International Society of Educational Planning, editor of the *International Journal of Educational Leadership Preparation,* and published in numerous peer-reviewed journals. The second improved edition of *School Maintenance and renovation: Administrative policies, practices, and economics*, which she co-authored, was just published. She can be contacted at lindal@gwu.edu.

Dr. Michael Cieslak was a social studies teacher in Lansing, MI and Fairfax, VA. He has held a number of leadership positions and most recently was the Educational Specialist for Social Studies, Health and PE, and World Language for Fairfax County Public Schools. Michael earned his bachelor and master's degrees from Michigan State University. He earned his doctorate in Educational Leadership and administration at The George Washington University. Michael can be contacted at mjcieslak@fcps.edu.

Dr. Marguerita DeSander earned her Ph.D. in Educational Policy, Planning, and Leadership from the College of William and Mary and her J.D. from The Thomas M. Cooley Law School. Marguerita's research interests include educational law, personnel administration in education, educational policy and reform initiatives. She is the former assistant superintendent for human resources for Lincoln County (NC) schools and executive director of human resources and coordinator of personnel for Williamsburg-James City County (VA) Public Schools. She has presented and published on the topics of teacher evaluation and merit pay, tenure teacher dismissal for incompetence, and the incongruence of federal legislation regarding public education. Margie is past president of the Consortium for Educational Accountability and Teacher Evaluation. Marguerita can be contacted at desander@gwu.edu.

Dr. Jennifer K. Clayton is an Assistant Professor in Educational Leadership with The George Washington University. Prior to joining The George Washington University, she served as a Visiting Assistant Professor at Old Dominion University. She is a career educator and has taught at the middle and high school levels. She also served as a K-12 curriculum developer and evaluator, testing coordinator, and new teacher mentor. Jennifer earned her Ph.D. in Educational Leadership at Old Dominion University and focuses her research on areas that can be used to impact sustainable school improvement. She seeks to work in an area of nexus between policy and practice. Jennifer has served as a reviewer for AERA, UCEA, NCPEA, CREATE, and VERA. Additionally, she has a history of publication and presentation in all areas in which she concentrates her research. She can be contacted at claytonj@gwu.edu.

Chapter 8

The District's Role in Leading Improvement: Professional Learning Communities as the Starting Point

Rebecca A. Thessin and *Joshua P. Starr*

"I am a better teacher as a result of my work in PLCs because . . . I have had the invaluable opportunity to confer with colleagues and directors of curriculum in organized problem solving meetings."

"One way instruction in my classroom has changed this year as a result of my work in a PLC is . . . I've improved and broadened the activities my students do."

"Compared to when I started my work in a PLC, today I . . . feel my grade level seems to be 'on the same page.' We work collaboratively as opposed to individually."

In the face of increased accountability, many schools are implementing professional learning communities (PLCs) to support teachers in utilizing assessment data and student work to identify students' learning needs and meet them in the classroom. However, in some cases, the term "professional learning community" has come to refer simply to time for teachers to meet in teams, the newest quick fix in education for lagging student achievement results. Providing time for teachers to meet and work together certainly represents a shift from the traditional, isolated, self-contained classroom model in which most school teachers have worked independently from administrators and from the teacher next door for the last century (Elmore, 2004; Tyack & Cuban, 1995). However, time is not all that is necessary for teachers in PLCs to truly affect the instructional core, the relationship between the student, the teacher, and content in the classroom (City, Elmore, Fiarman, & Teitel, 2009; Elmore, 2004).

A significant body of research and literature exists on professional learning communities and on teachers' work within these communities. McLaughlin (1993) first identified professional communities as a key piece of school improvement. A professional community, otherwise defined as a community of practice, might consist of a cohesive group of teachers that engages in a process of working together to deepen teachers' expertise on a particular topic and to discuss common challenges, thereby exemplifying elements of the learning organization (Stoll & Louis, 2007; Wenger, McDermott, & Snyder, 2002). Stoll and Louis (2007), however, distinguish that professional learning communities have an agreed-upon objective of improvement. Dufour, Dufour, Eaker and Karhanek (2004) further clarify that PLCs establish specific, measureable goals to improve student learning.

While the research on the importance of teachers' collaborative work is clear, few first-hand accounts exist of the districtwide implementation of PLCs. This chapter tells our story of the districtwide implementation of PLCs in Stamford, Connecticut. We share the conditions, supports and preparation required to establish high-functioning PLC teacher teams, and we identify research-based supports that must be provided at the district level that allow teachers and principals to learn how to work in teams, account for differentiation in school needs, and, correspondingly, monitor results. Additionally, we provide a rubric (see appendix) that leaders can use in their own work to promote and cultivate PLCs in their organizations.

In Stamford, a mid-city district, we began the implementation of Professional Learning Communities (PLCs) in the district's twenty schools in the 2007-2008 school year – "Year I" of PLC work. PLCs were initiated as part of an overall system redesign led by Superintendent Joshua P. Starr and supported by a grant from the GE Foundation Developing Futures Program. When Dr. Starr arrived as the new superintendent in Stamford, teachers throughout the system told him that they needed more time to collaborate. While the current educational era has led districts to search for quick-fixes to address problems in teaching and learning, Stamford sought to establish opportunities for collective learning so that teachers might share best practices and work together to meet student learning needs (Schechter, 2011); hence, PLCs were established to enable teachers to learn from each other.

In preparation for PLC work, the district's assistant superintendents worked with school leaders to ensure that time would be established, starting in September, for teachers at every school to meet with other teachers to discuss their practice each week. While school leaders engaged in professional development on the what and how of leading PLCs during that first year of implementation, teachers sat together in PLC time confused and, in some cases, even frustrated by this new direction. We quickly realized that it was not enough to put well-meaning individuals together and expect them to magically collaborate to work toward achieving this goal without professional development and guidance.

After a somewhat halting start, we recognized that the *school system* needed to first serve as the locus of change. While each school had initiated PLC work from a unique starting place, by Year III, we had developed structures and expectations to further the development of processes for adult collaboration around instructional issues. Therefore, the district established three goals: (1) Facilitate building the capacity of principals and teacher leaders to lead PLC work; (2) Differentiate support for PLC work across the district considering the variability in implementation among schools; and (3) Monitor the outcomes to ensure that all schools could establish high-functioning PLCs. Through these efforts, we found that implementing professional learning communities in every school formed the basis for a comprehensive reform effort that led to improved student achievement.

By the time we kicked off Year III of PLC work at our August Administrators' Retreat, teachers and administrators throughout the district knew that the work of PLCs was a top priority. At the retreat, central office and school administrators reviewed our PLC accomplishments in the previous years and assessed our current state with PLC implementation. We clarified how PLCs would further achievement of school improvement plan goals and recommitted our work to leading the growth of PLCs in the coming year.

FACILITATING BUILDING CAPACITY

Our implementation plan emerged from three principles identified in the research. First, researchers agree that one essential aspect of using data for instructional improvement as a component of professional learning community work is the use of a well-defined school improvement process (Armstrong & Anthes, 2001; Boudett, City, & Murnane, 2005; Holcomb, 2001; Love, Terc, & Regional Alliance for Mathematics and Science Education Reform, 2002). Garvin, Edmondson, and Gino (March 2008) more broadly state that concrete learning processes and practices are an essential part of preparing an organization to learn. In Year I of PLC work in Stamford, many teachers expressed confusion and even frustration as to how to use their PLC time; they collectively articulated their need for explicit processes and tools to guide collaborative work for improvement, leading to the development of the Stamford PLC process, designed by the district's PLC Steering Committee (see Figure 8.1).

Figure 8.1. Stamford PLC Process

Second, the conditions must be established by which teachers can transition from searching for student deficits and how to address them through structural interventions, such as tutoring programs and test-prep classes, to studying and addressing problems of practice in the classroom. More specifically, a cultural shift to becoming a learning organization, an institution in which practice is continually examined and improved, is necessary for instructional improvement to occur (Boudett, 2007). Yet a school must *learn* how to examine instructional practice and student results collaboratively. Hord (2009) indicates that "Learning is not an add-on to the role of the professional. It is a habitual activity where the group learns how to learn together continuously" (p. 40). This process of learning how to work effectively in teams would need to be taught in professional development sessions planned for this purpose. In Stamford, administrators engaged in collective learning on PLC work beginning in Year I, and in Years II and III, teachers and administrators participated in explicitly designed PLC learning and professional development sessions districtwide.

Finally, high-functioning teams establish goals to guide their work to improve instruction and student achievement (DuFour et al., 2004; Stoll & Louis, 2007). Schmoker (2004) agrees with McLaughlin's earlier research that collaboration will only have positive outcomes on achievement when initiated in pursuit of common goals. In this district, every PLC team articulated an instructional goal that would guide the team's work for the year and that was aligned with school and district goals.

We also relied on existing research on the essential elements of high-functioning PLCs. In designing our own professional learning sessions to guide teachers' work, we strove to assist teachers in establishing PLCs with the essential characteristics of effective teams identified in the works of Hord (1997), Dufour, Dufour, and Eaker (2008), and others, including: (1) an ongoing nature; (2) emphasis on context; (3) alignment with current reform initiatives; (4) collaborative work; (5) shared vision and purpose to improve student learning; (6) evidence of student learning; (7) supportive and shared leadership; and (8) the presence of certain structural and cultural conditions.

First, research has indicated that PLCs must have an ongoing nature (Annenberg Institute for School Reform, 2004; DuFour et al., 2008; Kanold, 2006). By engaging in ongoing inquiry, teachers can learn continuously as they establish goals for improvement and work together to achieve them (Annenberg Institute for School Reform, 2004). PLC work must also be embedded within context-specific needs (Annenberg Institute for School Reform, 2004; Easton, 2004; Hipp & Huffman, 2007; Little & McLaughlin, 1993; O'Neil, 1995). Additionally, a focus on context allows locally shared interpretations of practice to be considered while teachers implement their own learning, see results, and get feedback about progress they are making toward their goals (Annenberg Institute for School Reform, 2004; Little & McLaughlin, 1993). Furthermore, these goals should be aligned with current district and school reform initiatives (Annenberg Institute for School Reform, 2004; DuFour et al., 2008).

Existing research on PLCs and on teams indicates that PLCs must be based on a collaborative, inquiry-based approach to learning in which teachers work interdependently to reach collective goals and common understanding of practices, thereby building internal accountability (Annenberg Institute for School Reform, 2004; Donnellon, 1996; DuFour et al., 2004; DuFour et al., 2008; Elmore & Consortium for Policy Research in Education, n.d.; Hord, 1997; O'Neil, 1995; Pappano, 2007; Schmoker, 2004; Stoll & Louis, 2007). This collaboration is led by a vision focused on a high level of student learning for all and on supporting every child to achieve it (DuFour, 2004; DuFour et al., 2008; Hord, 1997; Stoll & Louis, 2007). Moreover, evidence of student learning must be examined in PLCs in order to ensure that every child can reach this high learning standard (Annenberg Institute for School Reform, 2004; DuFour et al., 2008). Professional learning communities assess current levels of student achievement and set goals for improvement, in addition to studying evidence of student progress throughout the year, as shown on formative assessments (DuFour et al, 2004). In this way, data analysis is a key component of improvement.

Finally, supportive and shared leadership is necessary to foster PLCs (Annenberg Institute for School Reform, 2004; Hord, 1997). The principal must create an environment in which staff can learn continuously, support a culture of inquiry, and bring ideas in from outside the school in order to focus teachers' work on improvement. The school leader also plays an essential role in establishing supportive structural and cultural conditions for PLC work (Annenberg Institute for School Reform, 2004; Hord, 1997).

Following the research on instructional improvement and on professional learning communities, this district established time for teachers to meet in professional learning communities, developed an improvement process for teachers' use in PLCs, and instructed every PLC to establish a goal to guide its work in Year II. We also developed a PLC Rubric to serve as a resource to both school leaders and PLC teams in understanding where they were on the trajectory of PLC growth, so that they might establish next steps to improve their PLC practice (see Appendix A). Additionally, in Year II, professional learning sessions were planned to prepare administrators and teacher leaders to address the foci of PLC work that the district had articulated with the guidance of the PLC Steering Committee, and to establish the essential characteristics of PLC work. But in preparing to continue PLC work in Year III, we knew that Stamford still faced two key leadership challenges: 1) how to differentiate our support for PLC work across the district considering the variability in implementation among schools; and 2) how to monitor the outcomes to ensure that all schools could achieve the goal of having high-functioning PLCs despite present differences in PLC growth.

DIFFERENTIATING SUPPORT

In May of 2009, the Stamford Public Schools administered its first district and communitywide survey. Since the beginning of this superintendent's tenure, many Board members had expressed an interest in having an annual survey. This first annual survey was intended to gather perceptual data on the district's overall reform efforts. Teachers, students (seventh and tenth graders), administrators, instructional support personnel, and parents were all asked to participate in the survey and thereby provide feedback on the progress of improvement efforts. The survey was aligned to the district's strategic plan and offered an important data set to the Board and the community regarding the perceptions our stakeholders had of the district's current reforms.

The survey also provided an opportunity for us to "drill down" on important issues with school administrators. By gathering perceptual data from stakeholders, we were able to determine whether there were significant issues or concerns about particular areas, or if there were certain areas of strength that could be celebrated. In the area of student engagement, for instance, we wanted to go beyond the lagging indicator of a test score and look at leading indicators that helped us understand instruction. By asking students how they felt about the actual instruction they were receiving, we were able to dig a little deeper with school administrators about students' day-to-day experiences, which complemented our analysis of annual test score data.

Since PLCs were a cornerstone of our district work, we designed the survey to include a comprehensive set of questions to help us understand how PLC work was progressing both districtwide and at individual schools. We hoped that the data would help us to adjust our efforts and guide our future work. While teacher participation in the survey varied from 30% to 99% by school (also an indication of school culture and commitment to the district's work), across the system, about 70% of teachers responded, providing us with some important insights on which to base our collective next steps.

The survey results gave us multiple levels of data that helped us to understand the technical and adaptive aspects of PLC implementation in each school and districtwide. On the technical side, at the most basic level, we knew whether each teacher in the district was involved in a PLC. Teachers could only meet in PLCs if individual school principals had adjusted school schedules and provided the necessary coverage for teachers to meet regularly with one another in teams. Using the administrator survey data, we could also learn more about specific actions administrators had taken to support teachers' engagement in and learning about PLC work at school sites (see Figure 8.2). On the adaptive side, survey data informed us about the degree to which teachers were modifying their work by engaging in ongoing collaborative learning in teams. For instance, had teachers established and utilized an instructional goal to guide their work? Did teachers believe collaboration in PLCs was contributing to improved classroom practice? Survey questions also asked teachers to reflect on the processes they used to facilitate conversations, such as their use of norms and protocols and on their own PLC's focus and commitment to the achievement of every student (see Figure 8.3). While we were not able to track the growth within a school with only one year of survey results initially, this data set created a baseline for school growth and enabled us to disaggregate data by school and share results, which then led to sharing and learning among schools. Survey results also provided valuable information to help us differentiate support and accountability for individual school leaders.

At the beginning of each school year, the Deputy Superintendent and the Superintendent visited every principal at his/her school to set goals for the coming year. While student achievement data had always been reviewed during this process, the district now had an additional data set to utilize in understanding the conditions in each school that support adult collaboration. Therefore, following the Superintendent's establishment of goals for improvement with each principal in the Fall of 2009, the Director of School Improvement and Professional Development and an outside consultant supporting the district's PLC work joined the Deputy on additional school visits to continue the conversation begun at the August Administrators' Retreat on next steps for PLC work.

During these school visits, the visiting team and the school leader used the teacher survey results to discuss current PLC work at the school site, evaluate possible next steps to support PLC growth, and decide upon differentiated supports that Central Office could provide to this school site to further PLC work. At one of these meetings, on-site training was planned for teachers at Highpoint and Center Valley Elementary Schools,[1] schools at

---

[1] Pseudonyms have been created for all schools referred to in this chapter.

which data suggested that teachers were ready to engage in a regular process of examining instruction through peer observation. Based on PLC observations, survey results, and administrators' recommendations, many PLC teams across these two schools displayed evidence of engaging in numerous aspects of the district's PLC improvement process, but teachers needed additional preparation to learn how to implement the components of a peer observation process to further their work.

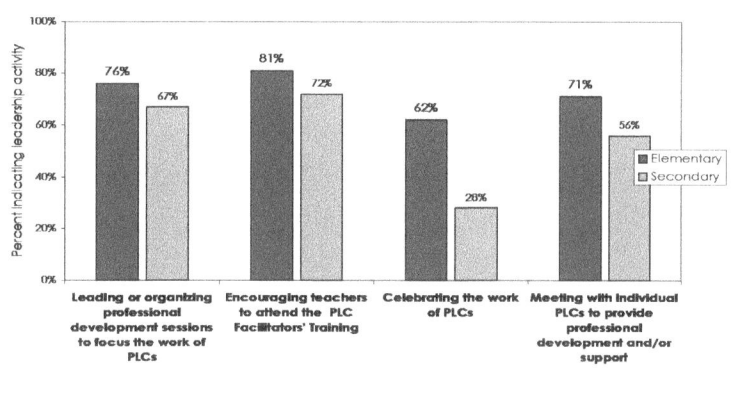

Figure 8.2. School Administrators as Leaders of PLC Work in Schools [2]

Instructional goal guides our work as a team

School Level	% Often or Almost Always
Elementary	66%
Secondary	54%

My PLC work improves my own classroom practice

School Level	% Often or Almost Always
Elementary	48%
Secondary	38%

My PLC focuses on supporting every student to reach a high level of achievement

School Level	% Often or Almost Always
Elementary	78%
Secondary	67%

Figure 8.3. Sample District-wide Teacher Survey Results

In contrast, at Longview Middle School, only 10% of the school staff had participated in the district's PLC Facilitators' Training sessions during the previous year

---

[2] Selected results of the 2009 Districtwide Teacher and Administrative Surveys found in Figures 2 and 3 were prepared by Amy Karwan, former Executive Director for Performance Management and Accountability for the Stamford Public Schools.

and the number of teachers who had responded to the district-wide survey was low as well. By all the evidence, this school was still at Stage 1 of PLC development. To address this school's need for support to move PLC growth to Stage 2, an introductory PLC professional development session was collaboratively planned by a lead teacher (who also served on the district's PLC Steering Committee), the school principal, and the district's PLC Consultant. The professional development session was scheduled to be held during one of the district's upcoming seven early-release professional development days dedicated to school-based work.

At the system level, the survey data served as a critical planning tool and a viable source of information on which to base the provision of needed supports. While the survey data were self-reported, thereby preventing us from drawing definitive conclusions, the data enabled us to ask more incisive questions of school leaders about how they were supporting PLC growth; moreover, the data illuminated district-wide trends. We now had information that showed patterns across schools and emerging successes at individual schools. Without this data, the district could not have justified allocating limited resources to offer school-based PLC training sessions at some schools and not others. By providing resources based on data that assessed schools' needs for teacher development, PLC development could be furthered across the district in Year III.

MONITORING OUTCOMES

One of the biggest challenges a superintendent faces when trying to reform an urban district is finding a balance between the context and culture of the community, the district he or she serves, and the mandates from the state department of education. While it is easy to categorize state departments as being too detached from the "real work" to be relevant, they too are in a difficult situation as they seek to find ways to implement federal and state legislative mandates in a time of standardized reform. The Connecticut State Department of Education had always taken a developmental stance towards districts regarding accountability; the classic "we're from the State and we're here to help" was a cornerstone of their message. In Stamford, the Board of Education and the community-at-large also needed to be convinced that the district's multiple reform efforts would have the appropriate return on investment. Moreover, in our case, our argument for the establishment of PLCs was strengthened through the support of a major corporate funder, the GE Foundation, which provided resources to support the district's PLCs through its Developing Futures program.

Most superintendents would agree that they have multiple masters. In our context, the State had imposed mandates for the district to follow as it was a school district in need of improvement under the federal No Child Left Behind legislation (NCLB); the local Board of Education needed to know that we were improving the district without creating too much controversy; and funders wanted to see a good return on their investment. Our challenge was to integrate and align State requirements, Board of Education goals, the funder's intended outcomes, and our own view of what we thought was best practice, given our context and culture.

In a recent study, Giles and Hargreaves (2006) found that schools that functioned as professional learning communities were able to sustain reform efforts by renewing their teacher cultures, distributing leadership, and planning for leadership succession.

These schools also involved their communities in decision-making, thereby gaining support for their reform efforts. We knew that supporting the development of PLCs in the district would not only lead to increased teacher learning, but would also serve as a key component of sustaining our other reform efforts. Stamford's Strategic District Improvement Plan (the "SDIP"), developed by the District Data Team, emerged as an effective umbrella for district efforts, attempting to shield the district from the downpour of multiple – and sometimes competing – demands.

During the district's first year and a half of PLC work, administrators across the district had expressed confusion as to how the pieces of the district's reform efforts, and the accompanying accountability requirements, fit together to support one another. At the same time that we were implementing PLCs, we were also revising the school improvement planning process to match new State requirements and streamline our efforts, and we were drafting districtwide expectations for all professional development sessions planned by both district- and school-based staff. When we initiated these improvement efforts, we knew that each one of these three efforts could not succeed without the others; however, even central office staff struggled to create a clear picture of exactly how they fit together. Only through the questions we were asked, and the ensuing conversations we had with administrators and teachers across the district, did we begin to see that both teachers' work in PLCs and the professional development in which teachers engaged should all support and be aligned to school goals for improvement. By tying these three reform efforts together through school improvement plans in Years II and III and through the SDIP at the district level, we sought to better align our work across the district while satisfying our own external accountability requirements to the State of Connecticut.

School Improvement Plans

While the District Data Team was first being formed in the 2008-2009 school year, we had initiated substantial revisions to Stamford's school improvement plans (SIPs) to align our process with State requirements and to focus our improvement efforts at each school site. Some schools' improvement plans were 40 pages in length in the 2007-2008 school year, articulating every possible tweak to a school's work that would be implemented in a given school year, even if that item would affect only one person in the school building. SIPs had also previously included a range of strategies, including technology upgrades, afterschool intervention programs, or implementation of a new schedule that would be designed and implemented by administrators. Put simply, we found that many of the changes described in our schools' SIP documents were structural, as opposed to *instructional,* improvements; we knew that some structural strategies might be necessary, but these strategies were not likely to affect the instructional core, the relationship between the student, the teacher, and content, in the classroom (City et al., 2009).

During State-led presentations we attended, the importance of focusing on a few improvement strategies, and doing them well, was repeatedly emphasized. We also knew that if a school improvement plan was not written with the intention of leading to changes in the everyday work of teaching and learning in classrooms, these plans would never become more than a document on a shelf, and no long-lasting changes would occur. The Superintendent always told district and school leaders that any plan has to be "dog-eared" or it is not likely to be useful. There is no point in putting something on paper if it isn't going to be used for organizing efforts and assessing progress.

Therefore, in the 2008-2009 school year, we sought to revise our School Improvement Plans (SIPs) to focus on a manageable number of specific strategies in the areas of Literacy, Mathematics, and Family and Community Engagement that would lead to changes in the everyday work of schools and, most importantly, improvements in instruction. At the Deputy Superintendent's suggestion, we initiated this process by sharing our own learning from attendance at State meetings with the district's principals during monthly principals' meetings. We developed a new template for schools to use in the school improvement planning process and held support sessions during which entire School Improvement Planning teams worked on revising their school's SIP with central office staff. And we worked with school teams to clearly connect the work of PLCs to schools' established instructional goals for improvement.

Strategic District Improvement Plan

The SDIP was nominally a mandate from the Connecticut State Department of Education, since we were identified as a district in need of improvement, according to the State's accountability system that reflected the NCLB legislation. The District Data Team (DDT), formed in response to another State mandate, assumed responsibility for drafting the document. Individuals were selected to participate on this team in two ways: We asked the Stamford Education Association and the Stamford Administrators Unit (the respective bargaining groups) to appoint people to the DDT. We also asked people who had been trained to utilize our district data warehousing system to apply for membership on the DDT. Finally, we invited teachers and administrators from across the district to apply to be on the team. We achieved a balanced membership by selecting teachers and administrators from different types of schools (magnet and non-magnet) and levels. The full team was composed of teachers and school and central office administrators, as well as representatives of the State.

In drafting the SDIP, as a district, we decided to go beyond the State requirements, which focused solely on Literacy and Mathematics, and incorporate our own priorities. Hence, our SDIP had four areas: 1) Curriculum & Instruction; 2) Professional Learning Communities and School Data Teams; 3) Instructional Grouping and De-Tracking; and, 4) School Culture. Each goal was intertwined – it was necessary to have rigorous curriculum and assessments in order to provide more children with access to a higher level of instruction in mixed-ability groups. In PLCs and school Data Teams, teachers had to work together to analyze multiple sources of data in order to develop new knowledge and skills that would help them to meet the individual needs of all students. And schools needed to have a positive culture that promotes teacher and student efficacy if we were to raise the standards and expectations for students and adults. The DDT was charged with developing and reviewing strategies, action plans and results indicators for each of the four areas of our SDIP.

The implicit Theory of Action of our SDIP was: "If adults learn new knowledge and skills to improve their practice, and if they are supported and held accountable for implementing those instructional practices, then more students will achieve at higher levels." Many districts skip the second step and fail to recognize that changes in adult behavior require time, the provision of supports, and accompanying expectations for improvement. It is not sufficient to simply teach adults something new and expect them to change their behaviors without explicitly supporting the change and articulating clear goals (Thessin & Starr, 2011). In order to properly support schools in an improvement cycle, it is necessary to have good data to understand where schools are relative to expectations for adult performance and to have a corresponding structure to monitor and intervene. By expanding a model we had piloted in the district's five traditionally lower-performing schools in the previous year, we were able to both meet State requirements and use Data Teams to build upon existing work.

During Year II of Stamford's PLC work, the Director of School Improvement and Professional Development had worked with central office and school leaders of the district's five traditionally lower-performing schools to design and implement the Stamford Excellence Team (SET Team). The team consisted only of the Director of Professional Development and School Improvement, one elementary English Language Arts coach and one secondary math coach who each supported multiple schools, and two consultant teams hired to provide additional instructional support and professional learning opportunities. As part of their responsibilities, the coaches facilitated selected PLC teams in their content areas of expertise and, accompanied by the Director, supported the work of a School Improvement Planning Team (SIP Team) at their school sites.

Similar to many districts, in most schools across Stamford, school improvement plans had often been written and shelved until the following fall when a new plan was required by central office. By establishing teams that met once per month to regularly review the school's School Improvement Plan (SIP) document, report on progress being made within individual PLC teams at the grade and subject-area levels, share data relevant to the school's goals, and collectively determine next steps toward schoolwide improvement, the work of individual PLC teams would not be lost at the "team" level.

During SIP Team meetings, team members shared student performance data and reported on the degree to which specific SIP strategies were being implemented across grade levels and subject area teams. At one high school's SIP Team meeting, the SET Team coach prepared and presented a list of 10th grade students at risk of not passing the State test later that year. He identified students by name that had both: (1) Placed at or below the proficient level on the State's 8th Grade State Math exam and (2) Received a grade of C+ or lower in the first quarter of 2008. Approximately 142 of 534 10th grade students, or more than 25% of the class, fell into this category. The entire SIP team was then challenged to determine how these students could be supported through the use of specific instructional strategies in the classroom during the school day, in addition to through the provision of one-on-one tutoring sessions and additional time for math instruction, as just two possible interventions. While looking for correlations in first quarter student grades and performance on a State test taken almost two years before would certainly not be a reliable predictor of all students' math performance that coming spring, in the absence of standardized districtwide math assessments for 9th and 10th grade students at that time, this information served as one more piece of data on which the school's SIP team could base its improvement efforts in the very near future.

At a middle school supported by the SET Team, early one Friday morning in December of 2008, the SIP Team together considered how to effectively monitor its newly crafted School Improvement Plan. With representatives of each subject area, the school librarian, two math coaches, and two school administrators at the table, the team considered how to both: (1) Gather data on the degree to which SIP strategies were being implemented in the classroom; and (2) Track the impact of these strategies on student learning. To determine the degree to which strategies were being utilized, both math coaches offered to create spreadsheets that included each of their school's math strategies in order to efficiently record their observations of strategies in classrooms they visited. While a coach might visit a specific classroom for only 10 minutes on a given day, if strategies were not observed over multiple days and weeks, then the coach could consider how to reallocate his time to provide necessary support to this teacher. The school's Assistant Principal, who supervised the school's English/language arts teachers, offered to try to use the same type of template to track strategy implementation across these classrooms as a means to determine where and to what degree professional development might be needed. Many districts are now providing administrators with handheld devices to track observations such as these. However, in a school with a dynamic principal leader and a teaching population of which approximately 90% had more than 10 years of experience (and most having many more), collaboratively developing a process by which teachers and administrators would collectively gather and track observational data was a significant shift in school culture and expectations.

To achieve their second goal related to the impact of these strategies, the SIP team acknowledged their need to utilize and/or develop common assessments to track student progress. The district was just beginning to implement common writing assessments in English/ language arts and common math assessments across the middle school grades. Results from these assessments could serve as indicators of student progress, and additional brief weekly or monthly assessments could provide data in between the administration of the districtwide assessments. In some PLC teams at the school, only one common assessment was crafted prior to the end of that school year six months later, while in others, numerous assessments were administered and analyzed. But collectively, across grade levels and subject areas, teachers were beginning to assume ownership for all students' learning.

While conversations such as these had typically been held only among administrative team members in prior years, with the implementation of a revised school improvement planning process in 2008-2009, schools began dedicating professional development time to schoolwide and grade-level or subject-area work articulated in the school improvement plan. By later including classroom teachers, school counselors, coaches, and other faculty members in the process of planning and monitoring the SIP document drafted by each school, the work of improvement could begin to be owned school-wide. Instead of pointing fingers at the teachers from the previous grade or school level who inadequately prepared students with needed knowledge and skills, by collectively analyzing data, determining where improvement was needed, and deciding upon strategies to address these needs, schools could acknowledge their shared goals and action steps and continually revisit these as a SIP Team and as an entire school faculty throughout the year.

Based on the work initiated in SIP Teams at the district's five schools identified for SET support in the 2007-2008 school year, the district's Data Team model began to emerge in Year III of PLC work. Grade-level and subject-area PLC teams would engage in ongoing learning in areas identified for improvement, and school-wide Data Teams would review the outcomes and recommendations of PLC teams' work. Data Teams would revise and revisit the school's improvement plan throughout the year to determine next steps school-wide, review a variety of data gathered across the school, and identify strengths and areas of improvement to be addressed in PLCs (Stamford Public Schools, October 2009). Data Teams would also work to align their schools' work with district-wide goals established in the SDIP.

In their study, Peterson, Murphy and Hallinger (1987) found that superintendents expected principals to coordinate district goals with classroom-level objectives. While we expected schools to establish their own goals for improvement that were instructionally-focused, and to align these goals with district goals, we also recognized that controlling school and classroom goals from the district level would not likely lead to meaningful or relevant instructional improvement at each of our schools. Through the establishment of the Strategic District Improvement Plan, the revision of the School Improvement Planning process, and the guidance that all PLCs should establish instructional goals aligned to school goals, we collectively began to see how the pieces of the district's improvement process could help to bring additional coherence to school and PLC improvement processes as well, as shown in Figure 8.4.

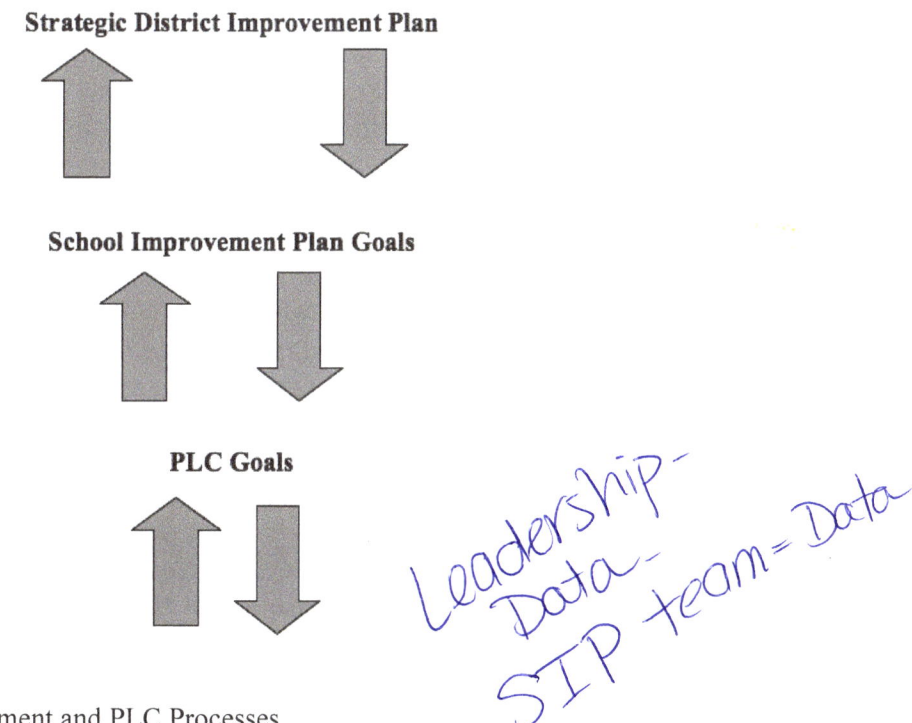

Figure 8.4. School Improvement and PLC Processes

There were still challenges to face ahead in implementing the SIP Team (now the Data Team) model district-wide in Year III. The process through which each school's Data Team members would be selected, and the time at which school teams would meet, was a point of contention with the Stamford Education Association, preventing the district's immediate implementation of the model. However, the lessons learned in the previous year's work at five schools informed the development and implementation process once it was underway. And as the result of having a venue in which to share the progress and challenges of improvement across a school, the learning of PLC teams could begin to benefit other grade levels and subject areas as well.

IMPLICATIONS FOR PRACTICE

While this district initiated the design and provision of differentiated support to schools in Year III of PLC work, we would suggest that districts planning to initiate PLCs should design a differentiated implementation plan in Year I that correlates with schools' and school leaders' readiness to engage in this work. The variation in the growth of professional learning communities that was observed in this district after two years of PLC work, and the confusion among many teachers regarding the work of effective PLC teams prior to receiving professional development, suggests that a district should determine schools' readiness to engage in PLC work and differentiate support to schools accordingly in Year I.

In order to determine each school's readiness for PLC work, a district might follow the guidance of this district's PLC improvement process (see Figure 8.1). While the process was developed to assist teachers in understanding student learning needs for the purpose of adjusting and improving instruction, the six steps of the PLC process could also be used to guide a district in designing a differentiated implementation plan for PLCs: (1) Inquiry; (2) Analyze Data; (3) Look at Student Work; (4) Examine Instruction; (5) Assess Student Progress; (6) Reflect.

1) *Inquire*: School and district leaders, both administrators and teachers, should be involved in the PLC development and implementation process. It is important to begin this collective learning about what a PLC *is* and *does* prior to the first year in which teachers begin meeting in PLCs. In the district studied, the PLC Steering Committee designed the district's improvement process and served as a valuable source of knowledge for school representatives who served on the committee and for central office representatives who were supporting schools in the implementation process. These representatives determined the district's next steps and brainstormed solutions to everyday challenges with PLC work. Additionally, Committee members assisted in gaining teacher support for PLC work at their own school sites.

2) *Analyze Data:* The district should survey teachers and administrators to determine schools' readiness to engage in PLC work. By designing and administering a short survey to preassess schools' readiness to engage in this learning, a district planning to implement PLCs can gather information on the extent to which the eight essential characteristics of PLC work already exist in each school. The survey should include questions about existing practices and professional development opportunities, school culture, and the readiness of school leaders and staff to engage in PLC practices. Asking teachers questions such as "How frequently do you work in teams?" and "What other professional development sessions may have prepared you to collaborate with other teachers?" will assist a district planning for implementation to determine which schools are ready to begin this work. A district may consider piloting PLC work at certain ready-to-go school sites, while other school leaders are supported in preparing their faculties with skills to engage in PLCs in subsequent school years.

3) *Look at Teachers' Collective Work:* If responses from the survey indicate that schools already have many of the eight characteristics of PLC work in place, and may even have engaged in aspects of an improvement process prior to the initiation of PLCs, the next step is to triangulate the data by following up with a visit to the school. As found at one of this district's schools, teachers may believe that they have been doing PLC work for years, while not realizing what a PLC actually *is*. By observing a few instances of teachers working together, such as during existing time for professional development, district leaders can assess teachers' familiarity with collaborative work. If no opportunities to observe teachers engaging in collective work are available, teachers and school leaders at this site may first need support in establishing structures for team work prior to establishing the eight PLC characteristics as a component of team functions.

4) *Examine the Culture of Instruction:* Prior to implementing PLCs, consider a school's culture by looking for initial indicators of a learning organization – Are classroom doors left open during instruction? Is student work displayed in the hallways? Do teachers have time dedicated to meet and plan for instruction? Are conversations in the teachers' room focused on sharing instructional strategies? Reflecting on a school faculty's readiness to begin to learn together prior to instituting PLCs may help district leaders better prepare a school to engage in this challenging work.

Teachers who have never before shared the instructional work that takes place inside their classrooms with one another should first learn how to organize for collaborative work by receiving support in establishing norms, utilizing protocols, setting goals, and writing agendas to guide their collaborative work. Then, as PLCs are formed at a school site, teachers working in PLCs should receive feedback on their work as it aligns to the eight essential characteristics of PLCs and to the district's improvement process through regular observations. Observations of PLC teams in action should be part of the larger district-initiated data-gathering process that is necessary to assess and support continued growth in PLC teams.

5) *Assess School Progress* and 6) *Reflect:* As the PLC implementation process gets underway, districts should continue to gather data, make adjustments, and differentiate support to PLC teams. An effective classroom teacher is constantly collaborating with colleagues to analyze student work and assessment data to determine which students need additional support and which students are ready to move on. In the process of implementing a new initiative, a district should also revisit school and individual team needs and subsequently provide differentiated support to assist PLC growth at each school site. Through the administration of annual surveys and the analysis of those results, observations of PLCs across the district, and the feedback provided by a representative committee, a district can make adjustments to its own PLC model to continue to improve its effectiveness. This work is best done collaboratively, in conjunction with teachers and administrators who are engaging in PLC work across the district.

In considering cost-efficient ways of providing differentiated professional development, districts might consider grouping schools together into Stage 1, Stage 2, and Stage 3 schools based on the results of data gathered and triangulated prior to implementation. Teachers at Stage 1 schools might participate in professional development focused on establishing basic components of collaborative work, such as creating norms, using protocols, and working toward a simple goal, while teachers at a later stage of growth might be supported in initiating the practice of peer observation. As school-based professional development would be most relevant to school teams' work, district administrators might also collaborate with school leaders in designing professional development sessions on PLCs to be led and held at individual school sites. By gathering data and visiting a school to observe teachers' collaborative work prior to planning professional development for a specific school site, this training could be developed with a particular school's needs for PLC growth in mind.

CONCLUSION

Stamford's results show that PLC time is providing teachers with the opportunity to work together to make a difference for their students. The 2009 Connecticut Mastery Test results illustrated strong improvements in achievement, especially in grades 6 and 8 in math, grades 5 and 8 in reading, and grade 8 in writing. Particularly, Stamford students in the White, African American, and Hispanic subgroups demonstrated higher overall achievement in the percentage of students scoring at/above "goal" when compared to students' performance statewide (Stamford Public Schools, 2010). In 2010, student performance on the State test continued on an upward trend, particularly in Math. In grades 3, 5, and 8, the gain in the percentage of students who scored at/above Goal in Stamford exceeded gains by the State. Overall, between the 2006-07 school year and the 2010 assessment, Math scores improved by 13 and 15 percentage points in grades 5 and 6 respectively (Stamford Public Schools, July 15, 2010).

Districts planning to implement professional learning communities should consider the role of district leaders in facilitating building the capacity of principals and teacher leaders to lead PLC work; differentiating support for PLC work across the district; and monitoring outcomes to ensure that all schools can establish high-functioning PLCs. In order for adult learning to contribute to improved learning for all kids, district leaders must take intentional actions to build the capacity of school and teacher leaders to lead others in learning and to differentiate support based on specific school needs. It is also critical for districts to specifically connect the work of PLCs to the process of school improvement. PLC work is not likely to lead to improved outcomes without an intentional focus on the achievement of an instructional goal aligned to school and district goals for improvement.

Future research is still needed, however, to determine how best to measure the outcomes of teachers' work in PLCs. While Stamford measured PLC work specifically through observations of PLCs in action and teacher survey results, a more systematic approach to determine to what degree student learning increased as a result of teachers' work in teams is needed. Teacher departures from a specific grade level, school or district, leading to few PLC teams including the same members from year to year, also make it difficult to tie student learning outcomes specifically to the work of one team. Future research may lead to new methods of tying teacher learning to student learning in the classroom.

No one reform can be cited for Stamford's improvements, but teachers were clear that PLCs contributed to their own improvements in practice. By Year III, we had established distinct structures and processes by which to achieve our goals of facilitating, supporting, and monitoring PLC work district-wide. However, we knew that structures and processes weren't sufficient to sustain this work over time. Only by providing continued opportunities to learn about and engage in PLC work would teachers and administrators recognize the importance of sustainment. While some teachers and administrators across Stamford had projected that PLCs, like other district initiatives, would come and go and could thus be "waited out," we sought to continue to embed PLC work in our ongoing work of improvement so that PLCs would become the means by which all other district reform efforts would take hold.

References

Annenberg Institute for School Reform. (2004). *Professional learning communities.* Providence, RI: Annenberg Institute for School Reform.

Armstrong, J., & Anthes, K. (2001). How data can help. *American School Board Journal, 188*(11), 38-41.

Boudett, K. P. (2007). Building learning organizations by using data wisely. In K. P. Boudett, & J. L. Steele (Eds.), *Data wise in action: Stories of schools using data to improve teaching and learning* (pp. 167). Cambridge, MA: Harvard Education Press.

Boudett, K. P., City, E. A., & Murnane, R. J. (Eds.). (2005). *Data wise: A step-by-step guide to using assessment results to improve teaching and learning.* Cambridge, MA: Harvard Education Press.

City, E. A., Elmore, R. F., Fiarman, S., & Teitel, L. (2009). *Instructional rounds in education: A network approach to improving teaching and learning.* Cambridge, Mass.: Harvard Education Press.

DuFour, R., DuFour, R., & Eaker, R. E. (2008). *Revisiting professional learning communities at work: New insights for improving schools.* Bloomington, IN: Solution Tree.

DuFour, R., DuFour, R., Eaker, R. E., & Karhanek, G. (2004). *Whatever it takes: How professional learning communities respond when kids don't learn.* Bloomington, Indiana: Solution Tree.

Donnellon, A. (1996). *Team talk: The power of language in team dynamics.* Boston, Mass.: Harvard Business School Press.

Easton, L. B. (2004). *Powerful designs for professional learning.* Oxford, OH: National Staff Development Council.

Elmore, R. F. (2004). *School reform from the inside out: Policy, practice, and performance.* Cambridge, MA: Harvard Education Press.

Elmore, R. F., & Consortium for Policy Research in Education. (n.d.). *Knowing the right thing to do: School improvement and performance-based accountability.* Washington, D.C.: NGA Center for Best Practices.

Garvin, D. A., Edmondson, A. C., & Gino, F. (March 2008). Is yours a learning organization? *Harvard Business Review,* 109.

Giles, C. & Hargreaves, A. (2006). The sustainability of innovative schools as learning organizations and professional learning communities during innovative reform. *Educational Administration Quarterly, 42*(1), 124-156.

Hipp, K. K., & Huffman, J. B. (2007). Using assessment tools as frames for dialogue to create and sustain professional learning communities. In L. Stoll, & K. S. Louis (Eds.), *Professional learning communities: Divergence, depth and dilemmas* (pp. 119). New York, NY: Open University Press.

Holcomb, E. L. (2001). *Asking the right questions: Techniques for collaboration and school change* (2nd ed.). Thousand Oaks, Calif.: Corwin Press.

Hord, S. M. (1997). Professional learning communities: What are they and why are they important? *Issues about Change, 6*(1), November 25, 2008.

Hord, S. M. (2009). Professional learning communities. *Journal of Staff Development, 30*(1), 40-43.

Kanold, T. D. (2006). The flywheel effect: Educators gain momentum from a model for continuous improvement. *Journal of Staff Development, 27*(2), 16-21.

Little, J. W., & McLaughlin, M. W. (1993). *Teachers' work: Individuals, colleagues, and contexts*. New York: Teachers College Press.

Love, N., Terc, & Regional Alliance for Mathematics and Science Education Reform. (2002). *Using data, getting results: A practical guide for school improvement in mathematics and science*. Norwood, Mass.: Christopher-Gordon Publishers, Inc.

McLaughlin, M. (1993). What matters most in teachers' workplace context? In J. W. Little & M. McLaughlin (Eds.), *Teachers' work: Individuals, colleagues, and contexts* (pp. 79). New York, NY: Teachers College.

O'Neil, J. (1995). On schools as learning organizations: A conversation with Peter Senge. *Educational Leadership, 52*(7), 20.

Pappano, L. (2007). More than "making nice". *Harvard Education Letter, 23*(2), 1-3.

Peterson, K., Murphy, J., & Hallinger, P. (1987). Superintendents' perceptions of the control and coordination of the technical core in effective school districts. *Educational Administration Quarterly, 23*(1), 79-95.

Schechter, C. (2011). Collective learning from success as perceived by school superintendents. *Journal of School Leadership, 21*(3), 478-509.

Schmoker, M. (2004). Learning communities at the crossroads: Toward the best schools we've ever had. *Phi Delta Kappan, 86*(1), 84-88.

Stamford Public Schools (October 2009). *Strategic district improvement plan.* Stamford, CT.

Stamford Public Schools (2010). *Stamford Public Schools Connecticut Mastery Test (CMT) and CT Academic Performance Test (CAPT) District Results.* Stamford, CT. Retrieved from http://www.stamfordpublicschools.org/filestorage/66/103/747/4252/SPS_CMT_CAPT_2010_Overview_071510.pdf.

Stamford Public Schools (2010, July 15). *Stamford Public School district continues upward trend on Connecticut Mastery Test*. Stamford, CT. Retrieved from http://www.stamfordpublicschools.org/filestorage/66/103/747/4252/CMT_CAPT_Results_2010.pdf.

Stoll, L., & Louis, K. S. (2007). *Professional learning communities: Divergence, depth and dilemmas*. Maidenhead: McGraw-Hill/Open University Press.

Thessin, R. A., & Starr, J. P. (2011). Supporting the growth of effective professional learning communities districtwide. *Phi Delta Kappan, 92*(6), 48-54.

Tyack, D. B., & Cuban, L. (1995). *Tinkering toward utopia : A century of public school reform*. Cambridge, Mass.: Harvard University Press.

Wenger, E., McDermott, R. A., & Snyder, W. (2002). *Cultivating communities of practice: A guide to managing knowledge*. Boston: Harvard Business School Press.

Dr. Rebecca A. Thessin is currently the Associate Superintendent for Professional Development and School Support for the Montgomery County Public School System in Maryland. Prior to her current position, she served as an Assistant Professor of Educational Administration at The George Washington University. In this role, she prepared aspiring educational leaders and served as a founding member of the DC-EdCORE consortium. Previously, she served as the Director of School Improvement and Professional Development in Stamford, Connecticut, where she led the district's implementation of an improvement process for professional learning communities and formed a professional development council to author a professional learning plan. She has also served as the Aide to the Deputy Superintendent in the Boston Public Schools, as an administrative intern at a Boston high school, and as a high school teacher in Connecticut, Massachusetts, and West Virginia. Thessin holds a doctorate in the urban superintendency from the Harvard Graduate School of Education. She can be contacted at rebecca_a_thessin@mcpsmd.org.

Dr. Joshua P. Starr is currently the superintendent of the Montgomery County Public School System in Maryland. Prior to his current superintendency, he served as the superintendent in Stamford, Connecticut. He has also previously been the director of school performance and accountability for the New York City Department of Education, where he helped design a comprehensive approach to measuring school performance. He has served as deputy senior instructional manager in the New York City Department of Education; the executive director of operations for the Freeport School District in New York; and the director of accountability for the Plainfield Public Schools in New Jersey. He began his career in education as a special education teacher in Brooklyn, NY. Starr holds a doctorate in the urban superintendency from the Harvard Graduate School of Education. He can be contacted at joshua_starr@mcpsmd.org.

Appendix A
SPS Professional Learning Community Rubric [3]

	Stage 1	Stage 2	Stage 3
Reflective Dialogue	• Unstructured discussion • Limited sharing of strategies or resources • Participation by some group members more than others	• Focused discussion • Regular sharing of strategies or resources • Engagement by most participants	• Respectful and focused discussion • Open and reflective problem solving focused on specific instructional concerns and resources • Active engagement by all participants
Shared Norms, Values, and Practices	• Norms not established yet • No agenda for meetings/purpose unclear • No or little evidence of use of protocols to guide group work • Discussion topic and focus varies • No minutes of meetings have been collected	• Group norms posted/shared and followed some of the time • Agenda used to focus meetings • Data, student work, and other resources used some of the time • Some use of protocols to guide group work • Focus and discussion about improving teaching and student learning • Minutes record decisions and agreements	• Group norms are posted and followed consistently • Meeting agenda prepared ahead of time • Data, student work, and other resources consistently used to focus discussion • Variety of protocols used to guide group work • Clear and consistent focus and discussion about improving student achievement • Minutes record decisions, agreements and next steps

---

[3] The characteristics described in the rubric are adapted from the article by Kruse, Louis and Bryk entitled "Building Professional Community in Schools."

Collaboration Toward Common Purpose	• Limited collective planning for future work and next steps to improve student learning • Individuals prepare materials and tasks to improve instruction, curriculum, and assessment on their own • Lack of specificity around implementation of strategies in the classroom • Strategies are selected based on what teachers indicate has worked over time	• Regular planning together for future work and next steps to improve student learning • Participants divide the work of preparing materials and tasks to improve instruction, curriculum, and assessment for the team • General conversation about what the teacher and students will be doing when strategies are implemented • Strategies are selected from identified best practices	• Systematic planning together for future work and next steps to improve student learning • Joint preparation of materials and tasks to improve instruction, curriculum, and assessment • Clear descriptions and expectations of what teachers and students will be doing when strategies are implemented • Strategies cited by research are selected in direct response to identified student needs
Collective Focus on Student Learning	• Some teachers seek to learn how to meet learning needs of some students • Discussion of instructional practices that individual teachers have used • No agreement upon common best instructional strategies that will be implemented in all classrooms	• Most teachers seek to learn how to address and meet learning needs of all students • Discussion of instructional practices that will engage students in learning • Beginning agreements upon common best instructional strategies that will be implemented in all classrooms	• All teachers seek to learn how to address and meet learning needs of all students • Discussion of instructional practices that will modify student thinking • Clear agreements upon common best instructional strategies that will be implemented in all classrooms

Data-Driven Decision Making	• Data and student work is examined sporadically or at the beginning of the year • Data, which may not be disaggregated, is reviewed but the connection between data and instruction is not made • Data is disaggregated by teacher performance and compared to GLEs • Some individuals establish goals; some are shared • There is limited follow-up discussion about implementation	• Multiple sources of data and samples of student work are examined periodically • Disaggregated data of student performance is used to guide conversation, but next steps for instruction are not agreed upon • Data is disaggregated by student performance and compared to GLEs • Some common goals are established to improve instruction • Successes and challenges of implementation are discussed	• Multiple sources of data and samples of student work are examined regularly and systematically • Disaggregated data of student performance is used to guide conversation and set next steps for instruction • Data is disaggregated by student performance and aligned to specific rubrics and GLEs • Clear goals are established to improve current levels of student achievement • Use of evidence to determine impact of implementation
Supportive and Shared Leadership	• Participants are reluctant and skeptical – they comply with attendance • A designated leader takes responsibility for the leading the PLC – members often show up unprepared • Administrators direct teachers' work on improvement	• Continued learning is valued by most PLC members • Co-leaders share leadership for PLC work – some members take responsibility for different aspects of meetings • Administrators support, but do not direct, teachers' work on improvement	• All PLC members are committed to continuous learning • Responsibility for the PLC's work is shared – all members participate in preparing for and the success of meetings • Administrators actively support teachers' work on improvement and promote teachers leadership
Structure and Culture	• Administrators observe PLC meetings once in a while, but no discussion takes place on the effective practices of PLC work • Structures have not yet been put in place for PLCs to share learning and achievements outside of their own PLC • Many teachers do not yet have the opportunity to participate in PLCs	• Teachers and administrators observe PLC meetings once in a while, but do not discuss effective practices to enhance PLC work • Some structures exist to allow PLCs to share their work, but achievements of PLCs are not yet shared on a regular basis • Most teachers have the opportunity to	• Teachers and administrators regularly observe PLC meetings and engage in discussion and learning about effective PLC practices • Structures exist to allow PLCs to share their learning and achievements in improving instruction schoolwide on a regular basis • All teachers participate

| | | with teachers of like grade levels or content areas regularly | participate in PLCs with teachers of like grade levels or content areas regularly | in PLCs with teachers of like grade levels or content areas on at least a weekly basis |

Part 3

Examining "Right Now" Reforms

Chapter 9

21ˢᵗ Century Learning: The Call for Change

Diane Hill and *Jean Maness*

We are educators, one leading a school and one leading at the district office level. We are as caught up in the turmoil and ambiguity that is the transition to Common Core State Standards as are other educational leaders across the state and nation. At the same time, we realize that this transition, one of great magnitude and breadth, is an opportunity to transform what we do as educators and how we support students in the process of 'schooling.' We do not claim to have answers to all the questions that current education reform policies have created. Instead, we contend that <u>now</u> is the time to change how we 'do' education in the most significant way that we have experienced throughout our collective professional lives in public education. We want to share our guarded excitement about this opportunity. We'd be negligent to say that we are not somewhat apprehensive, uncertain at times, and concerned about the readiness of ourselves and those we lead to meet the challenges that this new era of change requires. Our excitement is borne of our understanding that what can happen, what may happen, and what we hope will happen has potential to result in positive changes for students and for the future of public education. It is time for all of us in education to respond to the call for change, to embrace 21st century learning.

Public education in the United States has become a major topic for the nation's political leaders, including President Obama. Since the initial passage of the *No Child Left Behind Act* in 2001, the federal government has become more and more involved in public education policy and design, even more so after the Race To The Top funding program was developed in 2009 (U.S. Department of Education, 2010). Recently, there has been serious national debate about K-12 education, as Congress and President Obama develop ideas and strategies to address reforming education to meet the needs of 21ˢᵗ century citizenry in our global society. In *The Blueprint for Reform*, President Obama described the urgency and rationale that support his proposal for change:

> This effort will also require our best thinking and resources – to support
> innovative approaches to teaching and learning; to bring lasting change to our
> lowest-performing schools; and to investigate and evaluate what works and what
> can work better in America's schools…instead of investing in the status quo, we
> must reform our schools to accelerate student achievement, close achievement

gaps, inspire our children to excel, and turn around those schools that for too many young Americans aren't providing them with the education they need to succeed in college and a career. (USDOE, 2010, p. 2)

As we continue in the second decade of the 21st century, there is a great deal of support for the concept that preparing students for this century, and for their future, is a "moral imperative" (USDOE, 2010, p. 1). The education model most prevalent in the U.S. today is based on a concept of schooling developed more than a century ago to meet the needs of an industrial society and to prepare students for jobs and higher education programs that are no longer relevant (Robinson, 2010). This antiquated model of schooling is obsolete for students of this century (Saltrick, 2009). In order to move forward in the effort to reform education and to ensure students are prepared for success in their future, we must be able to describe 21st century learning and how the rigor and mastery required for this learning are different from the current educational model. We must also examine the role of educational leaders in supporting 21st century teaching and learning. This process is a paradigm shift for many teachers, students, administrators and other school stakeholders alike, and as such, necessitates a call for change.

PERSONAL PERSPECTIVES

As educational leaders, we struggle daily with addressing the managerial and administrative demands of our positions while also providing instructional leadership and support to principals, teachers and students as we prepare for the paradigm shift that will be required with the transition to the Common Core Standards. It is an ongoing challenge to find balance between the multitude of duties and responsibilities required by local, state, or federal mandates, and working with our schools in practices and activities that support 21st century teaching and learning.

> *Diane: As a principal new to my position, I am trying to learn the culture and dynamics of my school. However, I am also required to attend staff development related to Common Core and 21st century learning to help me be prepared to lead the change. I am torn being away from school but at the same time feeling the need to be knowledgeable as I lead my school into the unknown.*

> *Jean: At the district level, we feel the need to create a sense of urgency as we embark on the changes in curriculum requirements in every content area at all grade levels simultaneously. In our 28 plus years of experience, Diane and I believe this is the most significant era of change we have faced as educators.*

The move to Common Core Standards and 21st century teaching and learning requires more rigorous academic expectations for both teachers and students. Certainly, there may be teachers and students who are reluctant to embrace more challenging work and higher expectations. According to Dweck (2010), individuals sometimes "feel threatened by learning tasks that require them to stretch or take risks" (p. 18). Our goal is to work with those we lead to create the environment of trust and support necessary for adults and students to be successful learners.

The most significant changes impacting educators and students are the current emphasis on 21st century teaching and learning and the transition to the Common Core State Standards. The following sections of this chapter discuss the paradigm shift required by these transitions.

21ST CENTURY LEARNING

Preparing students to be successful now and in the future requires much more than mastery of the core subjects of reading, writing and math. "Learning in the 21st century is the fusing of the three R's and the four C's" (Shames, 2010, p. 1). Today's students must also demonstrate competency in creativity, critical thinking, communication, and collaboration. In 21st century learning, the core subjects are broadened to include subjects such as world languages and history. Students must also master interdisciplinary themes such as global awareness and civic literacy as well as 21st century skills including the use of information, media and technology. These three components of 21st century learning--the core subjects, the interdisciplinary themes, and the 21st century skills--are highly interwoven and interdependent. The demand of schooling now is to bring rigorous content together with activities and learning opportunities that have real world relevance for students (Saltrick, 2009).

> *Diane: A teacher at my school currently uses a multitude of worksheets, text based assignments and activities that require very little active learning from students to master content. Students have been successful on end of course assessments so the teacher feels this is evidence that he is doing a sound job. While proficient, over 50% of the students are not showing academic growth. We have ongoing conversations regarding instructional practices and the lack of rigor in his lessons. With the new standards, I worry about how I can help this teacher make the transition and increase the rigor of instruction in completely redesigned content.*

CORE SUBJECTS OF 21ST CENTURY LEARNING

The foundation for 21st century learning will be core content that moves beyond areas currently tested to meet state and federal mandates. While reading, writing, and math will be a crucial part of 21st century content for schools, students will be required to have knowledge and skills related to other areas. According to the Partnership for 21st Century Skills (2009), world languages, arts, economics, science, geography, history, and civics are also areas that 21st century students must master. The acquisition of knowledge and skills in these content areas must be driven by engaging, challenging instructional modes and techniques (Conley, 2011).

> *Jean: As I walked into Mrs. B's third grade language arts class, I thought I had stumbled into an archeological dig. Groups of students were combing through "the new neighbor's trash." This wasn't a science lesson. As students examined and discussed the artifacts, the expectation was to learn about the neighbor. The*

objective of the lesson was for students to experience how we make inferences in the real world, sometimes even from the neighbor's trash.

Thus, teaching and learning move beyond mere factual recall to include a more in-depth understanding of the learning process in each area and the ability to transfer the knowledge to authentic, real life situations. "Placing course content in the context of a real-world scenario helps a student remember specific details of a lesson because the context gives the information meaning" (McCain, 2005, p. 23). Connecting the content to real life situations that are personally meaningful to learners greatly improves student learning and retention of the content information (Saltrick, 2009).

INTERDISCIPLINARY THEMES OF 21ST CENTURY LEARNING

Another facet of 21st century learning includes five interdisciplinary themes: global awareness; financial, economic, business and entrepreneurial literacy; civic literacy; health literacy; and environmental literacy (Partnership for 21st Century Skills, 2009). This interdisciplinary work draws on a real world context. Designing content learning experiences that are relevant to students and that involve 21st century skills allows students to gain meaning and understanding at a deeper level (Saltrick, 2009). Global awareness centers on understanding and addressing global issues, working collaboratively with diverse cultures and understanding other nations and cultures that may be non-English speaking. Financial, economic and entrepreneurial literacy involves knowing how to make appropriate economic choices, understanding the role of the economy in society and determining how to use entrepreneurial skills for productivity and advancement. Civic literacy includes consideration of governmental processes, civic rights and responsibilities, as well as the implications of civic decisions. Obtaining and understanding basic health information and services, including preventive physical and mental health measures, making appropriate health-related decisions, and recognizing national and international public health issues are all part of health literacy. Environmental literacy includes knowing and understanding environmental issues as they relate to air, climate, land, food, energy, water, ecosystems, and society's impact on the natural environment (Partnership for 21st Century Skills, 2009). Demonstrating adeptness in processing, connecting, and applying these 21st century literacies within the context of the life of the individual is essential in preparing our students to be college and career ready.

21ST CENTURY LEARNING SKILLS

In order to be prepared for a more complex life and work environment, students must successfully master 21st century skills such as creativity and innovation, critical thinking and problem solving, communication, and collaboration, in addition to accessing and analyzing information. Creativity and innovation include the ability to create new ideas and "elaborate, refine, analyze, and evaluate their own ideas in order to improve and maximize creative efforts" (Partnership for 21st Century Skills, 2009, p. 3). Being able to communicate ideas to others effectively, as well as being open and responsive to group input and feedback are important 21st century skills. Students will be required to analyze and interpret effectively using various types of reasoning depending upon the situation. They must have the ability to use systems thinking which requires them to make judgments and decisions in an analytical and reflective manner, and to solve problems in both conventional and innovative ways (Partnership for 21st Century Skills, 2009). Having the confidence to take risks and confront possible failure are key to student and teacher learning for the future (Dweck, 2010).

Living in a media-suffused environment, successful learners must be able to "exhibit a range of functional and critical thinking skills related to information, media and technology" (Partnership for 21st Century Skills, 2009, p. 5).

> *Diane: At my school, students arrive every day with their cell phones, laptops, and iPads, and they are literally constantly connected for personal as well as academic reasons. Having access to all the information at their fingertips does not ensure they have the critical thinking skills needed to sift through all the available information in order to make meaning and to determine what is relevant or credible. Teachers and I struggle daily to support students in learning that everything "out there" is not equal.*

Students must know how to access, evaluate and manage information, media and technology in order to be successful. Additionally, students must be able to collaborate with others working towards a common goal.

Success in the 21st century is not solely based on content knowledge and thinking skills. Students also need to develop adequate life and career skills such as flexibility, initiative, self-direction, social and cross-cultural skills, productivity, leadership, and responsibility (Partnership for 21st Century Skills, 2009). This type of learning requires teachers to provide students with opportunities to see how the subject knowledge and skills relate to real world problems that require individuals and groups to access multiple areas of expertise and ability (Saltrick, 2009). Preparing students to be career and college ready requires that they develop abilities in interacting effectively with others, communicating clearly, and working cooperatively as well as independently. Contemporary learners must know how to manage products and produce results as well as guide and lead others. According to Christen (2009),

> Computer networking capabilities give educators the means to implement interactivity, creativity and information-sharing activities.......instructors can extend the classroom far beyond the four walls and reinforce the soft skills and critical thinking that students require to master complex tasks and compete for higher paying jobs. (p. 29)

Learning to master 21st century skills such as creativity and innovation, critical thinking and problem solving, communication and collaboration, and accessing and analyzing information is essential in preparing students for higher education or work in the contemporary global, economically competitive and knowledge-based society.

COMMON CORE STATE STANDARDS

The National Governors Association and the Council of Chief State School Officers developed a common core of state standards for proficiency in English-language arts and mathematics for grades K-12, as well as literacy in science, social studies, and technical subjects, an effort well known as the Common Core State Standards Initiative. The standards were developed in collaboration with teachers, school administrators and education experts. "The standards define the knowledge and skills students should have within their K-12 education careers so that they will graduate from high school able to succeed in entry-level, credit-bearing academic college courses and in workforce training programs" (Common Core State Standards: Messaging Toolkit, 2011, p. 2). Current standards, which differ widely from state to state, often lack rigor and make it possible for students to demonstrate mastery of state standards while not preparing the students for post-secondary school or work (Quay, 2010). As of this writing, forty-five states, four territories and the District of Columbia have adopted the standards for implementation. Adopting and implementing the Common Core standards simultaneously with a number of other states affords educators the opportunity to benefit from a wealth of shared knowledge. It may be challenging to direct district leaders, principals, and teachers to useful resources amidst the profusion of information that is available.

> *Diane: I have been working with my teachers in professional development all year around the transition to Common Core State Standards. Some of them are very concerned about the new literacy requirements. One social studies teacher lamented, "I don't know how to teach reading...I did not go to school for that...is someone going to show us how to do this?" Like the teachers, I sometimes find myself hoping for someone to show us how to do it. The reality is, I know we have to get in there and figure it out for ourselves. There is so much information, and a great deal of professional development has already taken place. Now we need time to let it all sink in...the information overload might just be more overwhelming than the actual work we need to do to implement the new standards and learn new ways of teaching for learning.*

The move to the Common Core Standards will incorporate "more rigorous content and application of knowledge through higher-order thinking skills" (Common Core State Standards: Messaging Toolkit, 2011, p. 6). The Common Core standards identify fewer content standards, which are clearer and more coherent across grades. They also incorporate higher cognitive demand and require greater depth of understanding on the part of students, and are better aligned with the knowledge and skills that are needed for success in college and careers. These standards will provide for more clarity and consistency in student learning across the country (Quay, 2010).

INNOVATIVE INSTRUCTION

> *Diane: In Mr. H's English class, 9th graders worked in groups creating comic strips using an online application and their laptop computers. Their comic strips had to illustrate different types of irony, without using words. Mr. H. circulated*

around the room, answering questions and checking the progress. Students stopped long enough to explain their ideas, then were right back to work. Some of them looked confused or even frustrated as they grappled with how to convey verbal irony without words. "Be creative, you know you can do this" encouraged Mr. H. As I left the room, I couldn't help thinking that irony would have made sense to me if I had been in that class.

Instruction to facilitate 21st century learning and implement Common Core Standards must be different than it has been for the last century. Teaching practices and instructional activities must be more rigorous and engaging for students if they are to obtain the habits of mind necessary for success as life long learners (Schmoker, 2011). As Silva (2009) stated, the emphasis must be on "what students can do with knowledge, rather than what units of knowledge they have" (p. 630). According to McCain (2005), students have successfully mastered school skills, which are lower level skills that enable one to do well on written tests and earn good grades; "School skills are mainly concerned with the assimilation of content. They are based on the notion that information alone is all we need to give students to prepare them for life" (McCain, 2005, p. 6). Brown (2006) writes that the "focus in education moves from building up stocks of knowledge to enabling students to participate in flows of actions, where the focus is on learning to be through enculturation and on collateral learning" (p. 23). Learning must involve doing--being part of the problem and the solution. Although acquiring and retaining the information or knowledge is important, "there is an increased need for educators to prepare students differently for success in life in the 21st century" (McCain, 2005, p. 7). Businesses have changed, and they need employees who can think independently, problem-solve, and work cooperatively with others, possibly on a global scale. "Today's workers in nearly all sectors of the economy must be able to find and analyze information, often coming from multiple sources, and use this information to make decisions and create new ideas" (Silva, 2009, p. 631). As educators we must not only teach the content but the skills to meet changing demands of 21st century employers. It is imperative to rethink how students are taught, as well as how they learn, if we want to prepare them for the 21st century.

The traditional lecture style of instruction will no longer meet our students' needs. According to McCain (2005), "We need an instructional approach that will equip students with real-world, problem-solving skills plus teach the content they must master to be an educated person" (p. 15). Learning must be authentic and multi-disciplinary. "Authentic learning focuses on real-world, complex problems and their solutions, using role-playing exercises, problem-based activities, case studies, and participation in virtual communities of practice" (Lombardi, 2007, p. 2). Authentic learning involves multiple disciplines, multiple perspectives or interpretations, and helps the student make connections to the real world. There should be numerous ways to solve a given problem, and the process should involve multiple people collaborating over an undesignated amount of time. Polished outcomes should be the by-product of learning that is deep and meaningful, which involves reflection and embedded assessments (Lombardi, 2007). Teachers must access a variety of rigorous, or cognitively challenging, instructional techniques such as simulation-based learning, student-created media, inquiry-based learning, peer-based evaluations, and working with remote instruments. Many of these techniques involve the use of technology as well as collaboration to support the learning process. All require the educator to prepare for and engage in non-traditional ways of teaching. The teacher must become a facilitator, guiding and supporting students as they take the lead in the learning process (Conley, 2011). The students in our schools today are not at all like we were as elementary or even high school students. They have never known school without computers, interactive whiteboards, DVDs, and other types of technology. But some of our teachers are still using the same teaching techniques they used before access to such technology. Our challenge is to change this mindset; rather than trying to help students to conform to our traditional, even archaic methods of teaching, we need to create opportunities for learning that fit the students we have today.

Authentic learning is not only more strenuous to teach, it is more rigorous for students as well. Lombardi (2007) states that "The reliance on traditional instruction is not simply a choice made by individual faculty—students often prefer it" (p. 10). This may be due to the fact that authentic learning often includes situations where there are not right or wrong answers but some that are better than others, depending on the context of the situation. Learning that includes ambiguity mirrors the "messiness of real-life decision making" (Lombardi, 2007, p. 10). This type of learning better prepares the learner for the uncertainty of the real world. It cannot be overstated that learning is optimized when students are deeply involved in rigorous activities that require them to use complex thinking and to apply knowledge to new or more challenging situations. Students are able to acquire new knowledge and understand concepts when they recognize the relevance to real life (Hess, Carlock, Jones, & Walkup, 2009).

REFLECTION AND CONCLUSION

In the second decade of the 21st century, we have the opportunity to revolutionize education in the best interest of students. However, we realize that leading the change that is called for will be no easy task. As a district level administrator and a principal in an innovative high school setting, we realize that we are asking teachers to embark on a journey into unchartered territory, and this can be challenging and frightening, even for the most accomplished teacher or educational leader. While teachers freshly minted from their preparation programs may be generally competent in embracing the four C's of 21st century learning - communication, collaboration, critical thinking and creativity (Shames, 2010), many of the nation's educators are veterans who will need to learn new methods for instruction and student engagement. Thus, as school and district leaders, our challenge will be to help our current staff improve their content knowledge and instructional techniques in order to teach the 21st century skills and content required for our students to succeed in our globally connected, fast-paced, digital world.

Moving forward, the focus of professional development will shift to "learning skills, 21st century tools, global awareness, and other elements of 21st century curriculum coexisting with the core content" (Salpeter, 2008, p. 3). Teachers and administrators will be expected to utilize technology as a tool on a daily basis, and school and district leaders at every level will be expected to model the use of technology as a regular part of the learning process. Students of today are digital natives and are very connected to each other and to the world through their electronic devices. It is logical and necessary to not only allow, but to encourage students to collaborate on real world, problem based learning activities aimed at preparing them for an uncertain future. Teachers must learn to utilize authentic learning and higher order thinking skills, and to incorporate rigorous learning targets. We realize professional development will not make a difference in instruction if the implementation is not supported and monitored by instructional leaders at the school and district level. Thus as educational leaders, we may be required to change how we approach working with our teachers as adult learners by modeling what we expect and monitoring teaching and learning in an ongoing effort to improve both.

The work that we are just beginning to undertake is daunting; it requires nothing less than courage from teachers as they take risks learning new content and standards and implementing new approaches to teaching and learning. For leaders at both the district and school levels, the challenges ahead require the expertise to provide support to teachers and students and the willingness to let go of having all the answers all of the time. We have to admit that we are not the "great and powerful Oz." As leaders, we are compelled to start the conversations across the district, in the school building, and in the community. At the school level, we can begin the dialogue by providing opportunities for teachers to collaborate through the implementation of purposeful professional learning communities (PLC). Successful PLCs are groups of teachers who meet regularly to focus on student data and student growth and to critically examine their teaching practices. According to DuFour and Eaker (2008), building the capacity in teachers to work together as a professional learning community will have the greatest impact on increasing student learning and eliminating gaps in achievement. If teachers are not isolated in their practice, the required transition to Common Core and 21st century learning may not be as threatening or seem as daunting.

As school and district instructional leaders, training and supporting our teachers to better teach 21st century learners are among our most important responsibilities. We embrace our roles as educational leaders and change agents. It is our responsibility to help teachers implement the more rigorous expectations that are a part of the new standards and to support teachers in developing learning opportunities that allow the use of a wide range of talents and abilities and involve students in challenging tasks that are relevant to real life (Matusevich, O'Connor, & Hargett, 2009). In order to achieve this goal, it is necessary to address not only *what* we teach--the aim of the new Common Core Standards, but also *how* we teach. Implementing the new standards and creating a new model of education will require drastic changes. The effort to deepen content and strengthen performance standards will not succeed without administrators and teachers working together to increase teachers' capacities to facilitate student learning and mastery of the new standards (Quay, 2010). In order to be a leader for 21st century teaching and learning, we must be knowledgeable of what 21st century learning is, and how it differs from current content and skills taught in our schools. It is also important for us to embrace the themes and tools that are involved in educating our students for the world in which they now live and for their future.

As we stated earlier, we do not pretend to have all the answers regarding how to make the transition to Common Core Standards and teaching and learning for the 21st century. For many of the students in our public schools today, the jobs of their future don't even exist. Preparing our students for life means preparing them for the unknown. We see this as a great opportunity to be involved in the *most important changes in public education in over a century. It requires us to move beyond modifying the status quo in the name of change. Instead, we are asking teachers and education leaders, students, and even parents to help us revolutionize the way we do school. This revolution is not just a great opportunity for us, it is even more important for our children.*

References

Brown, J. S. (2006). New learning environments for the 21st century :Exploring the edge. *Change*, 18- 24.

Christen, A. (2009). Transforming the classroom for collaborative learning in the 21st century. *Techniques*, 28-31.

Common Core State Standards: Messaging Toolkit. (2011). Retrieved from http://www.fldoe.org/board/meetings/2010_06_15/toolkit.pdf

Conley, D. T. (2011). Building on the common core. *Educational Leadership, 68*(6), 16-20.

DuFour, R. & Eaker, R. (2008). *Revisiting professional learning communities at work: New insights for improving schools*. Bloomington, IN: National Educational Services.

Dweck, C.S. (2010). Even geniuses work hard. *Educational Leadership, 68*(1), 16-20.

Hess, K., Carlock, D., Jones, B., & Walkup, J. (2009). *What exactly do "fewer, clearer, and higher standards" really look like in the classroom? Using a cognitive rigor matrix to analyze curriculum, lesson plans, and implement assessments.* (publication pending). Retrieved from http: http://www.nciea.org/publications/cognitiverigorpaper_KH11.pdf

Lombardi, M. (2007). Authentic learning for the 21st century: An overview [white paper]. Retrieved from http://net.educause.edu/ir/library/pdf/eli3009.pdf

Matusevich, M., O'Connor, K., & Hargett, M., (2009). The nonnegotiables of academic rigor. *Gifted Child Today, 32*(4), p. 45-52.

McCain, T. (2005). *Teaching for tomorrow: Teaching content and problem-solving skills.* Thousand Oaks, CA: Corwin Press.

Partnership for 21st Century Skills. (2009). Retrieved from http://www.21stcenturyskills.org

Robinson, K. (2010, October 14). Changing Education Paradigms [Video file]. Retrieved from http://www.youtube.com/watch?v=zDZFcDGpL4U

Quay, L. (2010). *Higher standards for all: Implications of the common core for equity in education.* Retrieved from http://www.law.berkeley.edu/files/Education_Roundable_Standards_Brief_4_10.pdf

Salpeter, J. (2008). 21st century skills: Will our students be prepared? *Tech & Learning,* Retrieved from http://techlearning.com/PrintableArticle.aspx?id=13832

Saltrick, S. (2009). *What holds up the rainbow: The intellectual and policy foundations of the 21st century skills framework.* [white paper]. Retrieved from http://www.pearsonschool.com/live/images/custom/21cl/pdf/framework.pdf

Schmoker, M. J. (2011). *Focus: Elevating the essentials to radically improve student learning.* Alexandria, VA: ASCD.

Shames (2010, May 6). Re: The 4c's of 21st century education [Web log message]. Retrieved from http://blog.entrepreneurthearts.com/2010/05/06/the-four-cs-of-21st-century-education/

Silva, E. (2009). Measuring skills for 21st century learning. *Phi Delta Kappan, 90*(9), 630-634.

US. Department of Education, Office of Planning, Evaluation and Policy Development (2010). *ESEA Blueprint for Reform,* Washington, D.C.

Diane S. Hill is an Ed.D. student in the Educational Leadership and Cultural Foundations Department at the University of North Carolina Greensboro. She serves as principal of an early college high school in a rural school district in North Carolina. Prior to her current position, Diane was a middle school principal for 3 years and a high school assistant principal for 4 years. She was a classroom teacher for 20 years, working at the high school and middle school levels. Diane's research interests include distributed leadership, innovative high school reform and equity in education. She can be contacted at dgshep426@gmail.com.

Jean H. Maness is an Ed.D. student in the Educational Leadership and Cultural Foundations Department at the University of North Carolina Greensboro. She currently serves as Executive Director of Elementary School Leadership in a medium sized district in North Carolina. Prior to her current role, she served for five years in other district office leadership positions in elementary curriculum and federal programs, and twenty-two years at the school level as a teacher, assistant principal, and principal. Jean is a member of ASCD and has served three years on the NCASCD Executive Board. She is interested in the leadership development of principals and teachers, with a specific interest in serving at-risk students. Jean can be contacted at jean_maness@abss.k12.nc.us.

Chapter 10

Curricular Consistency vs. Instructional Freedom: The Inherent Struggle that Exists with National Standards

Elizabeth M. Hodge and *Rhonda C. Schuhler*

National Standards have gained a great deal of leverage over the past year, with 45 of 50 states having adopted the Common Core Standards for reading and mathematics at the time of this publication (CCSSI, 2011). This shift has been accelerated by the introduction of Race to the Top, a national educational initiative aimed at providing states with competitive funding opportunities in exchange for meeting a specific set of criteria for school reform. This new federal initiative illuminates a focus on national standards as part of a model focused on consistency and accountability. This paper will explore the positive aspects of national standards, as well as provide cautionary words in the hope that the reader will carefully navigate implementation and will offset the potential negatives of large-scale legislation through effective leadership, whether at the district, school, or classroom level.

PERSONAL REFLECTIONS

As the Executive Director for Curriculum and Professional Development and a Curriculum Support Team Member charged with leading implementation of Common Core standards in a North Carolina school district, we find that the experience of moving forward with new standards evokes a range of emotions within ourselves as well as those whom we lead—enthusiasm, fear, empowerment, and stress, to name a few. We have worked to embrace this shift as an opportunity to revisit instruction in the classroom and to challenge teachers to collaborate and shift instructional practice in support of increased pedagogical understanding and improved teaching. In creating the space for this shift and in our desire to capitalize on this opportunity, we have had to slow down in spite of increased pressure and rapid changes, to make deep connections between instructional practice and student learning through professional development, and to integrate technology in new ways to effectively model the skills and experiences necessary to prepare students for college and career readiness in the 21st century. The changes associated with Common Core are staggering. We view the implementation of new standards as a unique opportunity to recalibrate, reflect on instructional practice, and increase the level of rigor and quality of learning in our classrooms through intensive professional development and support. This approach has the potential to help begin to transform an educational system that is in need of a "shot in the arm." In our current roles, we are on the front lines of this work and are excited about this opportunity.

What we find troubling in all of this work, however, is the parallel discussion that is taking place around accountability. As part of North Carolina's Race to the Top (RttT) plan, teacher performance will be directly linked to student achievement. The state is in the process of meeting with groups of teachers, principals and statisticians to help determine an appropriate way to link student achievement to teacher performance. This plan is currently unfolding, and the implications are staggering. Discussions swirl around ways to link teacher performance to student achievement in both tested and non-tested areas, and the state is moving closer to a model that will incorporate student achievement data into the teacher evaluation process. These concerns are echoed by our peers across the state. In a recent Teacher Effectiveness Vetting Session held by the North Carolina Department of Public instruction, conversations regarding the validity of these ratings, how best to calculate these ratings, and the implications for school culture were discussed. For example, scenarios around how much weight should be given to the individual teacher's student growth scores and the overall school growth scores were considered. Teachers attending the session were very concerned about the concept of their effectiveness being linked to a teacher's scores in another classroom (outside of their realm of control). However, only linking a teacher's effectiveness rating to that of her individual students without including a school level component seems to undermine the work taking place around Professional Learning Communities (PLCs) and frames teachers as independent agents in what is really a collaborative effort to serve students. These issues surrounding teacher effectiveness and student learning outcomes have dramatic implications for classroom instruction.

Depending on how this is executed, linkage between teacher performance and student achievement has the potential to lead to increased student outcomes. On the flip side, however, are issues of curricular reductionism, teaching to the test, gaming the system, cheating, etc. There is also a very real concern that powerful standards will be eclipsed by a testing model that may inform teaching more than the standards themselves. Additionally, although the Common Core standards clearly emphasize that they are not intended to tell a teacher "how to teach," it is concerning that there is already a great deal of discussion around development of instructional guidelines and resources at the national level that may be prescriptive in nature. For example, the Bill and Melinda Gates Foundation has emphasized the need to develop and broaden partnerships with universities, textbook companies, and other entities to provide teachers with teaching tools in support of implementation of new standards. "The Gates Foundation has sorted out the tasks ahead and placed its college-ready investments behind helping teachers improve their practice through intentionally designed tools, strategic partnerships, and incentives for the tools to go to scale." (Phillips & Wong, 2010, p. 39)

Consistency of instructional standards can be beneficial at the school and even district level, but it is troubling to consider that instructional decisions could be made at the national level and be felt directly in the classroom. A move towards consistency in not only standards, but resources and instructional tools, removes the teacher's capability to make situationally-sensitive instructional decisions based upon the unique needs of his/her classroom and students. In *Catching Up or Leading the Way* (2009), Zhao speaks to this possibility, drawing a comparison between the course that China is abandoning and the United States appears to be pursuing:

> I realized that what China wants is what America is eager to throw away—an education that respects individual talents, supports divergent thinking, tolerates deviation, and encourages creativity; a system in which the government does not dictate what students learn or how teachers teach and culture that does not rank or judge the success of a school, a teacher, or a child based on only test scores in a few subjects determined by the government. (p. vi)

These may appear to be harsh words, but we must work to ensure that they do not become the path that we take as a nation. This can only be accomplished by continuing to reflect upon the work that we do to ensure that our efforts at instructional improvement are aimed squarely at improving the quality of teaching in support of increased student learning.

THEORETICAL FOUNDATION

As we stated earlier in our writing, we are leading the charge in our district's implementation of Common Core standards. We perceive our state's adoption of what are effectively national standards as an opportunity for us to recalibrate instruction throughout our district, to build teacher leadership capacity around support of new standards, and to increase rigorous learning opportunities for our students in preparation for college and career.

We also have a front row seat to witness the challenges and potential pitfalls that come with new standards and the assessments that are guaranteed to follow. As we consider these challenges, we do so through the lens of critical pragmatism. We seek to explore the assertions and assumptions that exist around National Standards. The critical pragmatist recognizes that by "listening well, we can act to nurture dialogue and criticism, to make genuine presence possible, to question and explore all that we may do and yet become" (J. Forester, as cited in Zack, 2008, p. 98). We recognize that our work in leading implementation of new standards for our district creates its own set of biases, as we are so close to this initiative and committed to making this process a success that it is difficult for us to look at this reform in a balanced, let alone critical, manner. We are leading the charge in implementation of this initiative, and we are committed to making new standards work, regardless of some of the challenges (e.g., magnitude of shift, limited amount of time for professional development, lack of resources) that exist. This commitment, coupled with a tight implementation schedule, leaves little space for us to examine this mandate through a critically reflective lens. As a result, we are challenging ourselves professionally to take a proverbial "step back" and explore this issue with a critical eye and an open mind. Taking a careful look at the work that is taking place, and the complexity of the organization in which it must grow and thrive, will allow us to better address the challenges that exist through careful planning, monitoring, and support for our teachers. Cleo Cherryholmes (1996), father of critical pragmatism, describes the importance of understanding the role of pragmatism in school reform:

The aesthetics of pragmatism constitute another dimension along which educational reforms often glaringly exhibit unpragmatic tendencies. Reform proposals defy pragmatic logic and sentiment when they ignore the desires and fears and pleasures and pains of those whose actions are required to bring the reforms about and those who are the targets of reform. Lasting change, a pragmatist might observe, cannot be instituted on the basis of commandeered labor (see Sarason, 1990, for a longer discussion of this point). This argument is not to the point that all successful reforms or approaches to administration or textbooks or curriculum plans or classroom organization or assessment or preservice or in-service training must be pragmatic in every respect; no indeed. It is to the point that those who fail to take seriously consequences related to context and the aesthetics and pleasures of implementation may be headed for trouble (p. 17).

With these words in mind, we examine the context in which the Common Core standards were developed as well as what they mean for the people who will implement the standards and the students who are the targets of the standards.

WHAT ARE NATIONAL STANDARDS?

National education standards have gained momentum over the past several years, but they have been in the works for quite some time. As early as 1959, President Eisenhower called for "national goals" in education; President Nixon, apparently frustrated by the lack of national standards, declared the "fear of 'national standards'" one of the 'bugaboos of education'" (Finn, Petrelli, Winkler, 2010, p. 5). The introduction of 1983's *A Nation at Risk*, a hallmark report issued by the National Commission on Education Excellence, sparked a collective national dialogue around student achievement that has continued to influence state and national initiatives in subsequent decades (Barton, 2009, p. 3).

In 1989, the National Council of Teachers of Mathematics (NCTM) published recommended math standards. These standards created a common national language for math teachers for instruction, and they led to discussion on how comparable standards could be developed for other subject areas. In 1994, in order to create a common conversation around the elements necessary in a social studies curriculum, the National Council for Social Studies (NCSS) introduced their first set of national curriculum standards. The National Science Teachers Association (NSTA) introduced the *National Science Education Standards* in 1995 and 1996. These standards were intended to provide common goals for science education. In that same year, 1996, the National Council of Teachers of English (NCTE), along with the International Reading Association (IRA) introduced *The Standards for English Language Arts* in order to compliment other national, state, and local standards. Under the leadership of Assistant Secretary of Education in the administration of President George Herbert Walker Bush, Diane Ravitch led work on voluntary standards for science, history, geography, foreign languages, the arts, English and civics through the infusion of around $10 million dollars in grants to a variety of independent educational groups (Ravitch, 2010, p. 7). While these grants made the creation of these voluntary standards constitutionally permissible, as they were not federally imposed on states, these standards laid a foundation for many states to create their own standards (Barton, 2009, p. 5; Ravitch, 2010, p. 8).

The Clinton administration took the first official steps towards national standards with the initiation of Goals 2000, authorizing creation of the National Standards and Assessment Council in 1994. This council never actually got off the ground; 1994 was also the year in which the Elementary and Secondary Education Act (ESEA) was amended to require states to establish standards and to measure student achievement in these standards (Barton, 2009, p.6).

The 2001 enactment of No Child Left Behind (NCLB) put teeth into the ESEA's state requirements for standards and assessment. States were charged with determining a series of "stair steps" that would bring all students in all subgroups to 100% proficiency in both reading and mathematics by 2014. In support of reaching this goal, each subgroup of students was expected to make adequate yearly progress (AYP), with an emphasis on student growth.

The clear need for more rigorous curricula and consistent student performance led to The Common Core State Standards Initiative. This effort, coordinated by the National Governors Association Center for Best Practices (NGA Center) and the Council of Chief State School Officers (CCSSO), focuses on standards for English language arts and mathematics. To date, these standards, released in June 2010, have been adopted by 45 states, four territories, and the District of Columbia. The focus of these standards is preparing students to be career and college ready. According to the Common Core State Standards Initiative (November, 2011), the standards:

- Are aligned with college and work expectations;
- Are clear, understandable and consistent;
- Include rigorous content and application of knowledge through high-order skills;
- Build upon strengths and lessons of current state standards;
- Are informed by other top performing countries, so that all students are prepared to succeed in our global economy and society; and
- Are evidence-based. (para. 4)

While the NGA Center and the CCSSO coordinated their efforts towards national standards, President Obama was devising his educational agenda. In July 2009, the Obama administration introduced "Race to the Top," an initiative aimed at increasing standards and accountability in new ways through large-scale competitive grants to states. In the words of President Barack Obama on July 24, 2009:

> America will not succeed in the 21st century unless we do a far better job of educating our sons and daughters… And the race starts today. I am issuing a challenge to our nation's governors and school boards, principals and teachers, businesses and non-profits, parents and students: if you set and enforce rigorous and challenging standards and assessments; if you put outstanding teachers at the front of the classroom; if you turn around failing schools – your state can win a Race to the Top grant that will not only help students outcompete workers around the world, but let them fulfill their God-given potential. (White House Fact Sheet, 2009, para. 1)

A description of rigorous and challenging standards and assessments for districts includes "encouraging states to work jointly toward a system of common academic standards that builds toward college and career readiness, and that includes improved assessments designed to measure critical knowledge and higher-order thinking skills" (White House Fact Sheet, 2009, The Race to the Top, para. 6). These expectations provided impetus for states such as North Carolina to revisit their work on standards revision in favor of the new Common Core State Standards Initiative for English language arts and math.

The Obama Administration has also made a push towards reauthorization of the ESEA to more closely reflect the focus of Race to the Top. Although this effort has stalled legislatively, in September 2011 President Obama announced that states could request NCLB waivers to allow more flexibility with regard to meeting NCLB requirements (McNeil, 2011).

THE CASE FOR NATIONAL EDUCATION STANDARDS
NATIONAL EDUCATION STANDARDS AS A BEACON OF
CURRICULAR CONSISTENCY

The historical context for the shift to a national set of standards is clear: *A Nation at Risk* created a sense of urgency around national education reform, and fear that America was falling behind its international counterparts drove a number of federal initiatives aimed at infusing a greater level of consistency and rigor into public education in the United States. Most recently, introduction of a competitively-funded Race to the Top initiative and a presidential push for revision of ESEA in support of RttT-style educational reform has driven the majority of states (45 and counting) to adopt Common Core State Standards Initiative (CCSSI).

The implementation of Common Core State Standards provides states with a level of consistency of expectation in English Language Arts (ELA) and Mathematics. This standardization of expectation on a national scale is long overdue based upon indicators of college and career readiness, which point to wide variances in both academic demands and student performance. According to the Campaign for High School Equity (CHSE, 2009), students of color, students from low-income backgrounds, and students who are non-native English speaking are disproportionally negatively impacted by low standards. States with the highest concentration of learners that fall into one or more of these categories experience an even greater negative impact with regards to readiness for success after high school. This statement is supported by National Assessment of Educational Progress (NAEP) data indicating that students in the South, Southwest, and West are less well prepared for college and career (CHSE, 2009, p. 3). We must provide every student, regardless of their background, a level playing field on which to build future academic successes. Consistent standards will help to lay a foundation for this work.

Inconsistencies in quality of standards from state to state have been examined, and by comparison the Common Core standards are perceived to demonstrate greater levels of rigor, clearer statements of expectations, and less redundancy across grade spans than most states' standards (Carmichael, Martino, Porter-Magee, & Wilson, 2010). The Fordham Institute provides states with a report card based upon the quality of their current standards in ELA and Math, as compared to their analysis of Common Core standards. North Carolina received a "D" in ELA and Math standards, and the described areas of concern mirror those that we regularly hear from teachers- lack of clarity of expectation, redundancy from one grade level to the next, and language that is simply difficult to interpret consistently (Carmichael, Martino, Porter-Magee, & Wilson, 2010).

By contrast, the new Common Core State Standards are written in terms that are easier to understand. Literacy standards (reading, writing, speaking and listening) are integrated across all disciplines. Standards in English Language Arts build upon one another in a "spiraled" approach, increasing the depth of understanding of a particular concept from one grade level to the next without being repetitious. From kindergarten through high school, teachers in our district have echoed excitement and relief at the potential of these clear progressions. They see the potential for the creation of assessment that not only identifies specific break-downs in understanding or skill, allowing them to more accurately and efficiently intervene for struggling students, but that also identifies students for acceleration due to mastery. Math standards build upon conceptual knowledge long ignored or understated in favor of an approach that privileged mastery of math facts. In this way, a targeted set of concepts and ideas central to each discipline are identified, enabling knowledge to build upon knowledge, key to the goal of teaching students to think critically. While this renewed focus on the concepts of mathematical knowledge is causing many of the math teachers in our district to grapple with their own deep conceptual understandings, they realize that without that deep content knowledge, it is impossible for students to problem solve, reason, or analyze (The Albert Shanker Institute, 2011).

It is essential to acknowledge that even within the borders of the United States, students are not prepared equally. As we have previously mentioned, a wide array of standards has led states to produce a wide array of student achievement results. The lack of national consensus about standards has contributed to achievement gaps among states that cut across race and ethnicity gaps and affect all students. When test scores are compared between two states such as Maryland and Texas, for example, a wide discrepancy between what is taught and tested becomes apparent. On assessments of mathematics in 2001, 92% of students in Texas were found "proficient", while only 31% of students in Maryland had achieved this status; however, when comparing those scores to the more rigorous National Assessment of Educational Progress (NAEP) results, Maryland well outperformed Texas, suggesting that Maryland provided a more rigorous curriculum and/or assessment than did Texas (Schmidt and Prawat, 2006). This is but one example, but it is echoed by (McLaughlin, *et al.*, 2008) studies of NAEP data in comparison with state test pass rates: Statistical analyses suggest that if the same nationally representative sample of 4th grade students took the 2003 Louisiana state test and the North Carolina state test, "50 percent more would appear to show *consistent mastery* in North Carolina than would appear to demonstrate *mastery* in Louisiana (p. 23). In other words, the same set of students would be substantially more likely to pass the 2003 North Carolina state test than the 2003 Louisiana state test. A good deal of confusion and disparity arise when states teach, assess, and report on vastly different standards of student learning. Furthermore, these examples underscore the need to level the national playing field for our students in order to prepare them for our increasingly global world.

Adoption of quality standards in the core areas of ELA and math is certainly a step in the right direction, with the focus being on increased rigor through deeper understanding for all students. The opportunities that are afforded through networking, sharing of resources and ideas, and fine-tuning our work based upon collective implementation successes and challenges are also very valuable.

NATIONAL EDUCATION STANDARDS AS PREPARATION FOR GLOBAL COMPETITIVENESS

A critical impetus of the advent of national standards is that we must compete as a nation on the international stage. Our educational systems and standards must address the skills and knowledge needed to contend internationally. To be clear, this involves skills far beyond the use of the typically considered "21st century skills" of technology and collaboration. While these skills are certainly vital, it is of paramount importance that we understand the larger picture of globalization as well. In a marketplace where one in six jobs is tied to international trade, when events that happen on the other side of the world impact our local decisions, with populations in Asia, Latin America, and Africa on the rise, and misinformation and misunderstanding about the United States rampant throughout the world, there is no avoiding the culture, economies, and ideas of the rest of the world (Engler & Hunt, Jr., 2004). As a 2004 report issued by The Southern Growth Policies Board after more than 1,000 interviews and intense economic analysis states, "Global events used to be something that happened 'over there,' but today, globalization affects everyone's lives" (Engler & Hunt, Jr., 2004, p.198).

With indicators of college and career readiness suggesting the US lags behind our international counterparts, it is crucial that we examine our current processes and structures. As in other eras of renewed educational focus, the United States is examining our educational effectiveness against that of the world. One of the oft-cited international assessment measures, Program for International Student Assessment (PISA, 2009), places American students as average at best in literacy, math, and science in the most recent round of international assessment. The Trends in International Mathematics and Science Study (TIMSS) indicates similar findings for 4th and 8th grade students: Our rate of college graduates has fallen from the number one spot to number two behind Canada, and the entry rate for students entering college has fallen behind Australia, Finland, Iceland, Poland, and Sweden (Brown, Rocha, & Sharkey, 2005, p. 12). Although there is some debate as to the true meaning and implications of this data for education in the United States (Zhao, 2009), we agree that the current learning standards and assessment measures do not call for deep learning that accesses the critical understanding and thinking skills that will allow our students to be flexible and innovative players on a national stage, much less a global one.

A MORE CAUTIONARY VIEW OF NATIONAL STANDARDS

As with any major movement that is nationally and publically vetted, the national standards movement has its critics. While it is clear that some criticisms are drawn along political party or ideological lines, others are drawn from data and research evidence. Cautions have emerged as we have moved rapidly towards adoption of national standards, potential pitfalls associated with the accompanying high stakes accountability models have come to light, and the implications of the role of power, money, and control in state implementation of the standards have come to the forefront. In making decisions and creating meaningful curricular transformations, it is essential to understand and heed these voices.

Of major concern to many detractors of the current movement to national standards through the adoption of the Common Core State Standards is the sly way in which states have been "encouraged" to adopt these standards. While the CCSSI is not an overtly government institution, incentives and punishments through financial support or loss thereof, have been closely tied to the adoption of these standards through Race to the Top funding (Gewertz, 2010; Burke & Marshall, 2010). Not only does the lack of adoption obstruct states from RttT funding, but in February of 2010, the Obama administration announced a connection between Title I funding and adoption of common standards (Burke & Marshall, 2010). States that are financially challenged due to economic downturn have had to look to additional funding to make ends meet. Race to the Top offers such a financial boost; however, it comes with the cost of expectations tied to standardized testing, evaluation of teacher effectiveness, and other accountability measures. This is concerning to those who perceive this move to be a federal attempt to "open the door for the federal government to call for even more conditions, such as the use of national tests for accountability purposes" (Bryant, as cited in Burke & Marshall, 2010, p.3).

Further concern over government involvement revolves around the introduction of "publishers' criteria" for use in the implementation of the Common Core Standards. These criteria were developed by two of the writers of the CCSSI for the ELA standards with the intention of responding to "teachers' requests for support by helping them focus on the cornerstones of the standards and understand how classroom work will have to change to reflect them" (Gewertz, 2011, p.16). While critics of the criteria agree that it is important to articulate ways in which materials and resources should reflect the new standards, they are concerned that the publishers' criteria undermines teacher and local judgment of curricula by venturing beyond curriculum and into pedagogy (Gewertz, 2011). This concern is underscored by research that suggests that curriculum design should be locally controlled, as the nearer to the student curricular deliberation occurs, the greater the influence on learning (Tienken, 2011). In development of a plan for new standards implementation, we have worked to ensure that teachers are engaged in the unpacking of standards and development of tools and resources. It is our belief that if we have buy-in from our teachers, and their work is driven locally by our students' needs, we are more likely to have a positive impact on student learning.

Cautionary advice not only comes from those who are skeptical, but from those who support national standards implementation as well. A main tenant of common standards is college and career readiness; it is clear that our students need to be prepared through a more rigorous curriculum that allows for deep content knowledge and critical thought. It is also clear that historically, the wide variety of state standards in the United States have not consistently done so. Given the current standards and the rising expectations of new standards, great consideration must be invested in the design of new curriculum to help all of our students meet higher expectations. While there is excitement for standards reform among those who advocate for equity and access, there are also valuable lessons to be learned from districts that have pursued higher standards. One example of such a lesson is the 90's reform of Chicago Public Schools (CPS). In an effort to increase standards and access to college, CPS instituted reforms that required all students, regardless of exceptional child status or prior experience, to enroll in college preparatory English and Math courses--with devastating results. While this effort did give the appearance of preparing students for college readiness and increased rigor through larger enrollment in such courses, the failure rates increased, test scores and grades decreased, and students were no more likely to pursue college after these courses (Quay, 2010). Clearly, simply increasing rigor in standards and expectations is not sufficient. Implementation, professional development, and strong curricular development must be considered as well (Center on Education Policy, 2011).

CONCLUSIONS AND IMPLICATIONS

The concept of national standards appears to be here to stay, at least in the short term. This focus on curricular consistency on a national scale, coupled with accompanying assessments aimed at student achievement and teacher performance indicators, makes it difficult to imagine that the day will come in which we shift attention away from the national to local arenas. A focus on global competitiveness has created a sense of urgency reminiscent of the early days following *A Nation at Risk*. The idea that increased consistency and a level playing field may lead us to better performance on the national stage sounds appealing to many. There are dissenting voices out there, however. Zhao (2009) refutes claims that nations such as China are "leading the way," pointing to the detrimental effects of a nation laser focused on consistency and conformity. Ironically, China is moving away from the approach that we are now moving towards as a nation--national standards and assessments.

The jury is still out on whether this national standards movement will increase learning opportunities for students. An increased focus on rigor seems to be an important thrust of Common Core standards, and the benefit of this shift to higher learning expectations is difficult to refute. How this focus will actually translate into classroom practice remains to be determined. As it stands now, the CCSSI has clearly advocated for state and local autonomy in instructional practices as they relate to delivery of standards (CCSSI, 2011). If this approach continues, concerns regarding national control versus teacher autonomy may be abated.

In an effort to minimize the chance that national standards and assessments take the driver's seat in the classroom, state and local education agencies need to be thoughtful in the sharing and distribution of materials in order to keep the focus on state and local control rather than federal control. If states create strong curricula and support each other, the likelihood of a federal "take-over" of curriculum will lessen.

In the absence of strong state level curriculum development plans, local bodies should development rich implementation plans that focus on systems change, professional development in the areas of content knowledge and pedagogy, and school-level leadership development in the areas of change, curriculum, and sound instruction. The opportunity for districts to build internal capacity while adopting standards that are more rigorous and connected in nature should not be taken lightly. We have committed ourselves to this work in our district, thinking in terms of a focus on improved instructional practices in addition to new standards adoption, alongside development of school leadership capacity in support of change.

As curriculum leaders overseeing Common Core implementation, we recognize the value of the work that is taking place. We are engaging a broad base of teachers in this work, and we believe that the potential for instructional improvement is powerful. As educators, we must continue to learn and grow, and we must focus on providing quality instruction to students. If these considerations are made and instruction can reflect meaningful change, student learning will increase, critical thought and connections will increase, and performance tasks will show evidence of this. We believe that the pitfalls that are associated with implementation of new standards can be abated with thoughtful planning and support, and a focus on meaningful learning opportunities for all students.

In order to avoid such pitfalls in our district, we have been very intentional in our curriculum implementation and professional development plans, using the Common Core State Standards as just the starting point. Realizing that change is a complex process, that all stakeholders must have a deep understanding of the vision and purpose of the change, and even more so when the change is forced, we have purposefully included all stakeholders in this implementation process.

Beginning with teachers, because the central work of this change must occur in the classroom with instruction, we created teams of content specific teacher leaders at every level - elementary, middle, and high. The work designed for these teachers has been situated in learning communities in which the teachers have explored and investigated not only the new standards for implementation, but their own leadership and collaborative practices. As part of their work, the teacher leaders have unpacked and deconstructed the standards, and then led their colleagues through the same work during whole day professional development workshops. They have also explored the similarities and differences between the old state standards and the newly adopted ones, navigating the frustration with that which they are forced to leave behind and what to many feels like a repackaging of standards and expectations have come before, all while focusing on the possibilities this time of change has to offer. Because we feel that it is vital that all teachers are empowered to have a voice in this process, the teams of teacher leaders will lead the creation of curriculum and unit guides, while at the same time designing experiences in which their colleagues have opportunities to be heard and contribute meaningfully.

Additionally, it is clear that any change process must have strong administrative leadership and support. Through this implementation process, we have felt it essential to not only keep principals informed, but to develop their curriculum and instruction knowledge in order that they might be better prepared to support their teachers through this monumental shift. In order to accomplish this, our curriculum department designed seminars and mini-workshops for all school based administrators – both principals and assistant principals. These professional development sessions were focused on developing their understanding of the new standards, the shifts from the old, and the direction in which state and national assessment appeared to be heading. We provided further support through the creation of "implementation planning days", in which each principal was to bring a team of leaders from his/her school to work with the curriculum department with the purpose of thinking through the specific changes that would need to be supported to integrate the existing school programs with the new implementations. As part of a plan of ongoing support, these days would be followed up on and carried into the first years of implementation.

Mindful of all stakeholders, we were also purposeful in our outreach to the community. Many parent and community information sessions were offered, from school-based PTO/PTA meetings to the Chamber of Commerce and other local organizations. The purpose of these meetings was to provide general information about changes they should see in the coming year, but also to gauge the level of knowledge of the community in order to guide future work in this arena.

These are but a few examples of how our district has capitalized on the implementation of new standards and the changes that must accompany it to positively affect the culture of our district and schools, and ultimately student learning. We understand that we have only just scratched the surface of all that is to be uncovered in this work. From ongoing and deep investigations of district and department beliefs, to partnerships with local universities, and the development of long-term professional development plans, we constantly seek to use this time to create systemic change that transforms teaching and learning in our district.

References

Barton, Paul. (2009). *National education standards: Getting beneath the surface.* Educational Testing Service. Princeton, N.J.

Brown, C. G., Rocha, E., & Sharkey, A. (2005, August 23). *Getting smarter, becoming fairer*. Center for American Progress. Retrieved from http://www.americanprogress.org/issues/2005/08/b994995.html

Burke, L.M. & Marshall, J.A. (2010). Why national standards won't fix American education: Misalignment of power and incentives. *Backgrounder, 24*(13), 1-10.

Campaign for High School Equity. (2009). *Communities of color: A critical perspective in the common standards movement.* Washington, DC: Rockefeller Philanthropy Advisors.

Carmichael, S.B., Martino, G., Porter-Magee, K., & Wilson, W.S. (2010). *The state of state standards and the common core in 2010.*(July). Washington, DC: Thomas B. Fordham Institute.

Center on Education Policy. (2011). *States' progress and challenges in implementing Common Core State Standards*. Washington, D.C.: Same.

Cherryholmes, C. (1996). More notes on pragmatism. *Educational Researcher, 23*(16), 16-17.

Common Core State Standards Initiative. (2011). The Standards. Retrieved from http://corestandards.org/the-standards.

Engler, J. M., & Hunt, Jr., J. B. (2004). Preparing our students for work and citizenship in the global age. *Phi Delta Kappan, 86*(3), 197-199.

Finn, C. E., & Petrilli, M. J. (2010). *Now what? Imperatives & options for "common core" implementation & governance.*(October). Washington. DC: Thomas B. Fordham Institute.

Gewertz, C. (2011). Standards writers wade into curriculum. *Education Week, 30*(37), 1, 16-17.

Gewertz, C. (2010). States adopt standards at fast clip. *Education Week, 29*(36), 1-18.

McLaughlin, D. H., Bandeira de Mello, V., Blankenship, C., Chaney, K., Esra, P., Hikawa, H., Rojas, D., William, P., & Walman, M. (2008). *Comparison between NAEP and state mathematics assessment results*: 2003 (NCES 2008-475). Washington, D.C.: National Center for Education Statistics, Institute of Education Sciences, U.S. Department of Education. Retrieved from http://nces.ed.gov/pubs2008/2008475_1.pdf

McNeil, M. (2011). Obama gives go-ahead for NCLB waivers to states. *Education Week's Blog*. Retrieved from http.//blogs.edweek.org/edweek/campaign-k-12/2011/08/Obama_gives_go-ahead_for_waivers.html

Phillips, V. & Wong, C. (2010). Tying together the Common Core of standards, instruction, and assessments. *Phi Delta Kappan, 91*(5),37-42.

Program for international student assessment.(2009). *Mathematical literacy performance of 15-year-olds.* Institute of Education Sciences. Retrieved from http://nces.ed.gov/surveys/pisa/pisa2009highlights_3.asp

Ravitch, D. (2010). *The life and death of the great American school system.* New York, NY: Basic Books.

Quay, L. (2010). *Higher standards for all: Implications of the common core for equity in education.* Berkeley, CA: The Chief Justice Earl Warren Institute on Race, Ethnicity, & Diversity.

Schmidt, W.H. &Prawat, R.S. (2006). Curriculum coherence and national control of education: Issue or non-issue? *Journal of Curriculum Studies, (38)*6, 641-658.

The Albert Shanker Institute. (2011). A call for common content: Core curriculum must build a bridge from standards to achievement. *American Educator*. (Spring). Retrieved from http://www.aft.org/pdfs/americaneducator/spring2011/ASI.pdf

Tienken, C. H. (2011). Common core standards: The emperor has no clothes, or evidence. *Kappa Delta Pi Record, 47*(2), 58-62.

Zack, T. (2008). Critical pragmatism in planning: The case of the Kathorus Special Integrated Presidential Project in South Africa. (Doctoral dissertation). Retrieved from Wired Space. (URI:http://hdl.handle.net/10539/5682)

Zhao, Y. (2009). *Catching up or leading the way.* Alexandria, VA: ASCD.

Elizabeth M. Hodge is an Ed.D. student in the Educational Leadership and Cultural Foundations Department at the University of North Carolina Greensboro. She is also currently a district level Lead Teacher for Secondary (6-12) English Language Arts, Social Studies, and World Languages in a medium sized district in North Carolina. Prior to that, she served for three years as a middle school Curriculum Facilitator and taught for five years in both middle and elementary school. Elizabeth is passionate about teacher leadership, as well as curriculum and instructional design and leadership. She presents regionally on the topics of utilizing change implementation to build teacher leadership capacity and curriculum and instruction. She can be contacted at elizabethmarieh@gmail.com.

Rhonda C. Schuhler is an Ed.D. student in the Educational Leadership and Cultural Foundations Department at the University of North Carolina Greensboro. She currently serves as Executive Director of Curriculum and Professional Development in a medium sized district in North Carolina. Prior to her current role, she served for six years in other district office leadership positions in human resources and curriculum, and twelve years at the school level as a teacher, assistant principal, and principal. Rhonda is interested in the leadership development of principals and teachers, with a specific commitment to change leadership for instructional reform. She can be contacted at Rhonda.schuhler@gmail.com.

Chapter 11

Technology Leadership: A Digital Lever for Lasting Educational Reform

Justin Bathon

Technology leadership is just good leadership. One cannot be a great technology leader without exhibiting all the traits of effective school leaders, and in today's world, one cannot be an effective school leader without being a great technology leader. Technology has become core to the successful operation of schools. More importantly, it has become one of the vital levers for effective educational reform. Technologies can be the critical tool for opening windows for educational transformation. Until recently, a clear focus on technology as a critical element of school leadership has been absent (Schrum, Galizio, & Ledesma, 2011). There have been few leadership programs containing an explicit technology focus and few state or school level technology integration policies. There have also been few technology-based professional development programs for school leaders and few school leaders requiring technology integration on the part of their teachers. Generally, there has been an overall lack of attention to this vital issue even while it has eliminated entire industries and changed so much for the average citizen both in the workplace and at home. The lack of attention from within the educational system has been alarming.

Slowly, though, education is awakening to digital and informational changes and to the potential of technology to create opportunities for reforming learning institutions. For instance, a growing body of research has been examining this landscape, particularly the response of schools to the influx, or lack thereof, of new digital technologies invented in the past few decades. Recognizing this trend, the University Council for Educational Administration (UCEA) has even created and supported a program center to further this research and awareness. The Center for the Advanced Study of Technology Leadership in Education (CASTLE), for which I serve as a director, has been instrumental in leading research and practical awareness of technology leadership for the past several years. Further, because of the challenges and opportunities posed by technology, professional associations and other educational bodies have also taken a leading role in understanding and advancing technology in schools through leadership. For example, the National Educational Technology Standards for Administrators (NETS-A), published by the International Society for Technology in Education (ISTE), have solidified the importance and articulated the traits of high quality technology leadership amongst school administrators (ISTE, 2009). These early examples of the initial response to the challenge

of leading for technology are today beginning to merge into more formalized and systemic efforts to improve the technology awareness and leadership capabilities of school and district leaders.

This chapter is a brief introduction to technology leadership, including the growing response from the scholarly and practitioner communities. First, this chapter articulates some basic concepts around technology leadership. It then presents the elements of technology leadership as defined by the National Educational Technology Standards for Administrators. Next, this chapter reviews the literature base related to these elements. Fourth, a brief exploration of the digital conversations on technology leadership are explored, including tips and potential connections for future participants in this dialog. Finally, this chapter concludes by offering some practical advice for beginning technology leaders.

TECHNOLOGY, EDUCATION, AND IMPLICATIONS

Technology is a largely misunderstood concept. Few people have really given the idea of technology a great deal of thought even though it is, perhaps, a central element of what makes us human. As an example to help understand how fundamental technology is to the human experience, try the following thought experiment. Please pause, right now, and attempt to recite the alphabet backward from memory.

If you are like most people, you will struggle with this elementary task. We are good at remembering all of the data but only if the data is accessed in the pattern in which it was learned or used (Kurzweil, 2012). In our example, to compensate for this deficiency many of you probably reached for, or at least thought about, a pencil and paper to simplify the task. All of us can complete the task once we have the necessary tools (a pencil, paper, and an operable language with defined letters). These tools, reached for thousands of times a day, are human technologies built to supplement our daily interaction with the world (Kelly, 2010) and compensate for our various human limitations. Understood in this way, much of what a school principal does is technology leadership whether or not it is acknowledged as such. This realization even inspired an Internet meme (concept spread through the Internet) amongst educators called "#pencilchat" where they lampooned the education system's irrational natural tendencies against new technologies (Dwyer, 2011). Like pencils, learning technology is, in fact, a fundamental part of the school experience for all children. Learning to write is necessarily learning a technology. Once a school leader grasps this fundamental relationship between human learning and our technology tools, understanding their critical role as a technology leader becomes more apparent.

This relationship is lost on many school leaders, though, because this broad definition is counter to the everyday usage of the term technology. In fact, the very idea of a distinct concept of technology is relatively new. Although Aristotle referred to a "techne" in relationship to the "logos" in the *Rhetoric*, it was not until 1829 that the Harvard professor Jacob Bigelow used the word technology in the way we know it today, as a summary term for applied arts and sciences toward practical problems (Bigelow, 1831; Kelly, 2007). In common parlance, though, the concept is something closer to the everyday definition suggested by early computer scientist Allan Kay, who said, "a technology is anything invented after you were born" (as cited in Kelly, 2007, p. 1).

Although definitions are numerous, technology is a concept subjective to the individual user and his or her experiences. Many everyday devices contain electric motors, for instance, as the operative mechanical device. A ceiling fan might not be technology to most people but its cousin in a new electric powered automobile, such as the Toyota Prius, probably is to most consumers. The underlying mechanical and electrical concepts are not substantially different, but the scale and application are recent iterations made possible by new combinations of older technologies. This might be quibbling, and surely these are difficult questions, but when one is tasked with leading schools for technology integration it helps to know what tools an average person, such as a school board member, would consider a new technology.

Perhaps, at least for the last few decades, one can draw a box around digital technology as being distinct. Or, perhaps one can even draw a smaller box around computer-based technologies. Both of these narrowed concepts have definitional issues, as digital and computer technology are far older than most people would assume. However, there is a general sense that within the last few decades, at least within the lifetime of some current school leaders, there has been a dramatic shift in this particular species of technology. Digitally based information technologies facilitated by computers have had deep repercussions on our economy and our everyday lived experience.

In fact, from my own practice, when the term technology leadership is used by school leaders, university professors, or state policy personnel, it is typically to refer to leadership of the usage and implications of these recent information technologies in schools and classrooms. The challenge presented by these dramatic and disruptive information technologies are particularly relevant to schools as information-based organizations. These are not new challenges, but the sheer amount of change in the past decade is unique and unavoidable. For instance, for many years the debate raged over the usage of digital calculators in mathematics courses. In retrospect, this was quaint. By comparison, the phones in the pockets of our students today are supercomputers, capable not only of long division but of translating text or spoken language between cultures, creating works of art in music, movies, pictures, or poems, interpreting complex imagery, self-aware geolocation by connecting with satellites in space, algorithmic reasoning, real time video connections anywhere on the planet, and searching and browsing the greatest library of human information ever created. To think these new technologies were not going to fundamentally redefine the learning relationships between students, teachers, and parents was, and unfortunately still is for some people, beyond naïve.

In the face of such substantial change, it is irresponsible to ignore the issue or shirk from the challenge. Luckily, the educational infrastructure around the concept of technology leadership has begun to manifest within the past decade. Perhaps the clearest manifestation of thoughts around the elements of technology leadership, and the practical implications of those elements, was articulated in the National Educational Technology Standards for Administrators.

STANDARDS AND ELEMENTS OF TECHNOLOGY LEADERSHIP

To assist in further understanding the practical meaning of technology leadership in schools, it is helpful to look at the functional elements of technology leadership as defined by the NETS-A standards (ISTE, 2009). These five standards were first passed by ISTE in 2002 in consultation with a number of professional associations, state departments of education, university faculty, and other interested groups (Schrum, Galizio, & Ledesma, 2011). These standards were updated in 2009 after consultation with a similar set of educational entities providing input. The NETS-A is part of a broader set of technology standards that include additional standards for both teachers (NETS-T) and students (NETS-S).

The NETS-A standards provide a framework for classifying the actual performance standards that school leaders meet in their effort to be technology leaders. Each standard is followed by a description as well as three to five specific performances to meet the standard. Given the importance of these standards to the field and their role in classifying elements of technology leadership, a full reading is essential to gather a sense of the scope of the technology leadership challenge in schools. Thus, the following are the NETS-A standards in their entirety (ISTE, 2009):

1. **Visionary Leadership**. Educational Administrators inspire and lead development and implementation of a shared vision for comprehensive integration of technology to promote excellence and support transformation throughout the organization. Educational Administrators:
    a. Inspire and facilitate among all stakeholders a shared vision of purposeful change that maximizes use of digital-age resources to meet and exceed learning goals, support effective instructional practice, and maximize performance of district and school leaders
    b. Engage in an ongoing process to develop, implement, and communicate technology-infused strategic plans aligned with a shared vision
    c. Advocate on local, state, and national levels for policies, programs, and funding to support implementation of a technology-infused vision and strategic plan

2. **Digital Age Learning Culture**. Educational administrators create, promote, and sustain a dynamic, digital-age learning culture that provides a rigorous, relevant, and engaging education for all student. Educational administrators:
    a. Ensure instructional innovation focused on continuous improvement of digital age learning
    b. Model and promote the frequent and effective use of technology for learning
    c. Provide learner-centered environments equipped with technology and learning resources to meet the individual, diverse needs of all learners
    d. Ensure effective practice in the study of technology and its infusion across the curriculum
    e. Promote and participate in local, national, and global learning communities that stimulate innovation, creativity, and digital-age collaboration

distribute leadership

3. **Excellence in Professional Practice.** Educational Administrators promote an environment of professional learning and innovation that empower educators to enhance student learning through the infusion of contemporary technologies and digital resources. Educational administrators:
   a. Allocate time, resources, and access to ensure ongoing professional growth in technology fluency and integration
   b. Facilitate and participate in learning communities that stimulate, nurture, and support administrators, faculty, and staff in the study and use of technology
   c. Promote and model effective communication and collaboration among stakeholders using digital-age tools
   d. Stay abreast of educational research and emerging trends regarding effective use of technology and encourage evaluation of new technologies

4. **Systemic Improvement.** Educational Administrators provide digital-age leadership and management to continuously improve the organization through the effective use of information and technology resources. Educational administrators:
   a. Lead purposeful change to maximize the achievement of learning goals through the appropriate use of technology and media-rich resources
   b. Collaborate to establish metrics, collect and analyze data, interpret results, and share findings to improve staff performance and student learning
   c. Recruit and retain highly competent personnel who use technology creatively and proficiently to advance academic and operational goals
   d. Establish and leverage strategic partnerships to support systemic improvement
   e. Establish and maintain a robust infrastructure for technology including integrated, interoperable technology systems to support management, operations, teaching, and learning

5. **Digital Citizenship.** Educational administrators model and facilitate understanding of social, ethical, and legal issues and responsibilities related to an evolving digital culture. Educational administrators:
   a. Ensure equitable access to appropriate digital tools and resources to meet the needs of all learners
   b. Promote, model, and establish policies for safe, legal, and ethical use of digital information and technology
   c. Promote and model responsible social interactions related to the use of technology and information
   d. Model and facilitate the development of a shared cultural understanding and involvement in global communication and collaboration tools (p. 1-2).

The adoption of these standards by the education community has been spotty but significant. First, the NETS-A are broadly supported as the accepted set of technology leadership standards based upon the broad coalition constructed to create and then update the standards. Further, they have been adopted in some important places. For instance, these standards have been added to some regulations on the preparation of school leaders (16 KAR 3:050, 2012), and the standards consistently show up in the scholarly literature as a justification for the research (Richardson, Bathon, Flora & Lewis, 2012). However, these few integrations aside, the standards are still unknown by the majority of both school leaders and leadership preparation programs. This lack of knowledge by such a large percentage of professors, practitioners, and policy-makers results in a scarcity of focused attention to this group of tightly defined leadership activities needed for building and sustaining relevant schools in our digital society. Increased attention to both these activities and these standards would go a long way toward clarifying the digital responsibilities expected of school leaders. Luckily, as the following paragraph illustrates, such increased attention is beginning to emerge in the scholarly landscape.

SCHOLARSHIP ON TECHNOLOGY LEADERSHIP

Over the past decade there has been growing scholarly interest in the field of technology leadership. The publication of the NETS-A standards certainly contributed to this development. However, it has only been in very recent years that anything more than a trickle of research has begun to appear. In fact, two studies in recent years published through the work of CASTLE more closely examine this scholarly landscape. First, McLeod and Richardson (2011) looked for presentations and publications on technology leadership. They found that less than three percent of sessions at the American Education Research Association Conference and the UCEA conference were focused on technology leadership issues between 1997 and 2009. The National Council for Professors of Educational Administration (NCPEA), however, had a higher presence of technology leadership totaling over seven percent of all presentations in the same period. Further, in looking at the top 25 most cited journals in educational leadership (as identified by *Educational Administration Quarterly* and the *Journal of School Leadership*) only 43 of 8,925 articles—less than one percent—focused on issues of technology leadership (McLeod & Richardson, 2011).

An article published shortly thereafter (Richardson, Bathon, Flora & Lewis, 2011) looked at these publications in more detail to understand which of the NETS-A elements have received scholarly attention and which are still largely lacking a substantial research base. We found that all five standards have at least some treatment in the ERIC database but that this treatment was largely from non-peer reviewed articles. NETS-A Standard 2 and 3 (regarding both digital age learning and professional practice) received the most treatment with 20 articles touching on elements covered in the standard and, of those, seven coming from peer reviewed journals. Standard 5 (digital citizenship) received the least treatment with only twelve total articles and, of those, only four from peer-reviewed journals. Perhaps related to this lack of peer reviewed treatment was also a lack of empirical treatment of technology leadership, evidenced by the fact that only 32 percent of all the articles on NETS-A related issues in the ERIC database were either quantitative (9) or qualitative (3) in nature. Of these twelve articles identified by the Richardson, Bathon, Flora & Lewis (2011) review, two research teams were responsible for five of the published studies (Anderson & Dexter, 2000/2005; Afshari, et al., 2008/2009/2010). One clearly positive result from this review of the literature, though, was that technology leadership is receiving attention in international journals, particularly in Turkey and Southeast Asia (Afshari, et al., 2008/2009/2010; Deryakulu & Olkun, 2009).

While there has not been much volume in the scholarly research on technology leadership, there have been several noteworthy studies that have provided valuable information to school leaders in considering technology leadership. Anderson and Dexter (2000) provided some the earliest and most rigorous research in their nationwide examination of technology leadership characteristics. They followed up this study with an examination of the technology outcomes from the same schools and concluded that leadership played the central predictive role in positive technology outcomes (Anderson & Dexter, 2005). This study forms a large part of the foundational base of the field and has spurred a great deal of further interest in technology leadership. Lecklider, Clausen, and Britten (2009) also compared principals' stated priorities against actual observed technology usage in schools. Across the survey questions, the principals in the study rated technology highly in their prioritization of school functions, but under observation this stated priority was not manifested as an actual priority in practice.

In 2011, the *Journal of School Leadership* published a special issue on technology leadership topics, substantially adding to the scholarly base in technology leadership in the process serving as a substantial turning point in the legitimization of technology leadership as a distinct field of inquiry within the broader educational leadership landscape. First, as a foundational component of the special issue, McLeod and Richardson (2011), mentioned previously, conducted a substantial review of the broader technology leadership base both in the literature and in presentations at academic conferences. The underlying infrastructure of the field was also examined by Schrum, Galizio, and Ledesma (2011), who examined the technology preparation requirements of new school leaders and found little formal preparation. The researchers did find some amount of on-the-job technology preparation.

The special issue also examined the implementation of technology by school leaders. Dexter (2011) continued her scholarly leadership of the field by examining a component of effective technology implementation by using a cross-case analysis of middle school technology leaders to clarify our understanding of the importance of distributed leadership in technology implementation. Further, Doolittle and Gallagher-Browne (2011) used the broader view of technology, mentioned above, to examine the implementation of curriculum standards as the core technology of the classroom and the level of preparation for school leaders to be these types of instructional leaders. Their fourteen-school case study in New Jersey found missing implementation of the curriculum, poorly designed assessments, and a severe lack of instructional leadership amongst administrators. Finally, the special issue published an article by Rutkowski, Rutkowski, and Sparks (2011), who investigated classroom technology support policy levers internationally, finding few countries where the technology support policies actually impacted classroom level technology usage. Of the 18 countries studied, only South Africa, the Russian Federation, and Thailand evidenced a statistically significant connection between the policy and implementation.

In fact, international research around technology leadership has been very informative to the broader field and an obvious strength of this field of research. From a study conducted of school leaders in Iran, Afshari, Bakar, Luan, Samah, & Fooi (2008) found that principals used technology 2-3 days a week in completing administrative tasks and had a moderate level of technology literacy, dependent on issues such as access, competence, and negative perceptions of technology usage (Afshari et al., 2010). This is comparable to a similar effort in New Zealand, which found higher technology usage amongst primary school leaders translated into effective modeling for improvement of classrooms (Stuart, Mills, & Remus, 2009). The Iranian results were reflected in a nearby effort in Turkey that approached the question from the other direction, asking computer teachers their perceptions of their principals' abilities with technology (Deryakulu & Olkun, 2009). The teachers said that the school leaders lacked even basic knowledge and skills with technology. These challenges can be magnified in less-developed countries, such as in Cambodia where Richardson (2011) found that hardware, electricity and Internet access were all necessary technology integration ingredients that were missing in many schools. Finally, a recent study of technology policy practices amongst school leaders in the Flanders region of Belgium (Vanderlinde, van Braak, & Dexter, 2012) found that policy is distinctly developed within five different domains and that policy interacts very closely with the broader school culture.

There have also been several examples in the literature of technology leadership in action. Levin and Schrum (2012) profiled many technology leaders across the country, articulating particular strengths of each school and leader. This book comes on the heels of their previous work detailing specifics on leading 21st Century schools (Schrum & Levin, 2009). In another example of technology leadership in action from Kannapolis, North Carolina, technology leaders there made a major push to change their district to focus on technology-driven jobs after local community investment in a new research campus for the state (McCombs, 2010). This matching of broader community opportunities and challenges is a common theme amongst technology leaders in schools. For instance, a rural superintendent in Wisconsin was also profiled for embracing and promoting a variety of new digital technologies for classrooms (Butler, 2010). This included new digital workout machines, mixing both health and technology leadership for the improvement of the district. Another interesting thread through the literature was the usage of professional development institutes to strengthen the technology leadership skills of working professionals (Fletcher, 2009). A large-scale study of this type was conducted in Alabama by Parks, Sun, and Collins (2002) as well.

A few books have emerged that address the topic of technology leadership directly. Theodore Creighton (2002), Anthony Picciano (2010), and Rosemary Papa (2011) have all directly tackled technology leadership, with Creighton focusing on principals, Picciano focusing on infrastructure planning, and Papa editing a book on several elements of the NETS-A standards with a particular focus on leading changes to teaching and learning. These books assist in building the practical foundation for the field. ISTE has also published a very practical workbook specifically on NETS-A implementation (Brooks-Young, 2009). Susan Brooks-Young (2006) has also addressed leading schools for new literacies for teachers and students in another comprehensive overview book on technology leadership.

Leadership has also been a focus in several more general books about education and technology. For instance, Collins and Halverson (2009) specifically call for a rethinking of educational leadership to be proactive instead of reactive to technology change. Nussbaum-Beach and Hall (2011) address the critical elements of connected leaders as they call for leadership to transform systems in schools. Finally, even broader books about educational reform, such as the recent works by Wagner (2010, 2012), Khan (2012), Vander Ark and Wise (2011), and Christensen, Johnson & Horn (2010) have deep implications for embracing technology-driven change by school leaders.

In summary, the past decade has witnessed the birth of the new field of inquiry around school technology leadership. The recent increase in the number of books on the subject and the publication of the special issue of the *Journal of School Leadership* only further solidify this growing, global literature base. The next decade of research on school technology leadership promises to be even more exciting as a bevy of new researchers have begun to realize the importance of research on the role of the administrator as the technology leader in schools.

DIGITAL CONVERSATION ON TECHNOLOGY LEADERSHIP

One of the more interesting developments around the field of technology leadership has been the usage of digital technologies, particularly social media, as a source for conversation amongst practitioners, scholars, and policymakers. On this front, technology leadership is far ahead of more traditional school leadership strands in that more information is being exchanged more frequently between groups that typically struggle to engage in dialog in more traditional fields. On any given day, thousands of interactions between technology leaders are affecting real change in school environments, spurring new pathways for inquiry, and influencing policy conversations in state government. All of these leaders are connected in real time and have conversations about the best technology tools, the best leadership techniques, the latest policy initiatives, and so much more. The virtual platforms for these conversations vary considerably, but the relationships between leaders are very real. As an example, Alec Couros, a leading professor in the field at the University of Regina, on his fortieth birthday, received a YouTube video composed by 75 other technology leaders around the world collectively singing "Thank You for Being a Friend" (Shareski, 2011). The result of these technology enabled conversations amongst leaders is frequently a reflection on the very task of leading for technology itself. These conversations have been so prevalent and meaningful that it has even spawned physical books that document the best usages of these tools for school leaders (McLeod & Lehmann, 2011; Richardson, 2011).

It is difficult to explain the value and content of these conversations for technology leaders in this format. The easiest and most practical way to learn how these conversations can be helpful to all aspects of school leadership, including scholarship, is to simply begin to observe, or better yet participate in, these conversations. There are many hundreds of potential starting points for jumping into these conversations, but below I provide several recommended people and places that are both welcoming and highly informative.

1. Dangerously Irrelevant (http://dangerouslyirrelevant.org). A CASTLE blog written by founding director Scott McLeod, a university professor, that is a prominent outlet for thoughtful leadership around technology and educational reform.
2. Connected Principals (http://connectedprincipals.com/). A CASTLE blog written by over 50 practicing school leaders that serves as the vital conversation point for

practical discussion of technology leadership in schools. Also, follow the related hashtag #cpchat on Twitter.
3. Will Richardson (http://willrichardson.com/). Will, the author of several books, a frequent keynote speaker, and cofounder of a professional development company, provides thoughtful leadership to schools on the use of technology to transform learning experiences.
4. GETideas (http://getideas.org/). A social network built and operated exclusively for educational leaders interested in participating in global educational transformation (GET). The site has organized programs, resources, groups, news, and events specifically relevant to school leaders.
5. Hashtags: #edadmin, #edleader, #edleadership, & #cpchat. These hashtags organize Twitter into only the posts that authors deemed relevant to the field of education leadership—A great filter mechanism to save time accessing only relevant information.
6. Free Tech for Teachers (http://www.freetech4teachers.com/). Although not specifically focused on educational leadership, author Richard Byrne provides more information on learning tools than nearly anyone else. This includes specifically organized resources for the iPad, Android devices, Google tools and others.

In addition to these university, policy, or professional development resources, there are also hundreds of practicing school leaders that are daily providing resources and leading conversations about educational reform with a particular focus on technology:

1. Eric Sheninger (https://twitter.com/NMHS_Principal & http://esheninger.blogspot.com/). A New Jersey principal with over 30,000 twitter followers because of the highly useful connections that he provides to practicing school leaders.
2. Patrick Larkin (https://twitter.com/patrickmlarkin). An assistant superintendent who engages in deep conversations around technology leadership on twitter, including providing thousands of links and connection points to other relevant resources.
3. Chris Lehmann - (http://practicaltheory.org/blog/ & https://twitter.com/chrislehmann). The founding principal of the Science Leadership Academy in Philadelphia, he blogs on the daily trials of school leadership, frequently citing new technologies to improve learning for School 2.0.
4. George Couros - http://georgecouros.ca/blog/ & https://twitter.com/gcouros). With the official title of "Division Principal of Innovative Teaching and Learning," he is a school leader from Alberta who blogs and tweets on improving teaching and learning with a heavy emphasis on digital tools.

These examples are but a few of the common entry points for school leaders interested in participating in online discussion around technology, reform, and leadership in schools.

There are many ways to break into these conversations. Another useful technique for finding a digital conversation relevant to you is to use your local or state professional organizations as entry points. These organizations typically maintain a social media presence, and by participating in these environments—and by observing how these environments operate and how other professionals respond to them—leaders can learn strategies for their own use of social media, and leaders can connect with other local educators.

However one enters the conversation, the information will be more useful and the relationships richer if you are an active participant rather than a passive consumer. There are no rules against lurking, and many people choose to do only that. However, each school leader's voice is a valuable one. To a local parent or teacher, your voice is far more valuable than a remote voice with a million or more followers. Further, through the act of sharing one actually learns a great deal more for one's self.

Finally, remember that this digital conversation is free, with no barrier to entry other than the computer you already own. Millions of resources and relationships are waiting to assist in improving schools. These conversations around technology and leadership are the cutting edge of school reform globally. To tap into this global, free collaboration all one needs is to do is log in.

PRACTICAL STEPS TOWARD TECHNOLOGY LEADERSHIP

Given the broad definition of technology mentioned earlier, providing a limited number of practical strategies for technology leadership is daunting. Thus, as the NETS-A has provided structure to the broader field of technology leadership, it will also provide structure to these recommendations.

VISIONARY LEADERSHIP

The most vital first step for a potential school leader interested in leveraging technology for improvements in her school is to establish a personal comfort and understanding of digital technologies that permits a vision for how these technologies may positively impact the school environment. Attempting to inspire, promote, model, or facilitate technology in the learning environment without first having a consistent personal vision for technology may cause more harm in the long run. For instance, unblocking Facebook or other tools because neighboring districts have taken this step is a poor reason for doing so in your own school or district. If you are not personally committed to such steps, at the first substantial privacy violation or sexting incident you may be likely to revert to the old policy, especially under pressure from parents or the school board. It is in these moments that your vision, and your ability to lead technology, is tested. Failing these tests by wavering in your own convictions regarding technology will not only cause confusion, but you will also lose substantial trust with students and teachers who are more advanced with technology than you.

Building a personal technology vision is a harder task than it first seems. In our own teaching on technology leadership at CASTLE, we require our students to complete multiple drafts of this vision statement, as it changes substantially over time. Examining basic assumptions and decisions, such as a default policy of open access until proven inappropriate, is vital before questions arise. Finally, it is important to have a personal vision of how any particular technology project is going to integrate into the overall school improvement plan.

DIGITAL AGE LEARNING CULTURE

The most practical and useful advice I can provide on understanding digital teaching and learning opportunities is to do it. You can take a free online course, complete modules through the Khan Academy, learn to play the guitar on YouTube, or any other of the millions of things to learn online. You are quite literally a Google search away from learning something new. Do it. As an educator, you will not only learn the content, but you will also naturally pick up on the instructional elements. However, learning online is not enough for an educator; it is important to know how to teach online as well. Thus, you must take your digital learning adventure a step further and create a learning tool that others can use as well. You can upload your own instructional video to YouTube, write an explanatory blog post, create a photostream of one of your sports teams, or translate one of your PowerPoints into a narrated Prezi presentation. The critical step is not choosing the format but learning from the interactions with the tool. Better yet, be ambitious and try to teach a lesson or an entire course online. I recommend Instructure's Canvas platform as a good place to start, but there are many others. In short, one cannot understand the power of digital teaching and learning without engaging in digital teaching and learning. Like most things on the Internet, the preferred learning technique is to play. Try something new. I think you will be surprised at what you find.

EXCELLENCE IN PROFESSIONAL PRACTICE

Digital technologies are perhaps the greatest professional development tool in the history of mankind. With digital technologies at her fingertips, a school leader can gain additional information about nearly any topic of interest. In fact, these digital technologies have shifted the paradigm from one of information deficiency with limited access to materials to one of information overload with more materials available than can possibly ever be consumed (Tapscott & Williams, 2006). Such an environment changes many of the underlying assumptions about information and has far-reaching implications for structural elements of learning. For instance, the value in information lies not in its scarcity, which therefore must be protected, but instead in the attention and reputation it receives amongst the abundance. In this *attention economy*, it makes more sense to share openly to gain the necessary attention and reputation for your particular ideas to stand out. Further, an environment of potential information overload puts new demands on distinguishing or filtering valuable information from the massive amount of useless chaff. The useful information is highly valuable, but only if the task of distinguishing it is not overwhelming to all other necessary daily activities.

Luckily, personal learning networks have provided a viable mechanism for filtering valuable information (Richardson & Mancabelli, 2011). Every school leader should consciously maintain a personal learning network in this connected society. Of course, these personal learning networks go beyond digital technologies to traditional information relationships, such as the teachers' lounge down the hallway, but digital technologies, if properly geared for the desired outcomes, can drastically amplify the information base upon which to draw in making school leadership decisions. This information base can be used both for more passive professional development and for more active real-time problem solving. Either way, once developed, your personal learning network will become a central part of your school day, and it will be hard for you to remember how you ever functioned without it.

SYSTEMIC IMPROVEMENT

Improving the existing educational infrastructure for the digital revolution is perhaps the most mentally daunting task in the mind of a school leader. This standard covers so much territory, much of which has substantial price-tags, that it is easy to be overcome by the task. To be sure, these challenges, even the financial ones, must and will be overcome in the near future. For novice technology leaders, I recommend focusing less on multi-million dollar device initiatives and focusing instead on simple, cheaper opportunities as a way to build momentum in the school or district. One such element of technology leadership is the gathering and usage of new data in helping to drive decisions in organization. A multitude of free tools, such as Google Forms and Survey Monkey, distributed through simple techniques such as email, can collect opinions and provide simple analyses on students, teachers, parents, or community members. Further, many new mobile applications are particularly well suited for gathering formative feedback in classrooms, permitting more customization of the curriculum for the particular needs of each student. These options are even scalable into multi-grade student portfolios of their classroom work-products. Finally, existing data systems, such as the student information and management systems that most schools currently operate or purchase, can provide fine-grained data on students.

The result of all this additional easily available data to school leaders is the increased opportunity for feedback into the school. Simply asking students or teachers for feedback on various policies or practices can lead to very rapid decisions that already have the support of the school community. Simple questions, such as when to schedule a meeting for the convenience of most of the faculty, are answered both more easily and more accurately simply by employing free online data collection tools.

DIGITAL CITIZENSHIP

The simple advice for leading digital citizenship within your school or district is to be proactive instead of reactive in working with students as they explore and learn in new digital spaces. The typical approach amongst school leaders in working with students on Internet usage is to send home an acceptable use policy for parental signature and then punish any offending students who violate these usually broad and fairly undefined terms of "acceptable use." Such a reactive approach is insufficient. While there will always be a need for corrective actions with students, this should not be the only technique utilized in preparing students for coping with the challenges and opportunities of the digital world. These young people are facing a world of communication that previous generations would not have believed possible, and because schools are largely silent on digital citizenship, they are largely having to navigate these tricky waters alone or with their peers. It should thus be expected that they will occasionally violate some of these policies. In response, the Federal Communications Commission issued new guidelines in 2012 requiring schools receiving E-rate funding to, "provide for the education of minors about appropriate online behavior, including interacting with other individuals on social networking sites and in chat rooms, and cyberbullying awareness and response" (47 C.F.R. 54.520, 2012). In response to this new regulation, schools across the country changed their Acceptable Use Policies. Strong technology leaders will do more than just the minimal federal mandate in such an important area. New digital citizenship online learning options, such as those provided by Common Sense Media (2012) and the Digital Drivers License developed at the University of Kentucky (2012), provide additional training to students in the basics of digital citizenship. School leaders can also clearly celebrate the successes and demonstrate the shortcomings of particular usages of these technologies. Strong technology leaders, for instance, model appropriate technology and social media usage themselves and in doing so provide an example of moderating the risks of these platforms to reap the benefits.

CONCLUSION

The challenge of technology leadership is immense, particularly if one takes the broader interpretation of technology mentioned earlier. This challenge will only grow more intense over time as the progress of technology marches forward at an ever-increasing rate. Not only are the available tools for learning and leading a school different than they were only a few years before, but more importantly, the available career options for students are different—and ever-changing—as well. In this era of change, school leaders must not ignore the realities that this technological progress has brought to our communities. No longer are learning facts sufficient. Google, Wikipedia, or any other repository of information, increasingly kept in our pockets, is infinitely better at factual recall. The same can be said of basic calculation. Now you can simply verbally ask your phone a mathematical question, and it will tell you the answer. Advances in technology have real implications on our society and our students' future in it. Markets increasingly will not value, or pay people that are adept at, factual recall, basic calculation, assembly work or a bevy of additional tasks that can be replaced by new iterations of technology. Preparing students only for the society that the previous generation inhabited damns them to an uncertain future. Schools must provide more than that. Schools must meet the challenges of the constant change of technology and prepare creative, curious, adaptive, collaborative, entrepreneurial, and imaginative students (Wagner, 2008) ready to embrace and thrive in this uncertain future. To lead this type of school requires a new type of school leadership, one that embraces rather than avoids this technological challenge. This chapter provided only a brief introduction to the background, growing literature base, thriving digital conversations, and practical first steps. Embracing this challenge will require many additional steps where there is no clearly worn pathway to follow. Technology leaders are, necessarily, path makers. Despite this, I feel confident from my own experience and the experiences of the many great school technology leaders that I know, that not only will you find many new colleagues searching alongside you, but you will also be surprised at how many students, teachers, parents, and fellow school leaders are eager to follow.

References

16 KAR 3:050 (KY, 2012). (Professional certificate for instructional leadership – school principal, all grades).

47 C.F.R. § 54.520 (2012) (Children's Internet Protection Act certifications required from recipients of discounts under the federal universal service support mechanism for schools and libraries).

Afshari, M., Bakar, K., Luan, W., Afshari, M., Fooi, F., & Samah, B. (2010). Computer use by secondary school principals. *The Turkish Online Journal of Educational Technology, 9(3)*, 8–25.

Afshari, M., Bakar, K. A., Luan, W. S., Samah, B. A., & Fooi, F. S. (2008). School leadership and information communication technology. *The Turkish Online Journal of Educational Technology, 7(4)*, 1–10.

Afshari, M., Bakar, K. A., Luan, W. S., Samah, B. A., & Fooi, F. S. (2009). Technology and school leadership. *Technology, Pedagogy and Education, 18(2)*, 235–248.

Anderson, R., & Dexter, S. (2000). *School technology leadership: Incidence and impact.* Irvine, CA: Center for Research on Information Technology and Organizations. Retrieved from http://escholarship.org/uc/item/76s142fc

Anderson, R. E., & Dexter, S. (2005). School technology leadership: An empirical investigation of prevalence and effect. *Educational Administration Quarterly, 41(1)*, 49–82.

Bigelow, J. (1831). Elements of technology: Taken chiefly from a course of lectures delivered at Cambridge on the application of the sciences to the useful arts. Boston: Hillard, Gray, Little and Wilkins. Retrieved from: http://books.google.com/books?id=ed8JAAAAIAAJ

Brooks-Young, S. (2006). *Critical technology issues for school leaders.* Thousand Oaks, CA: Corwin Press.

Brooks-Young, S. (2009). *Making technology standards work for you.* Eugene, OR: International Society for Technology in Education.

Butler, K. (2010). A small district's big innovator. *District Administration, 46*(9), 78–80.

Christensen, C., Johnson, C. W., & Horn, M. B. (2010). *Disrupting class: How disruptive innovation will change the way the world learns* (2nd Ed.). New York: McGraw Hill.

Collins, R. & Halverson, R. (2009). *Rethinking education in the age of technology: The digital revolution and schooling in America.* New York: Teachers College Press.

Common Sense Media (2012). *Digital citizenship.* Retrieved from: http://www.commonsensemedia.org/advice-for-parents/digital-citizenship

Creighton, T. B. (2002). *The principal as technology leader.* Thousand Oaks, CA: Corwin Press.

Deryakulu, D., & Olkun, S. (2009). Technology leadership and supervision: An analysis based on Turkish computer teachers' professional memories. *Technology, Pedagogy and Education, 18(1)*, 45–58.

Dexter, S. (2011). School technology leadership: Artifacts in systems of practice. *Journal of School Leadership 21*(2), 166-189.

Digital Driver's License (2012). Retrieved from: http://otis.coe.uky.edu/DDL/launch.php

Dolittle, G. & Gallagher-Browne, E. (2011). Who moved my curriculum? Leadership preparation programs and the core technology of schools. *Journal of School Leadership 21*(2), 293-318.

Dwyer, L. (2011, Dec. 3). Why #pencilchat may the most clever education allegory ever. *Good.* Retrieved from: http://www.good.is/posts/why-pencilchat-is-the-most-clever-edcuation-allegory-ever/

Fletcher, G. H. (2009). A matter of principals. *T.H.E. Journal, 36(5),* 22–28.

International Society for Technology in Education (ISTE). (2009). *NETS for administrators 2009.* Retrieved from http://www.iste.org/docs/pdfs/nets-a-standards.pdf?sfvrsn=2

Khan, S. (2012). *The one world schoolhouse: Education reimagined.* London: Hodder & Stoughton.

Lecklider, D., Clausen, J. M., & Britten, J. S. (2009). Principals priority for technology as an indicator of observed use in schools. *Journal of Scholarship and Practice, 5*(4), 27-33.

Levin, B. B. & Schrum, L. (2012). *Leading technology-rich schools.* New York: Teachers College Press.

Kelly, K. (2007, Feb. 22). Everything that doesn't work yet. [Blog post]. Retrieved from: http://www.kk.org/thetechnium/archives/2007/02/everything_that.php.

Kelly, K. (2010). *What technology wants.* New York: Penguin Group.

Kurzweil, R. (2012). *How to create a mind: The secret of human thought revealed.* New York: Penguin Group.

McCombs, B. (2010). Culture of collaboration. *Learning & Leading with Technology, 38(3),* 10–13.

McLeod, S. & Lehmann, C. (Eds.) (2011). *What school leaders need to know about digital technologies and social media.* San Francisco, CA: Jossey-Bass.

McLeod, S. & Richardson, J. W. (2011). The dearth of technology leadership coverage. *Journal of School Leadership 21*(2), 216-240.

Nussbaum-Beach, S. & Ritter Hall, L. (2012). *The connected educator: Learning and leading in a digital age.* Bloomington, IN: Solution Tree Press.

Papa, R. (Ed.) (2011). *Technology leadership for school improvement.* Thousand Oaks, CA: Sage.

Parks, S., Sun, F., & Collins, B. C. (2002). Alabama Renaissance Technology Academy (ARTA) for School Leaders Survey Report. Paper presented at the Annual Meeting of the Mid- South Educational Research Association. Chattanooga, TN.

Picciano, A. G. (2010). *Educational leadership and planning for technology* (5th ed.). Upper Saddle River, NJ: Pearson.

Richardson, J. W. (2011). Challenges of adopting the use of technology in less developed countries: The case of Cambodia. *Comparative Education Review 55*(1), 8-29.

Richardson, J. W., Bathon, J., Flora, K. & Lewis, W. D. (2012). NETS-A scholarship: A review of published literature. *Journal of Research on Technology in Education, 42*(2), 131-152.

Richardson, W. (2011). *Learning on the blog: Collected posts for educators and parents.* Thousand Oaks, CA: Corwin Press.

Richardson, W. & Mancabelli, R. (2011). *Personal learning networks: Using the power of connections to transform education.* Bloomington, IN: Solution Tree.

Rutkowski, D., Rutkowski, L. & Sparks, J. (2011). Information and communications technologies support for 21st-Century teaching: An international analysis. *Journal of School Leadership 21*(2), 190-215.

Schrum, L., Galizio, L., & Ledesma, P. (2011). Educational leadership and technology integration: An investigation into preparation, experiences, and roles. *Journal of School Leadership, 21(2),* 241–261.

Schrum, L. M. & Levin, B. B. (2009). *Leading 21st-Century schools: Harnessing technology for engagement and achievement.* Thousand Oaks, CA: Corwin Press.

Shareski, D. (2011, Feb. 13). *Happy birthday Alec Couros* [Video file]. Retrieved from: http://youtu.be/idhsUy3SKE4.

Stuart, L. H., Mills, A. M., & Remus, U. (2009). School leaders, ICT competence and championing innovations. *Computers & Education, 53(3),* 733–741.

Tapscott, D. & Williams, A. D. (2006). *Wikinomics: How mass collaboration changes everything.* New York: Penguin Group.

Vander Ark, T. & Wise, B. (2011). *Getting smart: How digital learning is changing the world.* San Francisco, CA: Jossey Bass.

Vanderlinde, R., van Braak, J., & Dexter, S. (2012). ICT policy planning in a context of curriculum reform: Disentanglement of ICT policy domains and artifacts. *Computers & Education 58,* 1339-1350.

Wagner, T. (2008). *The global achievement gap: Why even our best schools don't teach the new survival skills our children need – and what we can do about it.* New York: Basic Books.

Wagner, T. (2012). *Creating innovators: The making of young people who will change the world.* New York: Scribner.

Dr. Justin Bathon is an Assistant Professor in the Department of Educational Leadership Studies at the University of Kentucky and a Director of the UCEA Center for the Advanced Study of Technology Leadership in Education (CASTLE). Justin focuses on the underlying code of education and the changes necessitated by the digital, global age. This work looks at the intersections of education, law, and technology and translates research into specific actions for local learning communities. Justin has legal and educational experience at the local, state, national, and international levels including as a high school teacher in southern Illinois. He holds a J.D. from Southern Illinois University and a Ph.D. in Education Policy from Indiana University. Justin can be contacted at justin.bathon@uky.edu.

Chapter 12

The Use of Value Added for Accountability and to Inform Leadership

Kimberly Kappler Hewitt

State achievement tests. Benchmark data. Common exam data. State graduation tests. ACT. PLAN. SAT. P-SAT. DIBELS. Cognitive Abilities Test. Iowa Test of Basic Skills. AIMSweb data. Formative assessment data. Graduation data. Attendance data. Discipline data. Today, as educators, we are inundated with mountains of data that we are supposed to use to inform decision-making. We have so many data reports, graphs, charts, and technical documents that we could wallpaper our classrooms, offices, and hallways.

And now we have value added data. What is value added data? What are its possibilities and limitations for accountability and leadership? How can it be used to inform the important work that we do as educators? How can it be part of our larger efforts to use data in efficacious and ethical ways to make schools more meaningful and equitable? These questions serve as the focus for this chapter.

WHAT IS VALUE ADDED?

Value added measures use sophisticated statistical processes to estimate the unique contributions of districts, schools, and teachers on student achievement gains (Harris, 2011; Jennings & Corcoran, 2009; Linn, 2008; Papay, 2011; Sanders, Saxton, & Horn, 1997). There are a number of different value added models (McCaffrey, Lockwood, Koretz, Louis, & Hamilton, 2004); essentially, though, value added models compute and compare estimates of progress students are *expected* to make to progress students *actually* do make, usually on state end of course and end of grade achievement tests.

Value added models are a type of student growth measure. Student growth measures are still relatively new in education and offer a different picture of student learning than more traditional status data, which for decades have been tracked and used for accountability purposes. Status data are "snapshots" of student performance on one test at one point in time and are strongly correlated to socioeconomic status (Coleman, 1968). Growth measures, which are more recent additions to accountability systems, incorporate student performance at more than one point in time to estimate student progress or *growth*. They provide a sense of what student learning looks like over time, or longitudinally. Because growth models take into account students' baseline scores, they allow an "apples to apples" comparison of a student's progress to her own starting point. A number of states and districts use value added measures as part of their accountability systems, including Tennessee, Ohio, North Carolina, Florida, Washington, D.C., and the Houston Independent School District.

Other Measures of Student Growth

There are other measures of student growth used by some states, the most popular of which is Student Growth Percentiles (SGPs), developed by Dr. Damian Betebenner. SGPs, used in Georgia, Hawaii, New York, Massachusetts, Rhode Island, and several other states, use past test scores to identify a percentile rank for a student and then compare the successive performance of all students at that same percentile rank. Advocates of the model argue that SGPs are a fair accountability measure because they compare the growth of students to their academic peers—those with similar past performance (Betebenner, 2009, 2012).

Another student growth model is the Growth Targets Model, used in Delaware. In this model, each student is assigned a target score, determined by growth made by students over two years on state tests and based on a couple of demographic factors (e.g., Students with Disability status, English Language Learner status) (Delaware Department of Education, 2012). A student whose spring test score equals or exceeds her target score is considered to have "met" the growth target.

While SGPs and the Growth Targets Model also warrant examination and research, this chapter focuses on value added, the longest standing growth model in use today. The following section provides brief background on value added.

Background on Value Added

In 1992, with the advent of its Tennessee Value Added Assessment System, Tennessee became the first state to incorporate student growth into its state accountability model (Ceperley & Reel, 1997). The use of educational value added was developed by Dr. Williams Sanders, then at the University of Tennessee, who took the idea from the field of agriculture (The Center for Greater Philadelphia, 2004), which uses value added measures to increase crop yield. In 1996, Tennessee began providing teacher-level value added data, and since 1998, value added has been one component of teachers' evaluations (Tennessee Department of Education, 2011).

Sanders eventually left the University of Tennessee for SAS, which now holds proprietary rights to several value added models, including the Multivariate Response Model and Univariate Response Model (Wright, White, Sanders, & Rivers, 2010). SAS has lucrative contracts with several states. Ohio, for example, paid SAS over $800,000 in 2009 for value added analysis (Stephens, 2010), and the Tennessee Department of Education has a five-year contract with SAS for almost $14,000,000 (State of Tennessee Contract Amendment, 2011). Thus from its beginnings as an agricultural strategy, value added is now a large—and expensive—component of numerous state and district accountability systems.

VALUE ADDED AS AN ACCOUNTABILITY TOOL

There are possibilities and limitations with the use of value added measures for accountability and for use in informing our work as educators. This section focuses on the use of value added as an accountability tool; the next section shifts to a discussion of the opportunities and challenges of using value added to inform teaching and leading.

The Policy Context

In 2005, Oakwood City School District in Ohio—in which I served as a district administrator—participated in a pilot of the Educational Value Added Assessment System (EVAAS) in Ohio. As part of a team of five educators from my district, I participated in five days of training on value added provided by Battelle for Kids, a powerful nonprofit headquartered in Ohio that identifies itself as a catalyst for change. During that training, we examined school-level and district-level value added data, and the instructors emphatically instructed us NOT to calculate or use teacher-level value added data. They informed us that the metric wasn't designed for the purpose of measuring teacher effects and that the data were too unreliable with small student samples sizes and without appropriate statistical adjustments.

A mere handful of years later, the caution of our instructors seems incredible, given the flurry of policy at the state and federal level that ties value added data to teachers' and principals' evaluations—and Ohio is one of these states. Bolstered by the Obama administration's Race to the Top program and a political climate focused on holding educators accountable for student learning, many states have passed legislation that ties educator evaluations to student performance data (Baker, Oluwole, & Green, 2013). Indeed, all Race to the Top (RttT) awardees must incorporate—"as a significant component" (US DoE, 2009, p. 9) student growth data into teacher and principal evaluations and to use those evaluations to make personnel decisions, including compensation, promotion, and dismissal. Some RttT awardees, including the District of Columbia and Colorado, are basing 50% of educators' evaluations on student growth data.

There is, after all, substantial research demonstrating the impact of quality teaching (Chetty, Friedman, & Rockoff, 2011; Rivkin, Hanushek, & Kain, 2005; Wright, Horn, & Sanders, 1997). Given the importance of quality instruction, it is imperative that each student be taught by an effective teacher. As such, it makes some sense intuitively to link student growth to educator evaluation.

Value added—A better way to evaluate educators?

Advocates of the use of value added for educator evaluation argue that traditional ways of evaluating educators have failed to adequately reflect teacher quality: "While many indicators suggest that there is a wide distribution of teacher effectiveness, in districts that use simple satisfactory-unsatisfactory evaluation ratings, the evaluation system places 99 percent of teachers in the satisfactory category" (Harris, 2011, p. 17). Such systems allow "chronically low-performing teachers [to] languish" (Weisberg, Sexton, Mulhern, & Keeling, 2009, p. 6) for years, affecting year after year of students. Advocates of value added measures of educator effectiveness argue that value added is superior to these traditional evaluation systems because it can be used to distinguish effective and ineffective teachers (Harris, 2011). Additionally, because value added estimates of teacher effectiveness hold teachers accountable for what is within their control—student learning—and address student "starting-gate inequalities" by comparing students to their own baseline performance, they are a fair way to evaluate educators (Harris, 2011). Kennedy, Peters, and Thomas (2012) argue that "it is safe to say that value-added analysis is a much fairer measure of what occurs in classrooms, schools, and school districts" (p. 11) than status measures because value added is substantially less strongly correlated to socioeconomic status. Nonetheless, there are a number of considerable challenges to using value added data to hold educators, schools, and districts accountable for student progress.

Challenges to the use of value added for educator evaluation

A growing body of scholarship has identified problems with value added estimates of teacher effectiveness that fall into five broad categories (see Figure 12.1): policy issues, issues of practice, test issues, technical issues, and equity and social justice issues (Hewitt, 2013b).

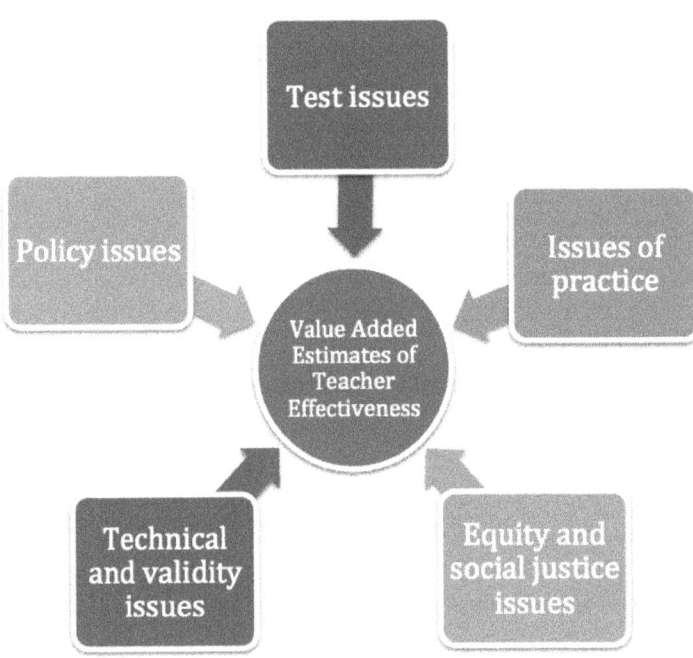

Figure 12.1. Challenges to the Use of Value Added for Educator Evaluation

Policy issues. Policy issues involve those decisions about how to use value added for accountability purposes, including what qualifications should be made about the data (e.g., how many years of teacher-level value added data must be used to calculate value added scores for teacher evaluations), as well as how value added should contribute to accountability models and how much of an educator's final evaluation should be based on value added. There are also more fine-grained policy issues, such as attribution. Attribution refers to determining which students should count towards which teachers' value added effects and raises questions about, for example, how to account for team- and co-teaching situations. It also raises questions about how much instructional time a teacher should have with a student before the student's learning is attributed to that teacher. Additionally,

> Districts/states must decide how to use value added data to evaluate teachers in non-tested subjects and grades; these individuals often account for the majority of teachers in a building. This raises equity issues between teachers who do and who do not get this data, and it also raises questions about the practice of using school level value added data to evaluate teachers outside of tested subjects/grades (as done in Tennessee). (Hewitt, 2012, p. 187)

Issues of practice. Regardless of what is intended by policy, unintended effects of policy can be powerful. Educators "in the trenches" make meaning of and respond to reform efforts and accountability and raise practice-related issues regarding value added. While the unintended policy effects of the use of value added for educator evaluation are still largely unknown, emerging data suggest that teachers may seek to change teaching assignments or schools under the belief that doing so will increase their value added scores (Hewitt, 2013a). Additionally, Amrein-Beardsley, Berliner, and Rideau (2010) found a "nontrivial" amount of cheating by educators occurs in schools. Research by Nichols and Berliner (2005) demonstrates that high-stakes testing is a causal factor for serious problems including cheating; *gaming the system* (e.g., pushing certain kids out of schools, extensive test preparation, and narrowing of the curriculum); the "abandonment of the ethic of care" as students are viewed as "score suppressors or increasers" (p. 166); and a pattern of teachers migrating out of tested grade levels and away from schools that serve impoverished students. They conclude that high-stakes testing distorts and corrupts test scores and educators themselves.

Test issues. Value added measures of teacher effectiveness are only as sound as the tests upon which they are based. While SAS (Wright et al., 2010) claims that almost all commercial and state-mandated tests meet specifications for use with value added measures, others disagree. Tests must have sufficient stretch (range of difficulty of questions) to accurately pinpoint students' performance (Amrein-Beardsley, 2008; Carey & Manwaring, 2011). Tests must also measure the same skills/content over time; otherwise there can be "construct-shift," which distorts value added measures (Martineau, 2006; Schmidt, Houang, & McKnight, 2005). Further, achievement tests measure a narrow set of skills/knowledge that does not represent the full range of learning that we expect teachers to cultivate (Corcoran, 2010).

Technical and validity issues. There are a number of technical and validity issues with the use of value added. This chapter introduces only some of them. For a more comprehensive discussion of these issues, see the workshop report of the Committee on Value-Added Methodology for Instructional Improvement, Program Evaluation, and Educational Accountability (National Research Council & National Academy of Education (2010).

Model selection. Using different value added models results in significantly different estimates of teacher effectiveness: Depending on the particular value added model used, up to 14% of teachers' effectiveness ratings would change by three or more deciles, 12-33% would change by two or more deciles, and 56-80% of teachers' effectiveness ratings would change by one or more deciles (Darling-Hammond, Amrein-Beardsley, Haertel, & Rothstein, 2012, p. 9).

Spillage. Spillage refers to the influence of other content area teachers on students' performance in a particular content area. Spillage can muddy teacher effects (Corcoran, 2010).

Persistence and decay. Teachers likely affect student learning beyond the year in which they teach them. This is known as "persistence" of teacher effects. Research suggests that the impact of persistence is nontrivial (Konstantopoulos & Chung, 2011) and that persistence decays over time (McCaffrey et al., 2004; Mariano, McCaffrey, & Lockwood, 2010). As yet, there is no definitive answer about how best to account for persistence and decay in value added models.

Non-teacher influences. Teaching in schools with more effective colleagues and stronger principal leadership can positively influence teacher effects (Corcoran, 2010), as can classroom composition (Hill, Kapitula, & Umland, 2011) and school characteristics (McCaffrey et al., 2004). As such, these factors can distort estimates of a teacher's "true" effect.

Selection bias. Generally, students and teachers are not randomly assigned to schools and classrooms. These unaccounted for imbalances can distort value added data (Braun, 2005). A study (Rothstein, 2010) conducted using a North Carolina data set illustrates this powerfully: The study indicated that a student's fifth grade teacher is a greater predictor of the students' fourth grade growth than is the students' fourth grade teacher. This is logically impossible and reflects the problem of nonrandom assignment of students and teachers.

Instability. Teacher-level value added data tend to vary considerably from year to year:

> In Houston, among those in the lowest 20 percent of value-added, only 36 percent remain among the lowest performers in the following year. Similarly, among those in the top 20 percent, only 38 percent remain among the top performers the next year. Twenty-three percent of last year's lowest performers are among the top performers in the following year, and vice versa. A similar pattern holds in an analysis of New York City Teacher Data Report data. (Corcoran, 2010, p. 6)

Sometimes changing grade level teaching assignments—from 8th grade to 6th grade, for example—can result in radically different value added ratings (Darling-Hammond et al., 2012). Instability of value added effects occurs not only across years but also across tests. Different tests of the same general content yield different teacher ratings (Jennings & Corcoran, 2012; Darling-Hammond et al., 2012).

Missing data. Missing student test data (due to absences, mobility, etc.) creates problems for value added models, and missing student data is all too common: Among 4th to 6th grade students in Houston Independent School District, only 66% had current and prior year scores, a "faction that falls to 62% for Black students, 47% for ESL students, and 41% for recent immigrants" (Corcoran, 2010, p. 21). Missing data can skew value added data (McCaffrey, Lockwood, Mariano, & Setodji, 2005)

Equity and social justice issues. While Ballou, Sanders, and Wright (2004) found that student characteristics and background factors have negligible influence on value added estimates, there is other research (Baker et al., 2010; Darling-Hammond et al., 2012; Kupermintz, 2003) that indicates that teachers tend to have lower value added scores when they teach substantial numbers of students with disabilities, when they teach gifted students, and when they teach grades in which "English language learners (ELLs) are transitioned into mainstreamed classrooms" (Darling-Hammond et al., 2012, p. 12). Transient students can also be further marginalized by value added. As discussed in the previous section, missing student test data can cause technical issues with value added estimates of teacher effectiveness. Beyond that, excluding students with missing data from calculations can serve as a perverse incentive for teachers to invest less time and effort into transient students "whose data will not contribute to teachers' and schools' effect estimates. This is an important social justice concern" (Hewitt, 2012, p. 187). Also, to the degree that missing data tends to be associated with certain racial or ethnic groups, then these inequities become institutionalized.

Possible Legal Challenges?

Pullin (2013) warns that although there has been little litigation thus far involving value added measures, "legal disputes are inevitable given potential high stakes individual and institutional consequences" (p. 3). While in general case law has upheld the use of student data in termination decisions, possible issues regarding constitutional and civil rights, coupled with social science evidence about the validity and reliability of value added measures of teacher effectiveness, suggest that the "potential for successful legal challenge to its use is high" (Pullin, 2013, p. 17). Baker, Oluwole, and Green (2013) foresee that teachers may legally "challenge the technical shortcomings of value-added testing policies on substantive due process grounds" (p. 10).

While this section has focused on challenges to the use of value added data to evaluate educators, many of the issues identified are applicable to the use of value added data for school and district accountability as well, as discussed in the next section.

Challenges to the Use of Value Added for School and District Accountability

While the use of value added data for educator evaluations is getting a good deal of attention in mainstream media and in academic domains, the use of school-level and district-level value added data for accountability purposes is problematic as well and is more longstanding than the use of teacher-level value added data for educator evaluation. For example, in Ohio, value added has been one component of the state's school and district accountability models since 2008, but the use of value added for educator evaluation will not be implemented statewide until 2013-2014. A number of the challenges to the use of value added data outlined in the previous section also apply to school- and district-level data, including various technical and validity issues (Institute of Education Sciences, 2010; Keeves, Hungi, & Afrassa, 2005; Timmermans, Doolaard, & de Wolf, 2011; Van de Grift, 2009), equity and social justice issues (Darmawan &

Keeves, 2006; Power & Frandji, 2010), test issues (Amrein-Beardsley, 2008; Carey &Manwaring, 2011), and while not as significant, perhaps, as those with value added for teacher evaluation, policy issues (Linn, 2008) and issues of practice (Nichols & Berliner, 2005). I focus here on illustrating the technical issue of instability of school and district data, using Oakwood and Ohio data as examples.

While Oakwood's 7th and 8th grade math were well above expected growth each year over 5 years, our 4th grade reading fluctuated at the district level from below expectations to above expectations and back again every year for 5 years. We were at a loss to account for this vast and patterned fluctuation in our 4th grade reading value added data when there were no substantial curricular, personnel, demographic, or operational changes over those years.

Perhaps even more troubling is instability at the district level across the state of Ohio. For the 2007-2008 school year, 45% of districts in the state had above expected growth; 23% met expected growth; and 32% of districts were below expected growth (see Figure 12.2). The following year (2008-2009), the percentage of districts above expected growth jumped incredulously to 72.6%; while the percentage of districts that met expected growth and were below expected growth fell to 15.7% and 11.6%, respectively. Then one year later (2009-2010), the percentage of districts above expected growth fell precipitously to 33.1%, and districts meeting expected growth and those below expected growth grew to 29.5% and 37.5%, respectively. Thus the percentage of districts not meeting expected growth increased 25.9 percentage points in just one year— in terms of effectiveness, over one quarter of all districts in the state of Ohio became "ineffective" in one year. Could so many districts really become more effective in one year only to have the next year see many districts regress? In 2010-2011, the percentage of districts that made above expected growth shrank further to 24.3%, the percent meeting expected growth swelled to 55.2%, and 20.5% made below expected growth, which was a drop from the previous year.

Many districts scrambled to attempt to make meaning of the drop in 2010 in their growth rating and to address Board and community concerns about these drops. Such enormous changes in district effectiveness seem unreasonable and almost inconceivable. Such data should raise red flags and initiate closer scrutiny. Indeed, in 2010, due to "unanticipated variability [sic] across grades and among years within a grade" (SAS, 2010, p. 1), the Ohio Department of Education charged SAS with developing "an additional procedure within its analytical process" (p. 1) to stabilize the data. In 2010, in an article in *The Columbus Dispatch* (Richards, 2010), Ohio Department of Education accountability expert Matt Cohen declared that the state had statistically addressed the cause of the instability of the data, that such an occurrence wouldn't happen again, and that the 2010 data were accurate. A value added specialist, Mike Thomas, explained in the article:

> Every year they have to have new tests, different tests, and it's really hard to make sure those tests are exactly equivalent to each other…you end up having an easier test or a test that is a little bit harder. What it ends up doing is, it looks like schools are gaining more than they are or producing poorer growth results than they actually are. (Richards, 2010, para. 13).

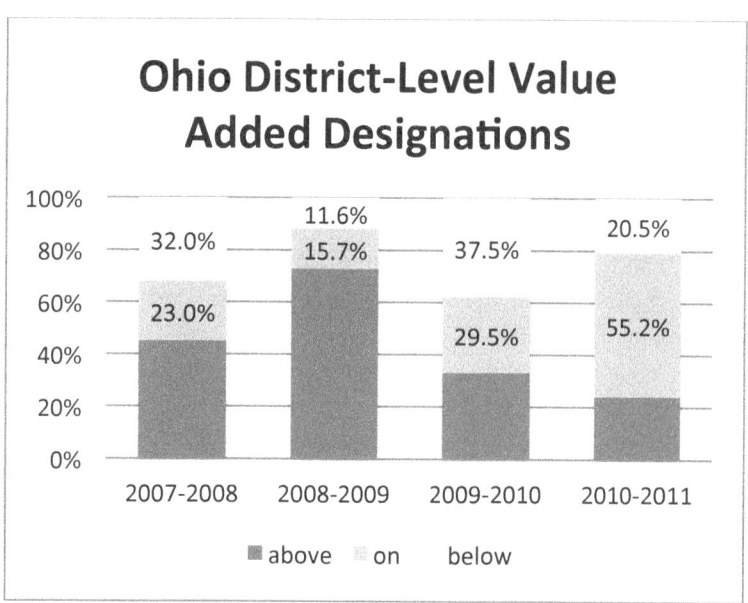

Figure 12.2. Ohio District-Level Value Added Designations, 2007-2011

As previously noted, in 2011—the year *after* SAS implemented the "scale stabilization procedure" (SAS, 2010, p. 3)—the percentage of districts making above and below expected growth shrank (by 17 percentage points and 8.8 percentage points, respectively), and the percentage of districts meeting expected growth swelled to 55.2% (an increase of 25.7 percentage points), suggesting continued instability of data (see Figure 12.2).[4]

Despite these concerns raised by research and practice, states and districts continue to use value added for school and district accountability, and a number are moving ahead with implementation of new educator evaluation systems that include value added estimates of teacher effectiveness. The following section examines whether and how school-level and district-level value added data can be used to inform leadership. Due to the highly problematic nature of teacher-level value added data, it is not discussed in the following section.

VALUE ADDED AS A LEADERSHIP TOOL

The preceding section identified a number of challenges to the use of value added for accountability and teacher evaluation purposes. What does this mean for its use as a tool for informing leadership? While some of the aforementioned concerns are particular to accountability issues, such as policy challenges, others are relevant to the use of value added data to inform leaders, including technical issues, test issues, and issues of

---

[4] Data for 2012 have not yet been officially released by the Ohio Department of Education (ODE), due to an ongoing investigation by the State Auditor's office of irregularities in the reporting of attendance data by some districts (ODE, 2012).

practice. Given these issues, should value added data be used at all to inform leadership? Used critically and carefully, yes. The remainder of this chapter establishes ways to use value added data ethically and efficaciously to improve teaching and learning.

Setting the Stage

The use of any educational data should be framed by commitments to do so ethically. As a district leader, I helped to establish our district's data commitments, and these were revisited each time before digging into data:

Using Data: Our Beliefs

- *Data should always be used as a tool and never as a weapon.*
- *When we look at data, we ask ourselves:*
  - *What does this data say?*
  - *What does this data NOT say (cannot say)?*
  - *What questions does this data raise? (Often data raises more questions than it can answer.)*
  - *One measure of student learning (one type of data) will NEVER be sufficient.*

While these may seem straightforward—even self-evident—such commitments are important for developing a healthy culture of inquiry and data use. Perhaps key amongst these is the commitment to use data solely as a tool and never as a weapon. Being open to making meaning of data—to critically examining data—puts people in a vulnerable position. Some wonder, "How is this data going to be used against me? How is this data going to make me look?" As such, it is imperative that leaders build people's trust, and key to doing this is establishing and upholding the ground rule that data will never be used as a weapon. The focus is on taking from data what we can in order to strengthen and improve our collective work as educators. This mindset is key.

Doing Interpretive Work Collectively

While providing access to data to all relevant educators is appropriate, expecting them to critically examine the data on their own is less than ideal. We can come to more accurate and deeper understandings of data if we have the opportunity to collaboratively examine the data in teams. There may be some aspect of the data that I overlook or cannot see that others see as obvious.

For example, Figure 12.3 shows a sample school-level value added summary report. When I shared this with colleagues and asked them which grade level they believed warranted the most support, based on these data, people differed in their responses. Most members of the group believed that 7th grade warranted the most support, since its three-year value added average school effect (-0.6) was significantly below the state average. Several other people felt that 6th grade warranted the most attention. They argued that for the two most recent years (2009 and 2010) 7th grade had a school effect not detectably different than average growth in the state, while the most recent (2010) 6th grade school effect (-0.3) was significantly below average growth in the state. As such, they felt that 7th grade was showing a positive trend in its data over the three most recent years, while 6th grade's pattern was possibly shifting in a more negative direction.

In this example, a group of highly educated people was interpreting the same data set differently, leading to potentially different decisions about how to use limited resources. By being able to work collectively to explain their reasoning and pose questions, groups of individuals may come to better, more productive conclusions about data than could individuals working on their own.

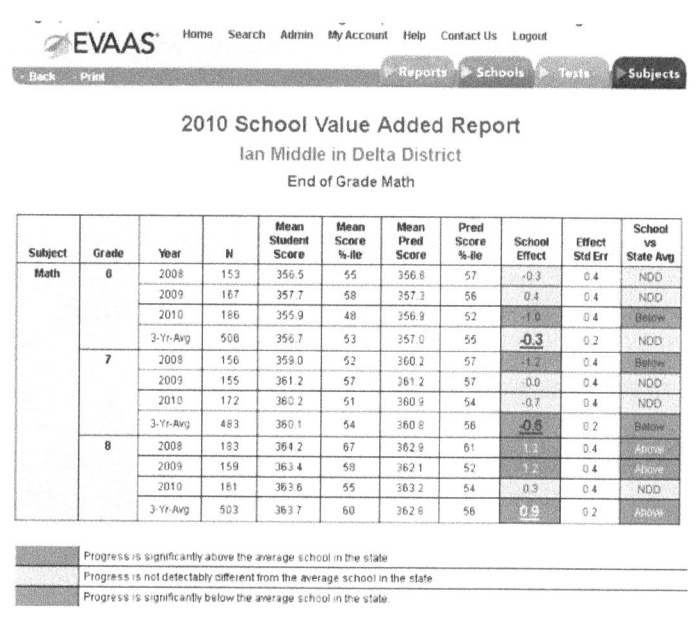

Figure 12.3. School-level Value Added Summary Report.

Additionally, when we collectively make meaning of data, there is a sense that we all own the data and are all responsible for using it to strengthen the work that we do as educators. We can be less defensive and more vulnerable to the data—more open to what the data say and how we can use data to inform practice—if we work in small teams in which trust has been established.

Making Data Accessible

Making meaning of data is not self-evident, and for some people it is a laborious, even painful, process. A brilliant and creative middle school social studies teacher once said to me, "Kim, numbers just don't speak to me." Her words echo in my head to this day. As a leader, I work to compile data for teachers and to use symbols and colors to code data in order to make it more accessible. For example (see Figure 12.4), the Oakwood Junior High 2009 school-level value added data have been color-coded (although this is difficult to tell, given that it is in black/white here), and symbols have been used to indicate for each grade/content level whether the performance is "above" expected growth (in green and indicated by a "+" sign), "below" expected growth (in hot pink and indicated by a "—" sign), or "met" expected growth (although not relevant here, in yellow and indicated by an "=" sign).

The use of symbols in Figure 12.4 makes it fairly quick and easy to see patterns. For example, it is clear that 8th grade math has consistently had above expected growth over five years.

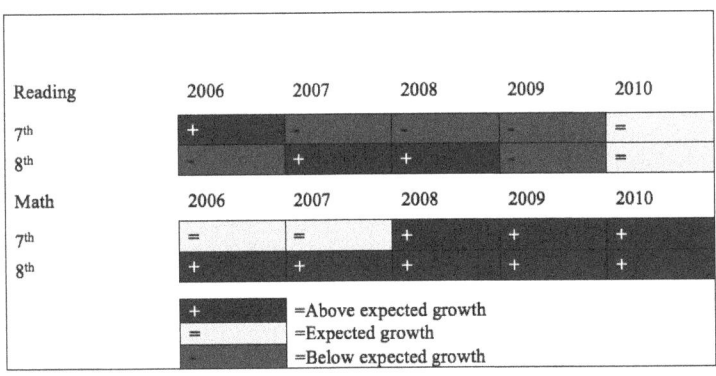

Figure 12.4. Oakwood Junior High School Value Added Ratings, 2006-2010

Observations, Interpretations, and Conclusions

In order to use data to inform decisions, we must accurately read and make meaning of the data. In order to do this, it is important to make observations, interpretations, and to draw conclusions—in that order. Doing so allows us to identify "facts" upon which to ascribe meaning to data. Observations are basic, factual statements about the data. Observations may seem self-evident—often because they are. Yet it is important to intentionally begin with observations as the basis for interpretations and conclusions. Using Oakwood Junior High value added data presented in Figure 12.4 as an example, here are some observations from the data: Eighth grade math has consistently made above expected growth, as has 7th grade math from 2008-2010 Reading is a more complicated picture. Seventh grade reading made above expected growth in 2006, but the following three years made less than expected growth. Then in 2010 met expected growth. In 2006, 8th grade reading was below expected growth. The next two years (2007 and 2008) 8th grade reading made above expected growth. In 2009, 8th grade made less than expected growth. In the following year (2010), 8th grade met expected growth.

Interpretations pull together multiple observations to make a statement concerning the data. For example, one interpretation from this data is that 7th and 8th grade math consistently rate above expected growth. Another is that 7th grade reading, from 2006-2010, has overall had the lowest value added ratings of Oakwood Junior High content areas/grades. Another interpretation is that 8th grade reading value added data has been the most inconsistent of the content areas/grades reported.

Conclusions build upon interpretations and require value judgments. For example, one might conclude that overall 7th and 8th grade math are strong programs. Another conclusion may be that 7th grade reading requires more attention and exploration to determine the root causes behind the weaker value added data. In isolation, the value added data discussed here may be of limited usefulness. However, by combining it with contextual information and by triangulating data, the value added data can be more powerful.

Contextualizing Data

It's important to provide background or contextual information that situates the data. For example, the data in Figure 12.4 includes data from value added pilot years (2006 and 2007), when a value added prediction model was used, as well as data using a normal curve equivalent model (2008-current), which was implemented when value added "went live" as part of the state accountability system in 2008. While both are value added models, research (Hill, Kapitula, & Umland, 2011; McCaffrey et al., 2004; Timmermans et al., 2011) has shown that the use of different value added models can result in different value added ratings. As such, comparisons that bridge 2006 and 2007 to 2008 and beyond can be problematic.

Contextual information may also be in the form of comparison data from the state or from similar districts or schools. For example, when Oakwood Junior High 8th grade reading dropped two levels from above expected growth in 2007 and 2008 to below expected growth in 2009, 71% of districts in Ohio had below expected growth in 8th grade reading; 23% met expected growth; and 6% made above expected growth. Compared to the previous year, when only about 15% of districts were below expected growth in 8th grade reading, the statewide value added performance dropped precipitously in 2009. This is an important contextual detail when making meaning of the 2009 8th grade reading data. Given that the previous year 8th grade reading had "above expected growth" and that 71% of districts across the state similarly had "below expected growth" in 2009, this contextual information helped us to decide not to take any corrective action or make substantial changes based on the data.

Contextual information can also pertain to changes or other considerations regarding curriculum, personnel, demographic, or other factors that could influence the data. For example, having several first-year teachers in a particular grade/content area in one year might influence data, as can the adoption of new textbooks or supplemental software. Additionally, larger school-wide issues might be noteworthy, such as construction in a particular year that disrupts schedules or causes a great deal of disruptive noise. In another year, winter storms may cause school to close for 10 days. On the other hand, a technology grant may mean the influx of rich technology resources and related professional development for teachers. Such contextual information must be considered when making meaning of data; however, it should not be used to dismiss or negate data.

With regard to 7th and 8th grade reading, there were no personnel changes, nor were there any major curricular changes (e.g., new adoptions; new standards; etc.) in English/language arts courses from 2006-2010. Additionally, there were no major changes in student demographics during this period. Given this contextual information, changes in value added data over this time period seem perplexing. In order to get a fuller sense of student learning and program/instructional quality, it is important to use multiple data sources to triangulate data.

Triangulate Data

Triangulation is an orienteering technique used to identify one's location—or a close approximation of it—on a map. See Figure 12.5 for a visual representation of triangulation. Triangulation involves finding one's location anywhere, using nothing more than a topographic map and a compass, by plotting three different points in the field of vision on the map and, using one's compass, aligning and then drawing straight lines from each. The result is a triangle, and one can be confident that one's actual location is somewhere within that triangle. Obviously, the larger the area within the triangle, the less precise is the location. The same can be true with educational data: Lack of consistency in findings across measures decreases both the precision and credibility of any inferences made based on those data points.

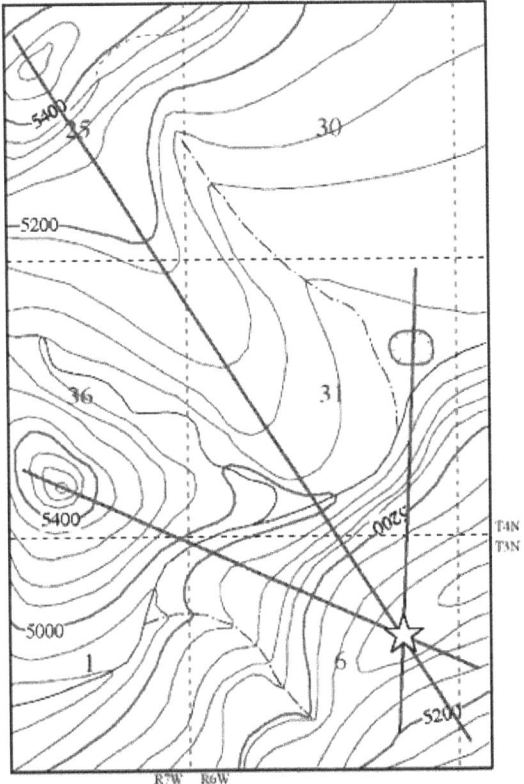

Figure 12.5. Triangulation Using a Topographic Map

No one measure of student learning or teacher/school/district quality can ever capture the full picture. However, by triangulating data and looking for patterns over time, we can be more confident that the inferences we make about student learning or teacher/school/district quality are warranted and credible. We can triangulate data by using more than one data source or data type to get a more precise sense of where we are (Bernhardt, 2004; Holcomb, 2004). For 7th grade reading in Oakwood, other data include nationally norm-referenced achievement data, state achievement test data, and perceptual data from surveys administered to students regarding their feelings about their English/language arts teacher and course.

Figure 12.6 shows the difference between actual student performance and predicted student performance on the Iowa Test of Basic Skills (ITBS), in the areas of vocabulary, reading comprehension, and combined reading total. Predicted student performance is based on students' ability scores on the Cognitive Abilities Test (an aptitude test taken with the ITBS). Positive numbers indicate that actual student performance outpaced predicted student performance by a statistically significant margin. Negative numbers would signify that actual student performance lagged predicted performance by a statistically significant margin. As illustrated in Figure 12.6, from 2008-2010, 7th grade actual student performance outpaced predicted performance each year by a range of 2-9 scaled score points, where the mean score is 100 and the standard deviation is 15 points. Detailed analysis of this data is beyond the scope of this paper, but this data does suggest that from 2008-2010 student performance in reading was strong. It is important to note (as contextual information) that unlike the state achievement tests used to calculated value added, ITBS is a nationally normed test and was not developed from the Ohio 7th grade reading standards; as such, there is not perfect alignment between test content and Ohio's 7th grade curriculum. Additionally, unlike the state achievement tests, which include multiple choice and constructed response items, the ITBS is comprised entirely of multiple choice items.

	Vocabulary Acquisition	Reading Comprehension	Total Reading
2010	+5	+2	+3
2009	+9	+7	+7
2008	+7	+6	+5

Figure 12.6. Statistically Significant Differences between Oakwood Junior High 7th Grade Actual and Predicted Scores on the Iowa Test of Basic Skills, 2008-2010

Another data source is the comparison of Oakwood Junior High state achievement test data to that of districts with similar demographics. Again, this is contextualized data, as it provides comparison to a comparable group. Figure 12.7 indicates that, compared to districts with similar demographics (a more rigorous comparison for Oakwood than comparing performance to state averages), Oakwood Junior High performed as well—and more commonly better—than similar districts in both percent of students who pass the test (score proficient or higher) and percent of students who score above proficient (accelerated or advanced), from 2008-2010. Again, this data warrants more thorough analysis, but again it helps us triangulate the reading performance of Oakwood 7th graders over a three-year period of time.

	% Passing	% Above Proficient
2010	+	=
2009	+	+
2008	=	+

+ = performance better than demographically similar districts
= = performance statistically equivalent to that of demographically similar districts
- = performance weaker than demographically similar districts

Figure 12.7. Oakwood Junior High Achievement Test Performance Compared to Similar Districts, 2008-2010

Another data source is students' perceptions of their 7th grade English/language arts courses and teachers. Although not detailed here, this data for 2008-2010 overall indicated student satisfaction with their teachers and courses.

Thus while the 7th grade reading value added data for 2008-2010 was the weakest of Oakwood Junior High grades/content areas, it should be noted that for 2010, the school met expected growth, and other data sources—including differences between actual and predicted ITBS data, state achievement test comparisons to similar districts, and student perceptual data—indicate no striking weaknesses or problems. On the contrary, the other data sources suggest that 7th grade reading is pretty healthy. Given this triangulation, it would be erroneous to conclude that there is a big problem with 7th grade reading, and it would be foolish to make radical personnel, curricular, or programmatic changes based on this value added data. That said, in a culture of inquiry and continuous improvement, teachers and school leaders will want to reflect further on all of the aforementioned data to identify goals for further improving 7th grade reading.

Triangulation, as in the example here, can help to answer key questions:

1. How is our district (school) doing in [content area/grade/program/demographic group], as compared to...
    a. Our district's previous performance?
    b. Our similar districts' performance?
    c. State averages?
    d. College expectations?
    e. How we were predicted to perform based on value added?
    f. Where we would like to see our performance?
2. What are students', teachers', parents' and community members' perceptions?
3. What are areas of strength for our school?
4. What are our challenging areas (weaknesses)?
5. What patterns do we see in the data?
6. Where should we place our priorities?
7. What questions do we have based on these data?
8. What, if any, additional data do we need?
9. What should our goals, informed by this data, be?

In order to triangulate data, we must regularly collect multiple types of data from a variety of sources. At the same time, it is important to avoid the "DRIP" syndrome—being *data rich but information poor*. DRIP syndrome occurs when we collect mounds of data but fail to take the time and energy to fully analyze it and use it to inform decisions. Collecting data that does not get analyzed and used is a waste of educator time and energy and undermines larger efforts to cultivate a culture of inquiry and data use.

Disaggregating Data

In their book *How to Use Value-Added Analysis to Improve Student Learning: A Field Guide for School and District Leaders*, Kennedy, Peters, and Thomas (2012) argue that a "good curriculum does not work well for all students and an ineffective curriculum works well for some students" (p. 60). As such, they advocate for disaggregating value added data (e.g., by achievement level, racial subgroup, gender, by Students with Disabilities status or gifted status) and looking for "any kind of consistent pattern in the data" (p. 62). Unfortunately, such consistent and informative patterns are not common in disaggregated value added data, which may not be surprising, given the instability of aggregate value added data. That said, disaggregated data can be used as a tool to examine issues of equity and social justice. For example, Figure 12.8 displays North Carolina's Green Middle School (a pseudonym) 6th grade reading value added data for Hispanic students.

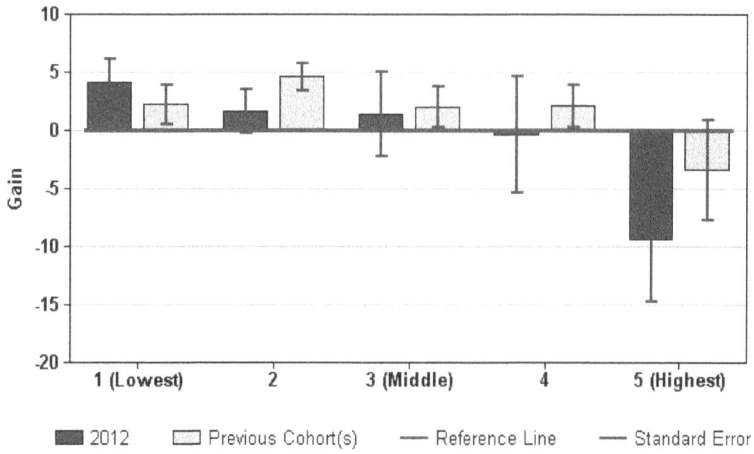

			Prior-Achievement Subgroups				
			1 (Lowest)	2	3 (Middle)	4	5 (Highest)
Reading		Reference Line	0.0	0.0	0.0	0.0	0.0
	2012	Gain	4.1	1.6	1.4	-0.4	-9.4
		Standard Error	2.0	1.9	3.6	5.0	5.3
		Nr of Students	30	30	15	6	5
		% of Students	34.9	34.9	17.4	7.0	5.8
	Previous Cohort(s)	Gain	2.2	4.6	2.0	2.1	-3.4
		Standard Error	1.7	1.2	1.8	1.8	4.3
		Nr of Students	75	57	41	24	11
		% of Students	36.1	27.4	19.7	11.5	5.3

Figure 12.8. Green Middle School 6th Grade Reading Value Added Data Disaggregated by Hispanic Subgroup

The 6th grade Hispanic students' data is broken into quintiles based on students' previous year's achievement. In other words, if all of the 6th grade students in North Carolina were lined up in order from the lowest to highest achievement on the previous year's state achievement test and then divided into five equal-sized groups, you would have quintiles. Quintiles allow us to see whether the progress of some achievement groups is different from that of others. In Figure 12.8, the darker columns indicate the most recent year's value added data for each quintile, and the lighter bars represent the growth of previous years' cohorts (past years' 6th grade students). The thick horizontal line at the "0" point on the Y-axis is the reference line indicating expected progress. Columns extending above it indicate more than expected growth or progress, and columns extending below it indicate less than expected growth or progress. The more that the column extends above or below the reference line, the greater the magnitude of growth above or below expected growth. The "I" bar superimposed on each column indicates the standard error. In those cases in which the "I" bar crosses the reference line, growth is not detectably different than expected growth. The size of the "I" bar—the magnitude of the standard error—is based on the number of students in the subgroup and the amount of variation in those students' growth. For example, the smaller the subgroup size, the larger the standard error and therefore the bigger the "I" bar will be. The more variation in subgroup students' growth, the bigger the "I" bar will be. In Figure 12.8 the lowest quintile of Hispanic 6th grade students made above expected growth in reading in 2012, whereas the middle quintile made expected growth (as indicated by the fact that the standard error "I" bar crosses the reference line), and the highest quintile of Hispanic students made below expected progress in 2012. The table below indicates that 30 6th grade Hispanic students (34.9% of the 6th grade Hispanic population at Green) fell into the lowest quintile, whereas 5 (5.8%) fell into the highest quintile.

In 2012 as well as in previous years, the lowest quintile of Hispanic students has made the most progress, and the highest quintile of Hispanic students has made the least. That said, it is important to note that in 2012 as well as in previous years, with the exception of the highest quintile in 2012, Hispanic students in 6th grade have met or exceeded expected growth in reading. Initial interpretation of this data may lead educators to wonder whether high achieving Hispanic students are being underserved. This is an important question, and contextualizing the data can help answer the question.

Figure 12.9 shows the reading value added results for the entire Green Middle 6th grade student population. In 2012, the lowest quintile of 6th graders at Green Middle made the most growth, and the highest quintile made the least growth. This pattern mirrors that of the disaggregated Hispanic students' data (although it should be noted that for past cohorts of Green 6th graders, the lowest quintile did not make the most growth in reading, whereas that is the case with the lowest quintile of Hispanic students). From an equity standpoint, this may be reassuring, although the data warrants further examination to determine why the highest quintile is making the least progress and what can be done about it.

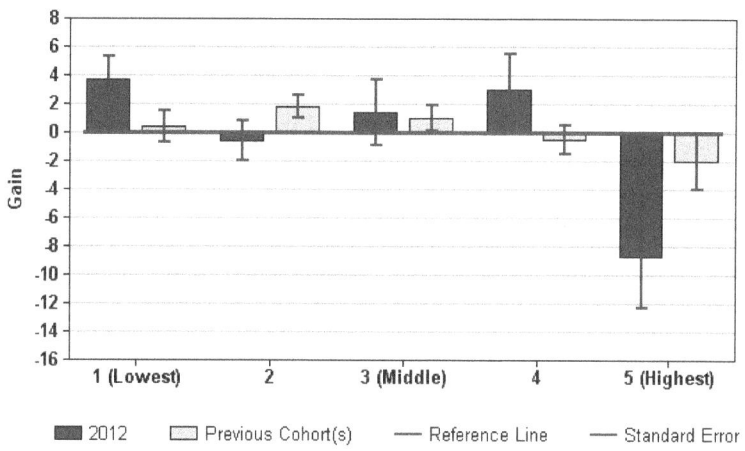

			Prior-Achievement Subgroups				
			1 (Lowest)	2	3 (Middle)	4	5 (Highest)
Reading	Reference Line		0.0	0.0	0.0	0.0	0.0
	2012	Gain	3.7	-0.6	1.4	3.0	-8.7
		Standard Error	1.6	1.4	2.3	2.5	3.6
		Nr of Students	62	61	34	25	8
		% of Students	32.6	32.1	17.9	13.2	4.2
	Previous Cohort(s)	Gain	0.4	1.8	1.0	-0.5	-2.0
		Standard Error	1.1	0.8	0.9	1.0	2.0
		Nr of Students	175	167	142	105	42
		% of Students	27.7	26.5	22.5	16.6	6.7

Figure 12.9. Green Middle School 6th Grade Reading Value Added Data

Closer examination of the data, however, does suggest an equity issue. Figure 12.10 shows that Hispanic students are underrepresented in the highest two quintiles, indicating that their achievement (NOT their growth) lags behind that of the whole 6th grade population. Specifically, while Hispanic students represent 45.3% of the 6th grade at Green, they represent only 33.3% of the top two quintiles. Thus while the growth rates of Hispanic students are consistent with—and in some areas exceeding (see differences in the scales of the Y-axis in Figures 12.8 and 12.9)—the growth rates of the entire 6th grade population at Green, Hispanic students are still underrepresented in the top quintiles.

The next section exhorts educators to respond to such data, taking care to avoid simplistic technical fixes that potentially ignore more powerful underlying equity issues.

	% of 6th Grade Population	% of Top Two Quintiles (Top 40%)
Hispanic	45.3%	33.3%
African American	26.3%	27.3%
White	22.6%	33.3%
Other	5.8%	6.1%

Figure 12.10. Achievement Demographics of Green Middle 6th Grade

Beware of Technical Fixes

Educators might respond to the aforementioned data by assuming that the achievement gap between Hispanic students and the full 6th grade population (note, this is not a growth gap) is due to language issues, and as such educators might redouble their efforts to highlight content vocabulary and increase pullout time for English Language Learners to work with specialists. Such technical fixes may be unproductive or even counter-productive. Sometimes equity gaps reflect deeper systemic inequities that must be addressed in order to close a growth gap or achievement gap.

In their book *Data Strategies to Uncover and Eliminate Hidden Inequities: The Wallpaper Effect*, Johnson and La Salle (2010) argue that as educators we must increase our "equity muscle" (p. 223) by challenging what is taken for granted as "normal" and "natural." For example, an educator might look at the aforementioned data and think, "Well, that makes sense. Hispanic students usually have lower achievement because they're still learning the language." Such a statement is problematic on at least four fronts. First, it incorrectly assumes that all Hispanic students are English Language Learners. Second, it suggests that being an English Language Learner "naturally" relegates one to lower achievement, that language issues are the root cause of lower achievement. Third, it suggests that because Hispanic students "usually" or "normally" have lower achievement that lower achievement is therefore "natural" for Hispanic students; it is perceived as so commonplace it is taken for granted as acceptable or unproblematic (Noguera & Wing, 2006) and relegated as unworthy of further analysis or urgent, righteous indignation. Fourth, such discourse "others" and marginalizes Hispanic students and insulates us as educators from facing the hard reality that our schools—and our society—are inequitable places.

Johnson and La Salle (2010) point out that much of what schools do to decrease achievement gaps (e.g., provide add-on programs that give students "more of the same" in an effort to improve learning; focus on program implementation as opposed to outcomes/impact; provide an ever-increasing number of uncoordinated programs) merely wallpapers over more systemic inequities. Systemic inequities based on race, class, and gender include the sorting, "stratifying and segregating of students" (Murphy, 2010, p. 150); providing more limited access to high-level, rigorous coursework; differences in qualification and effectiveness of teachers (known as distributional inequity); "anemic instructional designs, inordinate focus on lower-level skills, inappropriate learning contexts, and lower teacher expectations for students" (p. 150); and dissonance between teachers' pedagogical styles and learners' preferences (Murphy, 2010).

The deficit model, which "views the providers of a service as advantaged and the recipients as disadvantaged" (Hess, Lanig, & Vaughan, 2007, p. 32), is prevalent in schools today (Harry & Klinger, 2007). Educators often myopically focus on students' deficits and try to remedy them through remediation and intervention instead of focusing on students' strengths and capabilities and leveraging these to maximize student learning. The deficit model is a powerful form of systemic inequity and disproportionally affects some groups: "When a habit of looking for intrinsic deficit intertwines with a habit of interpreting cultural and racial differences as a deficit, the deck is powerfully loaded against poor students of color" (Harry & Klinger, 2007, p. 20).

While technical adjustments to discreet instructional strategies (e.g., explicit teaching of content vocabulary) may be warranted, as educators we must step back and look critically at the larger context in which data are situated. It may be the case that the focus needs to be on cultivating culturally relevant pedagogy and attending to school culture, including the way in which all stakeholders, including parents, are treated by the school. Thus we need to allow data to speak to larger issues of serving students justly and not just at discreet, technical issues of instruction.

Conducting Root Cause Analysis

As educators, how do we know whether what we see in the data is a function of the pedagogical approach or specific instructional strategies teachers are using versus larger issues of systemic inequity and school culture? "In many cases, student performance data, and especially achievement data, are equivocal" (Kennedy et al., 2012, p. 114). While it is unlikely that this question can be answered with certainty, root cause analysis can help. To address the source of what we see in the data and not just the "symptom" of it, we need to get at the "deepest underlying cause, or causes, of positive or negative" (Preuss, 2003, p. 3) findings. This process involves making hypotheses about the root of what we see in the data and then, ironically, involves testing those hypotheses by collecting and analyzing relevant data. For a two-part video introduction to root cause analysis, see Hewitt (n.d.) at http://screencast.com/t/NMjPQNLY (Part I) and http://screencast.com/t/XIU99sWE0Uxp (Part II).

CONCLUSION

While the use of value added data involves a number of challenges, including test issues, issues of practice, equity and social justice issues, technical and validity issues, and policy issues (Hewitt, 2013b), when used critically and carefully, it can inform leadership. The following recommendations will promote the ethical and efficacious use of value added data:

Recommendations

1. Set the stage by consensually developing and maintaining data commitments.
2. Do interpretive work collectively, focusing on accurately analyzing the data and building group trust in order to be vulnerable to what the data say.
3. Make value added data accessible to educators (e.g., by using color-coding and symbols to display data).
4. Cultivate data literacy by:
    a. Interrogating the strengths and limitations of all data sets
        i. considering not only what the data say but also what they do not say and cannot say
        ii. considering cautions or limitations regarding the data
    b. Making observations, interpretations, and drawing conclusions from data.
    c. Using multiple measures to triangulate data.

d. Looking for patterns in data sets over time. Remember that "one year does not a pattern make."
   e. Disaggregating data, especially with an eye for equity issues.
5. Contextualize data by considering background information regarding the test itself and testing conditions, comparing data to that of similar schools/districts, comparing data over time, and considering other pertinent information (e.g., regarding curriculum, personnel, demographic, or other factors).
6. Conduct root cause analysis as needed to identify and address the underlying causes of what is seen in the data.
7. Use value added data with caution:
   a. Avoid making too much of any one year's data.
   b. Be mindful of the limitations (both technical and practical) of value added data.
   c. Act on trends that are stable over time and are triangulated with other data.
   d. Take great care in how teacher-level value added data is interpreted and used. Do not act on it in isolation from other data sources.

Our overarching ethical commitment as educators is to do what is best for students. Data—including value added data—can serve as an important tool to fulfilling that commitment.

References

Amrein-Beardsley, A. (2008). Methodological concerns about the education value-added assessment system. *Educational Researcher 37*(2), 65-75.

Amrein-Beardsley, A., Berliner, D. C., & Rideau, S. (2010). Cheating in the first, second, and third degree: Educator's responses to high-stakes testing. *EPAA, 18*(14), 1-35.

Baker, A. L., Barton, P. E., Darling-Hammond, L., Haertel, E., Ladd, H. F., Linn, R. L., Shepard, L. A. (2010). Problems with the use of student test scores to evaluate teachers. *EPI Briefing Paper*. Washington, D.C.

Baker, B. D., Oluwole, J. O., & Green, P. C. (2013). The legal consequences of mandating high stakes decisions based on low quality information: Teacher evaluation in the Race-to-the-Top era. *EPAA, 21*(5), 1-65.

Ballou, D., Sanders, W., & Wright, P. (2004). Controlling for student background in value-added assessment of teachers. *Journal of Educational and Behavioral Statistics, 29*(1), 37-65.

Bernhardt, V. L. (2004). *Data analysis for continuous school improvement*. Larchmont, NY: Eye on Education.

Betebenner, D. (2009). Norm- and criterion-referenced student growth. *Educational Measurement: Issues and Practice, 28*(4), 42-51.

Betebenner, D. (2012). *The Hawaii growth model: A technical overview of the student growth percentile methodology*. Dover, N.H.: The National Center for the Improvement of Educational Assessment.

Braun, H. (2005). Value-added modeling: What does due diligence require? In Lissitz (Ed.), *Value added models in education: Theory and applications* (pp. 19-38). Maple Grove, MN: JAM Press.

Carey, K., & Manwaring, R. (2011). *Growth models and accountability: A recipe for remaking ESEA*. Washington, D.C.: Education Sector.

Ceperley, P. E., & Reel, K. (1997). The impetus for the Tennessee value-added accountability system. In J. Millman (Ed.), *Grading teachers, grading schools: Is student achievement a valid evaluation measure?* (pp. 133-136). Thousand Oaks, CA: Corwin Press, Inc.

Chetty, R., Friedman, J. N., & Rockoff, J. E. (2011). *The long-term impacts of teachers: Teacher value-added and student outcomes in adulthood* (Working Paper 17699). Cambridge, MA: National Bureau of Economic Research. Retrieved from http://obs.rc.fas.harvard.edu/chetty/value_added.pdf

Coleman, J. S. (1968). Equality of educational opportunity. *Equity & Excellence in Education, 6*(5), 19-28.

Corcoran, S. P. (2010). Can teachers be evaluated by their students' test scores? Should they be? The use of value-added measures of teacher effectiveness in policy and practice. *Education Policy for Action Series*. Providence, R.I.

Darling-Hammond, L., Amrein-Beardsley, A., Haertel, E., & Rothstein, J. (2012). Evaluating teacher evaluation. *Kappan, 93*(6), 8-15.

Darmawan, G. N., & Keeves, J. P. (2006). Accountability of teachers and schools: A value added approach. *International Education Journal, 7*(2), 174-188.

Delaware Department of Education. (2012). Component 5 questions and answers. Dover, DE: Author. Retrieved from http://www.doe.k12.de.us/csa/dpasii/files/QandAComp5_v3AK.pdf

Harris, D. N. (2011). *Value-added measures in education: What every educator needs to know*. Cambridge, MA: Harvard Education Press.

Harry, B., & Klinger, J. (2007). Discarding the deficit model. *Educational Leadership, 64*(5), 16-21.

Hess, D. J., Lanig, H., & Vaughan, W. (2007). Educating for equity and social justice: A conceptual model for cultural engagement. *Multicultural Perspectives, 9*(1), 32-39.

Hewitt, K. K. (n.d.). Introduction to root cause analysis: Part I and Part II (video clips). Retrieved from http://screencast.com/t/NMjPQNLY (Part I) and http://screencast.com/t/XIU99sWE0Uxp (Part II).

Hewitt, K. K. (2012). Is value added a socially just route to increased student learning? An analysis of Tennessee's Value Added Assessment System. In J. Ballenger, B. Thornton, & S. Harris (Eds.), *Social justice, competition, and quality: 21st Century challenges* (pp. 185-202). NCPEA Publications.

Hewitt, K. K. (2013a, April). *Using value added to evaluate educators: Escalating the opportunity gap*. Paper presented at the meeting of the American Education Research Association, Chicago, IL.

Hewitt, K. K. (2013b). *A conceptual framework for challenges to the high stakes use of value added data for accountability and evaluation*. Manuscript in preparation.

Hill, H. C., Kapitula, L., & Umland, K. (2011). A validity argument approach to evaluating teacher value-added scores. *American Educational Research Journal, 48*(3), 794-831.

Holcomb, E. L. (2004). *Getting excited about data: Combining people, passion, and proof to maximize student achievement*, (2nd ed.). Thousand Oaks, CA: Corwin Press.

Institute of Education Sciences. (2010). *Error rates in measuring teacher and school performance based on students' test score gains*. Washington, D.C.: U. S. Department of Education.

Jennings, J. L., & Corcoran, S. P. (2009). "Beware of geeks bearing formulas": Reflections on growth models for school accountability. *Phi Delta Kappan, 90*(9), 635-639.

Jennings, J. L. & Corcoran, S. P. (2012). Beyond high-stakes tests: Teacher effects on other educational outcomes. In S. Kelley (Ed.), *Assessing teacher quality: Understanding teacher effects on instruction and achievement* (pp. 77-95). New York: Teachers College Press.

Johnson, R. S., & La Salle, R. A. (2010). *Data strategies to uncover and eliminate hidden inequities: The wallpaper effect*. Thousand Oaks, CA: Corwin.

Keeves, J. P., Hungi, N., & Afrassa, T. (2005). Measuring value added effects across schools: Should schools be compared in performance? *Studies in Educational Evaluation, 31*(2), 247-266. doi: 10.1016/j.stueduc.2005.05.012

Kennedy, K., Peters, M., Thomas, M. (2012). *How to use value-added analysis to improve student learning: A field guide for school and district leaders*. Thousand Oaks, CA: Corwin.

Konstantopoulos, S., & Chung, V. (2011). The persistence of teacher effects in elementary grades. *American Educational Research Journal, 48*(2), 361-386.

Kupermintz, H. (2003). Teacher effects and teacher effectiveness: A validity investigation of the Tennessee Value Added Assessment System. *Educational Evaluation and Policy Analysis, 25*(3), 287-298.

Linn, R. L. (2008). Methodological issues in achieving school accountability. *Journal of Curriculum Studies, 40*(6), 699-711.

Mariano, L. T., McCaffrey, D. F., & Lockwood, J. R. (2010). A model for teacher effects from longitudinal data without assuming vertical scaling. *Journal of Educational and Behavioral Statistics, 35*(3), 253-279.

Martineau, J. A. (2006). Distorting value added: The use of longitudinal, vertically scaled student achievement data for growth-based, value-added accountability. *Journal of Educational and Behavioral Statistics, 31*(1), 35-62.

McCaffey, D. F., Lockwood, J. R., Koretz, D., Louis, T. A., & Hamilton, L. (2004). Models for value-added modeling of teacher effects. *Journal of Educational and Behavioral Statistics, 29*(1), 67-101.

McCaffrey, D. F., Lockwood, J. R., Mariano, L. T., & Setodji, C. (2005). Challenges for value-added assessment of teacher effects. In Lissitz (Ed.), *Value added models in education: Theory and applications* (pp. 111-141). Maple Grove, MN: JAM Press.

Murphy, J. (2010). *The educator's handbook for understanding and closing achievement gaps*. Thousand Oaks, CA: Corwin.

National Research Council, & National Academy of Education. (2010). Getting value out of value-added: Report of a workshop. Report of the committee on value-added methodology for instructional improvement, program evaluation, and educational accountability. Washington, D.C: The National Academies Press.

Nichols, S. L., & Berliner, D. C. (2005). *The inevitable corruption of indicators and educators through high-stakes testing.* East Lansing, MI: Great Lakes Center for Education Research & Practice.

Noguera, P., & Wing, J. Y. (Eds.). (2006). *Unfinished business: Closing the racial achievement gap in our schools*. San Francisco: Jossey-Bass.

Ohio Department of Education. (2012). *Additional preliminary district and school report card data released*. Retrieved from http://www.ode.state.oh.us/GD/Templates/Pages/ODE/ODEDetail.aspx?page=3&TopicRelationID=1&ContentID=131230&Content=135557

Papay, J. P. (2011). Different tests, different answers: The stability of teacher value-added estimates across outcome measures. *American Educational Research Journal, 48*(1), 163-193.

Power, S., & Frandji, D. (2010) Education markets, the new politics of recognition and the increasing fatalism towards inequality. *Journal of Education Policy, 25*(3). doi: 10.1080/02680930903576404

Preuss, P. G. (2003). *School leader's guide to root cause analysis: Using data to dissolve problems*. Larchmont, NY: Eye on Education.

Pullin, D. (2013). Legal issues in the use of student test scores and value-added models (VAM) to determine educational quality. *EPAA, 21*(6), 1-21.

Richards, J. S. (2010). Fewer kids get a full year's education, revised figures show. *The Columbus Dispatch,* (September 13, 2010). Retrieved from http://www.dispatch.com/content/stories/local/2010/09/13/value-of-schools-drops.html

Riesterer, J. (2008). *Finding self on a map.* Retrieved from http://geology.isu.edu/geostac/Field_Exercise/topomaps/self_finding.htm

Rivkin, S. G., Hanushek, E. A., & Kain, J. F. (2005). Teachers, schools, and academic achievement. *Econometrica, 73*(2), 417-458.

Rothstein, J. (2010). Teacher quality in educational production: Tracking, decay, and student achievement. *The Quarterly Journal of Economics*, *125* (1), 175-214. doi: 10.1162/qjec.2010.125.1.175

Sanders, W. L., Saxton, A. M., & Horn, S. P. (1997). The Tennessee Value-Added Assessment System: A quantitative, outcomes-based approach to educational assessment. In J. Millman (Ed.), *Grading teachers, grading schools: Is student achievement a valid evaluation measure?* (pp. 137-162). Thousand Oaks, CA: Corwin Press, Inc.

SAS. (2010). *SAS EVAAS technical report: Ohio scale stabilization process*. Raleigh, NC: Author.

Schmidt, W.H., Houang, R. T., & McKnight, C. C. (2005). Value-added research: Right idea but wrong solution? Lissitz, R. (Ed.), *Value added models in education: Theory and applications (pp. 145-164)*. Maple Grove, MN: JAM Press.

State of Tennessee. (2011, August 31). Contract Amendment. Contract #FA1030469-02.

Stephens, T. M. (2010, October 9). Value-added measurement unreliable. *The Columbus Dispatch.* Retrieved from http://www.dispatch.com/content/stories/editorials/2010/10/09/value-added-measurement-unreliable.html

Tennessee Department of Education. (2011). Tennessee Value-Added Assessment System (TVAAS). Retrieved from http://www.tn.gov/education/assessment/test_results.shtml

The Center for Greater Philadelphia. (2004). *Value-added assessment.* University of Pennsylvania. Retrieved from http://www.cgp.upenn.edu/ope_value.html.

Timmermans, A. C., Doolaard, S., & de Wolf, I. (2011). Conceptual and empirical differences among various value-added models for accountability. *School effectiveness and school improvement, 22*(4), 393-413.

U. S. Department of Education. (2009). *Race to the Top program executive summary.* Washington, D. C.: Author.

Van de Grift, W. (2009). Reliability and validity in measuring the value added of schools. *School effectiveness and school improvement, 20*(2), 269-285.

Weisberg, D., Sexton, S., Mulhern, J., & Keeling, D. (2009). *The widget effect: Our national failure to acknowledge and act on differences in teacher effectiveness.* Washington, D.C.: The New Teacher Project.

Wright, S. P., Horn, S. P., & Sanders, W. L. (1997). Teacher and classroom context effects on student achievement: Implications for teacher evaluation. *Journal of Personnel Evaluation in Education, 11*, 57-67.

Wright, S. P., White, J. T., Sanders, W. L., & Rivers, J. C. (2010). SAS EVAAS statistical models. Raleigh, NC: SAS Institute, Inc.

Dr. Kimberly Kappler Hewitt is Assistant Professor in the Educational Leadership and Cultural Foundations Department at the University of North Carolina Greensboro. Prior to that, she served for 8 years as a district-level administrator in Ohio and also as a building principal. She has worked in both affluent and high need communities, including an urban Appalachian district in Ohio. She serves in an elected position on ASCD's Leadership Council and has been selected as a 2010 Emerging Leader by ASCD. Kimberly specializes in the ethical and efficacious use of data, implementation of change/reform, and instructional leadership. She is the author of *Differentiation is an Expectation: A School Leader's Guide to Building a Culture of Differentiation* (coauthored by D. K. Weckstein, Eye on Education, 2011). Kimberly can be contacted at kkhewitt@uncg.edu.

Conclusion

Practitioner Scholar, Instructional Leader, Public Advocate

Carl Lashley and *Aaron Woody*

When first we read this book's title, *Postcards from the Schoolhouse,* two thoughts came immediately to mind. The first was *memories*, memories of times gone by, simpler times, times when schools were respected institutions and when postcards were sent and received from idyllic summer vacations, joyous trips to faraway lands, and family vacation spots at the beach. Memories of *Wish you were here!* and *School's out, school's out! Teacher let the bulls out!*

Our second thought was *anachronism*— something that is out of date, old-fashioned. Both *postcards* and *schoolhouses* fit the bill. Postcards have been replaced by the camera in your phone, Facebook, or Instagram--electronic functionaries that give us instant gratification and the widest possible coverage. Postcards are somehow quaint reminders of our deliberate, snail mail past.

The *schoolhouse* brings to mind a community center to which children walked to learn their letters and cipher. A little red building on the edge of town where a schoolmarm held forth over students of all ages, where some learned, many didn't, but most entered a world where they would survive and even thrive. The schoolhouse has been replaced by brick and mortar buildings that are bureaucratically organized and where students are processed through a curriculum and instruction regimen that has been developed and stamped approved by a committee in some far away state capital.

And many find even the brick and mortar school to be anachronistic. Education futurists today foresee a time when learning occurs anywhere and everywhere, and the school is a space where children and adults gather when it's necessary for learning, recreation, and custodial care. Web 2.0, smart phones, tablets, and apps certainly make such a future seem possible. Perhaps the schoolhouse has passed its prime as a cultural image.

Given these idyllic and anachronistic perspectives on postcards and schoolhouses, why then create this collection of chapters in which practitioner-scholars discuss their ideas about making 21st Century schools responsive to the needs of all children? What does it take to be a practitioner-scholar, to be transformative, and to simultaneously navigate the system and disrupt it? Where does a school leader find the time, energy, resources, allies, and personal and political power to sustain him/herself, especially at this time of high-stakes accountability, public criticism of schools, and economic uncertainty? What relevance do these *Postcards from the Schoolhouse* have for the intrepid among us who are determined to renew and transform schools into educative organizations that serve all students and their communities?

We write this concluding chapter to describe the leadership challenges faced by 21st Century principals and to discuss the necessity for transcending the system in which our leaders find themselves. We believe that surviving as a transformative leader means challenging the inappropriate uses of power and privilege that create or perpetuate inequity and injustice in schools and society. Transforming requires the skills to keep management and leadership in dynamic balance so the school community can create space for authentic learning experiences, for social progress, and for moral growth. Furthermore, we contend that transformative leaders must facilitate the visioning of educational and community values instead of affirming the psychometric, bureaucratic, standardizing values that support assessment systems, the accountability movement, and indeed most of our thinking about what a *good school* is.

As many of the chapters before have outlined, the role of a practitioner-scholar has become critical to re-shaping the landscape of American education. To lead in this way requires one to "become a reflective practitioner, which means developing the capacity to be alone in dialogue with one's own soul" (Palmer, 2011, p. 155). We contend that 21st Century schools work in flurries of activity that need to be balanced by meaning and purpose. Principals and teachers are faced with ever-increasing demands for student performance productivity in a standardized environment, for a disciplinary environment that is conducive to learning in an increasingly permissive society, and for publicized accountability that scrutinizes practice as an exercise in basic skills. Faced with these challenges, principals are apt to "lose heart" as Palmer (2011) says – "breaking into a thousand pieces manifesting itself in anger, depression, and disengagement" (p. 10).

Everyone believes that the education of the young is something that all principals and educators alike should be committed to. We can do it well, or we can do it poorly. The public lays blame fairly and unfairly on the shoulders of educational leaders as our policies constantly attempt to produce better quantifiable results, knowing full well that this is but one indicator of a child's learning. The American ideal of educating every student to his/her potential is as important as ever. At the same time, a similar and arguably more important goal of education is to create and facilitate an educated citizenry—*a public*—that contributes to the growth and revitalization of our democratic republic.

PARALYSIS IN THE PRINCIPALSHIP

Because we are experienced school administrators whose university work prepares students for school leadership roles, we often espouse that the principalship is key to both school improvement and a thriving democracy. We believe this because it aligns with our vision of equity and socially just communities. However, we are increasingly disenchanted and heartbroken--*broken into a thousand pieces*--as we talk with principals about their sense of the future. Principals feel shackled, paralyzed, stifled by a system that requires them to serve standards and values that run counter to what they believe to be the well-being of children and the love of learning.

One variable that seems to stifle the outlook of hard working principals is the level of responsibility required to do this work well. The various responsibilities required for success as an educational leader in the 21st century are staggering. Bugbee (2006) addresses how the principal's role has evolved to be the highly political position it is today. The pressures from the community, the state and federal government, the superintendent, staff, parents, and teacher unions require principals to be involved in many activities and to keep up-to-date about current issues affecting schools. Principals are expected to be visionaries, instructional leaders, assessment experts, disciplinarians, public relation gurus, and crisis interventionists.

When the United States Secretary of Education was asked to describe the role of principals in improving student achievement, Arne Duncan (2011) stated,

> Nothing is more important. There's no such thing as a high-performing school without a great principal. It is impossible. You simply can't overstate their importance in driving student achievement, in attracting and retaining great talent to the school . . . . Principal leadership is so critically important, and we want to support principals as they grow and develop. We want to do everything we can to help those great leaders at the local level make a difference in their communities (Connelly, 2010, para. 9-10).

According to West, Peck, and Reitzug (2010), "principals typically exert limited control over phenomena ranging from consistent demands to high-intensity events. This generates formidable pressures because a single episode can place the organization and personnel under significant distress" (p. 246). The current state of the principalship requires a school leader to handle daily affairs while simultaneously staying focused on the strategic plan for continual success and negotiating what "successful" means to the various constituencies s/he serves. *Success* to the superintendent may mean solid test scores, while success to one parent may be a scholarship to a prestigious university and to another parent it may mean getting through another day when the phone doesn't bring a call from an assistant principal about trouble at school. Principals juggle all of these demands while keeping the doors open and the lights on, the classrooms staffed, and the after-school events running.

Davis, Darling-Hammond, and Meyerson (2005) have clarified the multi-faced job of the principalship:

> More than ever, in today's climate of heightened expectations, principals are in the hot seat to improve teaching and learning. They need to be educational visionaries, instructional and curricular leaders, assessment experts, budget analysts, facility managers, special programs leaders, and expert overseers of legal, contractual, and policy mandates and initiatives. They are expected to broker the often conflicting interests of parents, teachers, students, and district office officials, and they need to be sensitive to the widening range of student needs. (p. 5)

These themes have been well documented and researched in various other recent studies (Ginsberg, 2008; Leithwood, Harris, & Hopkins, 2008; Louis, Leithwood, Wahlstrom, & Anderson, 2010; Powell, Higgins, Aram, & Freed, 2009), indicating the importance of how principals use their time to ensure they focus on what is most important. Leaders need to be hopeful, and they need to be able to foster this hope in others. Walker (2006) communicates this variable by stating, "principals must do this in spite of the complexities of our times, the rigidity of our thinking, and the deadlock of tensions of our diverse values and aspirations" (p. 543).

According to Lunenburg and Ornstein (2004), "the school principal has been cited as the most influential person in promoting school reform, change and innovation, and developing the overall culture of the school community" (p. 375). The principal is looked to for the promotion and implementation of school reform and practice. While teachers may be the most important people in the performance of students, principals influence learning environments through their roles in organizing, maintaining, and sustaining schools' climate, culture, time, and resources.

As the principal's job becomes more demanding, many who are connected to educational systems in America are concerned with the rate of turn-over and leadership sustainability. There is ample evidence that the demands of leadership within the schoolhouse are almost impossible to meet, and it is difficult to tell how well principals are supported across American school districts. Researcher Ed. J. Fuller (2009), who conducted a national study at the University of Texas, shares this sentiment in relation to principal tenure as he states, "Current research points out that the job of the principal has outgrown the ability of one person to handle it…nobody is staying long enough to make connections or shepherd a reform through" (Fuller, 2009). When our school administrators are scrutinized, challenged, and pushed to exceed the results from previous years, an environment of manipulation is created as opposed to authentic intentionality. The emotional and physical strains a principal faces become more than one person can stomach.

There are additional notations in the literature to describe the current tenure rate among principals in the country. Debra Viadero (2009) cites, in a research report for *Education Week*, a recent Texas study that turnover in the principalship has detrimental effects across the country. In the study of employment data from 1995 to 2008, which looked at more than 16,500 public school principals, the average tenure was about five years for elementary school principals, four and a half for middle school, and slightly less than three and a half years for high school principals.

Within the urban district where our graduate students work, we informally determined that the average term of an elementary principal is about 3.6 years. This implies that few of these leaders actually remain in their schools long enough to see effective implementation of programs and reforms. Coupled with top-down district mandates and political pressures from the larger community, the task of leading a school toward democratic collaboration is almost unattainable.

Very little research has been conducted about how principals make sense of the job. According to Duke and Salmonwicz (2010), how leaders think about what they do, and why they do it, has received little attention in the education world. Principals believe they have little time to work deliberately and think deeply about their practice. While they sometimes examine what they do, they are disinclined to reflect about beliefs, perspectives, and ways in which their practice influences the practice of others, or how "what they do" influences what we as a community become. This must be explored and brought to light. Palmer (2011) suggests:

> The heart is where everything begins: that grounded place in each of us where we can overcome fear, rediscover that we are members of one another, and embrace the conflicts that threaten democracy as openings to new life for us and for our nation. (p. 10)

Emphasis and discovery must take place in considering the *heart* of our schools. Because of the enormous emphasis placed on the principal, we must begin with the heart of the school's leadership. A failure to see the imperative of an inquiry into heart as a viable notion in leadership will result in our continuing to do what we have always done.

THE CHALLENGES OF THE 21ST CENTURY PRINCIPALSHIP

The principalship requires an ever changing, multi-layered, globally relevant approach to teaching and learning in the local schoolhouse. There is also a demand for principals to be change agents, motivators, inspiring communicators, and all things to all people. However, for the sake of this paper, we seek to look closely at what we believe to be the most pressing challenges to pursuing democracy that principals face as they relate to the work of the *heart* in the school. We have named these obstacles: 1) Overwhelmed by context, 2) Raging against the machine, 3) Finding the balance between raging and healing, and 4) Deconstructing the moral elements of leadership.

Overwhelmed By Context

With so much emphasis placed on the external demands of the job, often principals become consumed by the tedious work of the school and fail to recognize the importance of their role in the real work of teaching and learning going on around them. The task of leadership seems increasingly convoluted as principals seek to make sense of discipline issues, parent concerns, staff growth, financial constraints, and district policies. Palmer (2011) explains that to "effectively lead in this environment one must become a reflective practitioner, which means developing the capacity to be alone in dialogue with one's own soul" (p. 155). The *heart* that drove the educator to seek the role as principal cannot be sacrificed in the reality of overwhelming obstacles.

Some of these obstacles are insurmountable when principals try to find deeper meaning behind the daily responsibilities they are charged with. For instance, Doyle and Rice (2002) claim that principals experience as many as 50-60 individual events an hour, some of which include physical plant problems, discipline decisions, paper purchases, and requests from others. They also found that just 11% of these interactions could be classified as instructional leadership. In another study, Miller (2001) found that principals devote about eight hours per week to parental concerns alone. Given the expanse of principals' responsibilities, finding the time needed for strategic planning, instructional leadership, and critical reflection becomes extremely difficult.

Section III of this volume deals with four currently popular school reform vectors—21st Century learning, the Common Core Standards, technology, and value-added assessment. Each of these reforms taken individually offers considerable promise to improving schools. They also add to the already overwhelming burden that principals and teachers feel as reform is handed down to them. As many researchers and educational pundits have argued, involving those who have to do the work of reform is essential if reform is to be successful. This requires an opening of the mind and the heart to possibility. Unfortunately, accountability pressures are sufficiently counter to the values of schools that the tendency to shut down rather than rise up plays out as schools confront all they have to do.

In the midst of so many demands and accountability structures, principals are also consumed by the realities of their students and community. Many children come to school with few resources, little support, diminished hope—often greeting us in the morning with heartbreak and entrenched levels of cynicism. Their hearts are shattered in spite of their often reported resiliency. Staff members, also in need of healing, may need spaces of authentic inquiry, motivation, and emotional support. The principal must find a way to create space for healing.

Freedom, access, and opportunity are major components of democracy. Along with individual rights and freedoms comes a collective responsibility to ensure that we are all doing our best, and we are all treated fairly. Palmer (2011) reminds us that schools and district level leaders are charged with creating schools where all students have equitable access and opportunity to instruction, curriculum, and resources. Many students, and staff, he argues, are deprived of this access. Schools are one of the primary venues where a person's heart is shaped. Schools, and the process of schooling, determine how students view their personal role in citizenship and democracy.

Mendels (2012) indicates that principals experience better success rates when instead of using authoritative control, "they make good use of all the skills and knowledge on the faculty and among others" and "encourage the many capable adults who make up the school community to step into leadership roles and responsibilities." (Mendels, 2012, p. 56) This is also validated by other studies (Horng & Loeb, 2010; Protheroe, 2011) that argue a school principal's leadership and influence on teachers' motivation and working conditions has more impact on student achievement than their influence on teacher's knowledge and skills. School leaders can have a tremendous effect on the teachers they hire, and the students they support, simply by being reflective about their own personal approach to the decision making process.

Within the context of a local school, a principal must be able to move beyond the walls of the building to embrace the higher order skill of critical analysis. Instead of always being driven to action, to do something, to make something happen, principals who engage in meaningful personal reflection can help themselves see the importance of being mindful, deliberate, contemplative, and oriented toward the matters of the *heart*. The process of moving beyond the walls can build a bridge between how the little things in the school connect to the bigger approaches and accomplishments. How can we balance the flurry of activity in our individual contexts with the creation of meaning and purpose? How do we answer the question of what it is we want our students and staff to be instead of what we want them to do? These are the questions that can be explored as one walks the road to the heart of the school.

Raging Against the Machine

In the first section of this volume, the authors discuss the need for new approaches to thinking about children and how we serve them. Moore's (Chapter 1) ideas about culturally relevant pedagogy, Aleman's notions of connecting to communities (Chapter 2), response to intervention described by Palladino (Chapter 3), and the Eadens, Ray, Eadens, and Shirer (Chapter 4) treatment of deficit models all point to the need to disrupt how we think about the human capabilities of children and their possibilities. For many years, the mantra *all children can learn* has been mouthed by educators and policymakers as we promise *no child left behind*. However, the promise of those words has been contradicted by our policies and practices that attempt to homogenize children, label children's characteristics as pathologies, and separate children from one another according to often arbitrary groupings that are more related to socioeconomic status than to capabilities.

Palmer (2007) describes a tragic tale regarding the failures of a hospital to save a relatively healthy patient who went in for a routine procedure. In his descriptions and analysis he compares the problems organizations encounter when they qualify the personal approach to humanity with systemic routine approaches. He contends that a deeper layer of tragedy exists in the face of indignity when the self-preservation of the system overwhelms the logic of the human heart. When we strip organizations of their ability to value human dignity, we create systems that value productivity, efficiency, and the bottom-line. This comparison is applicable as we think about the approach principals and teachers take to the task of educating all children while navigating the structures of the *system*.

The rush to keep everyone accountable in our schools, primarily through high-stakes testing, has had a variety of effects upon our students and our communities. Many believe that this narrow approach to basic knowledge and skills has resulted in academic mediocrity and a lack of inspiration (Orfield, Losen, Wald, & Swanson, 2004; Stipek, 2006). This problem has been studied nationally by many researchers and care agents (Goodlad, 1984; Millikan, 2007; Wolk, 2007) as they look at the effects of high stakes testing on students. At its core, the research indicates that the effects of these tests, in limiting the purpose and value of schools, also limit the possibilities of children.

For instance, as we head into an age of national Common Core standards, there is little evidence that previous federal legislation like NCLB has "increased student learning in any significant way" (Nicholas & Berliner, 2008, p. 14). In contrast, a wealth of documentation indicates that the negative effects of these tests are pervasive and a cause of concern (Bloom, 2012; Jones, Jones, & Hargrove, 2003; Orfield & Kornhaber, 2001). One district teacher went so far as to say, "We are so focused on reading, writing, and mathematics assessments, we don't do any community outreach like visiting the nursing home, or cleaning up a park we had adopted" (Taylor, Shepard, Kinner, & Rosenthal, 2003, p.51).

To be fair, teachers and principals naturally focus on teaching skills and attributes that they can readily measure. However, the current ritualized focus on test scores only exacerbates that tendency. No one asks whether a school makes adequate yearly progress in increasing students' proficiency at caring for others, making meaning in their community, or giving a project their all. Likewise, multiple-choice tests can't measure such components as caring, tenacity, integrity, and creativity. If educational leaders continue to ignore these essential skills necessary for success in life, we will find a sea of young people ill-prepared for lives of caring, compassion, and democratic leadership.

The kind of leadership necessary for changing this paradigm will take courage and will. Educators must promote and build meaningful relationships for all students and stakeholders in the community. They must show willingness for vulnerability and open communication. This has been noted in multiple studies as researchers found all students need caring and competent educators in their lives (Nichols & Berliner, 2008; Stipek, 2006) and that positive relationships in the schoolhouse can improve individual student achievement (Wimberly, 2002). These variables reflect a desire by students to trust, depend upon, and respect the adults in their lives (Cottrell, Neuberg, & Li, 2007).

In Section II of this volume, the authors discuss teachers who gain a voice to lead. Cultivating teacher leadership through PLC utilization and shared decision making are steps in the right direction toward sharing power, knowledge, and networks. When these efforts to democratize schools are driven by a vision for access, equity, and diversity, teachers become more capable of responding to the needs of all students. And an important benefit is that teachers also feel more connected to their school and their colleagues. Wes-Burhham (2009) suggests that the future role of school leadership is likely to undergo a radical change from being inwardly focused on school improvement initiatives to recognizing the need and potential for schools to become more involved with their communities. To achieve this, he argues that school principals will begin to shift their focus away from "institutional improvement" that characterized school leadership initiatives of the 1990's and towards "community transformation" through the building of social capital. He suggests that taking a role in the building of social capital will have positive spin-offs for schools and create "rich networks of interdependence" between schools and their local communities: "If academic standards are to be raised in a sustainable way and broader educational aspirations achieved, then educationists will have to see their role in terms of creating social capital, rather than just improving classroom practice" (p. 137).

Principals in the 21st century will need to know how important building and sustaining good community relationships are to the well being and culture of their school. Building these relationships will better prepare the school community for sustaining meaningful networks and partnerships. Michael Fullan (2000) speaks to this as he says:

> Schools need the outside to get the job done. These external forces, however, do not come in helpful packages; they are an amalgam of complex and uncoordinated phenomena. The work of the school is to figure out how to make its relationship with them a productive one (Fullan, 2000).

This unique challenge requires a principal to maneuver his/her way through political waters. Principals have historically been involved at varying degrees in "community or public relations." They spend time organizing parent meetings, speaking at civic and business meetings, meeting with community leaders and citizens, and engaging in other acts that are clearly political as they seek support for their school community. The political powers and the strategies principals use as they navigate political waters affect whether a policy is implemented, changed to meet unique needs of their school, or completely abandoned. Keen interpersonal skills and strong values are must haves for the political arena, and it weighs heavily on the emotions of a principal.

In his book, *The Moral Imperative of School Leadership*, Fullan (2003) talks about moral purpose. He states, "The highest form of moral purpose is not altruistic martyrdom but a mixture of selfish and unselfish motives" (p. 17). If leaders embody moral purpose, they can show tremendous levels of energy, enthusiasm, and hope, as well as provide comfort to make people feel that even the most difficult problems can be tackled in a productive manner. These leaders spread hope and optimism with an attitude of never giving up. Their responsibility is to rage against the machine—to point out the school's role in crafting a society that values human dignity, to create ways of working that build on the capabilities of students, staff and community, and to assure that the instrumentalities of power understand the nature of the educative enterprise.

Finding Balance Between Raging and Healing

A principal's role should include a balance of managerial and instructional focus in order to provide an ideal educational environment for students and staff. However, finding the right balance is often difficult because of overt and covert forces at play that manipulate the actions and emotions of the leader. As we have discussed, the role of a principal can become easily consumed with daily managerial duties that risk hijacking innovativeness and preventing a leader from thinking critically about passions, conviction, or the actions that lead to success.

Principals stand at a crossroads and must choose the path that leads to either a shattered heart or a heart broken open. Instead of facing the emotional and political forces that cause bleeding with a heart shattered, reflective leaders can choose to take an alternate route by investing the self into the work of the school. This is done by developing people and enabling staff to be effective and vulnerable. It is also achieved by setting direction for the organization by developing a "collective" vision on how to get where they need to go. Lastly, it is accomplished by transforming schools into more effective organisms instead of organizations--places where themes of social justice, caring, and collegiality are valued at the expense of standardization.

Because principals must take on the responsibility of helping create an appropriate school climate, they must know their staff and their students. Furthermore, they must recognize that the cultivation of interpersonal relationships and an emphasis on academic achievement are the dual purposes of schooling. "Principals and teachers together craft a leadership relationship that promotes an educational program characterized by focus, coherence, and consistency" (Printy, Marks, & Bowers, 2009, p. 505). In understanding this, it becomes critical that the principal delegates tasks and responsibilities effectively. Not only does this serve the organization of the school more efficiently, it ensures that the right work is being done by the right people.

Few schools take seriously the substantial capacity associated with shared and distributive leadership. In fact, most principals continue to avoid discussing their personal strengths, weakness, and preferences with administrative partners. Instead of having the principal and the administrative team complement each other's strengths, team members have traditionally assumed well-defined roles in school decision making. As we have seen in this volume, PLCs show tremendous potential for developing collaborative relationships that leave the tradition of division of labor behind.

Marzano, Walters, & McNulty (2005) have stated that no one questions the amount of work that takes place within a school. The questions ultimately come down to who is doing the "right" work within the building.

> These falsehoods include believing that schools fail because the people in them – administrators, teachers, and students – don't work hard enough and that they are lazy, unmotivated, and self-serving. However, as we have seen, the problem in low-performing schools is not getting people to work, it is getting people to do the 'right work.' (p. 76)

All educational leaders must devote a great deal of thought and critical analysis to protect the most important aspect of teaching and learning--the students--and the type of instruction and connections they need. Delegating is a critical aspect of shared decision-making but the nature of leading democratically is far more consuming. The creation of a meaningful learning community is not an easy endeavor because it takes considerable amounts of reflection, communication, planning, and ultimately energy. The notion of the school as a community engaged in a collaborative partnership represents a fundamental shift in the ideology that shapes the understanding of schools and of professional practice. Because of this paradigm, principals must look toward their staff and find collective goals, values, and plans to support students. To find collective success and personal fulfillment, principals should practice leadership that is neither passive nor hierarchical but rather is proactively democratic. In addition to leadership decisions, power and authority should be shared with all members of the school community.

Fullan (2008) describes this process of capacity building as essential for leadership and school success. He believes that leaders who embrace this model hire talented people then go out of their way to lead them toward developing cultures of purposeful collaboration. When done effectively, according to Fullan (2008), "principals regain the instructional leadership role and members of the community (the staff) become system strong as opposed to individually strong" (p. 71). Theoretically, a principal who can develop this type system could again be freed up to work on the cultivation of relationships and positive partnerships that enhance the school's programming. This aspect of leadership could lead to greater fulfillment and less cynicism, emotional disconnection, and burnout.

Working to establish democratic partnerships, particularly in schools identified as at-risk of failure, takes an enormous amount of time and energy. Because the efforts are rooted in organizational strategy and relationship building, the work is oftentimes slow. It takes place in the larger activities of the school but more subtly and crucially in the individual interactions of the principal and teachers. Word of mouth from parents and community members becomes the primary avenue for transferring this information and reputation. Because of this aspect, the energy level, awareness, and behavior of the principal and staff must be on point at all times. This requires everyone on staff, and particularly the principal, to model enthusiasm and transparency. These are two variables of an individual's personality that typically require extra amounts of energy. In order to alleviate the risk of derailment, a principal must work to provide a pace that pushes the community forward but also eliminates risks of internal distress.

We are hopeful practitioner scholars and believe in the work of our schools. Our collective experiences as educators, citizens, and as academic researchers have helped us see the potential we have to improve our schools and our far-reaching communities. In reflecting on our personal journeys, we know that there were deliberate steps that led us to where we are today. Over the past few years, we have witnessed a troubling trend in educational leadership and behavior. Engaging in discussions away from the schoolhouse, we find a growing hostility against public education. In an effort to respond with results, educational leaders face the temptation to become involved in doing what is *expected* while bypassing what is *best* for children. To overcome these obstacles, principals must communicate the school's outrage at educational injustice while they foster individual, school, and community growth and development through democratic processes and decision making.

Deconstructing the Moral Elements of Leadership

In light of the many technical aspects of educational leadership, it is important to note that leadership is **always** a moral act. This is why the principal position is so distinct and emotional. While characterized as school executives, principals are more often considered middle management, and they are held to a standard a step below clergy. Principals must be willing to approach their tasks, roles, and positions with an open heart ready to embrace and confront the emotional difficulties of the job. In order to explain our position here we must take a moment to deconstruct what we mean when we say that leadership is a moral act.

Quite frankly, schools are not only laboratories for social justice; they are the places where our civil and communal inequities are brought forward with glowing clarity. President Barack Obama has expressed his concern about inequities in various speeches regarding this issue. In one of his campaign speeches quoted by Darling-Hammond (2011), he describes the "large race and class based achievement gaps we experience as morally unacceptable and economically untenable" (Darling-Hammond, 2011, p. 3). This point is driven home more vividly in the same text as Darling-Hammond notes a recent study of southern high schools that found that the socioeconomic status of the school had as much impact on their achievement as their own personal socioeconomic status. Twenty-first century segregation in public schools exists and is often tied to resources and quality instruction. A principal must be willing to fight this trend, expose this truth, and argue with precision the need for change.

At the same time, principals must unpack many of the common clichés used to describe their work--things like, "doing what is best for kids," or "striving for excellence" and "making sure that we believe all kids can learn." What does this really look like in practical terms? How do we know when we have met the mark, achieved the goal, or lived the standard? Only through a clear interrogation of our practice can we better reform the behaviors needed to find justice, and this can be done neither in isolation, nor hastily.

This is where our intentions and our behaviors intersect to create transformational change. It is in the space created to evaluate our moral purpose and focus that we unpack the themes and desires of our hearts. This involves staying true to the collective vision, to the motivations within our hearts that guide our decision-making processes. It also requires that we honestly evaluate our behavior and the behaviors of the "system" in which we work. In short, we must lead with integrity of purpose and a vulnerability of openness that exposes truth.

BREAKING OPEN THE HEART TO INVITE HEALING

In our work together, we have come to the conclusion that how a principal greets students at the beginning of a day is a powerful indicator of his/her heart. A principal who expresses his/her enthusiasm for each child, who welcomes children and parents as integral to the school community, who approaches the school day as an opportunity for joyousness and blossoming—this is a principal who has opened his/her heart to children, learning, and the love of schooling. Palmer (2011) argues that:

> If (the heart) breaks *open* into greater capacity to hold the complexities and contradictions of human experience, the result may be new life. The heart is what makes us human—and politics, which is the use of power to order our life together, is a profoundly human enterprise. Politics in the hands of those whose hearts have been broken open, not apart, helps us hold our differences more creatively and use our power courageously for the sake of a more equitable, just, and compassionate world. (p. 18)

In this volume, we have heard practitioner scholars express their views that our discourses about children must shift to include cultural relevance, community, needs responsiveness, and human capability. What we now need is a movement that encourages educators to break open their hearts to these ideas–a movement to reclaim democracy (Palmer 2011) and notions of caring that have been foundational to progressive education. Breaking open our hearts means taking a look at the myths and legends that surround our work, comparing them to the realities we encounter everyday, and closing the gap between our heartfelt aspirations and our corrupted realities. Our heartfelt work links us to "communities of congruence" (p. 186) in which we join with others to create hope and change.

Breaking open our hearts also encourages us to look at reforms like 21st Century learning and the Common Core with a lens of possibility rather than a lens of action. Proposals and programs become more understandable when we take the time to reflect on their purposes and look at them as tools for accomplishing our valued, heartfelt becomings rather than lists of compliances and activities that keep us busy, confused, and unproductive.

As we look at these *Postcards from the Schoolhouse,* perhaps we should allow ourselves the luxury of recalling those idyllic, anachronistic days when (we think) we understood our moral purposes as educators and we believed that we had undertaken a sacred mission. Modernity has buried those discourses under rationalism, technique, strategy, and cost-benefit. As practitioner scholars, it's time to re-invent a moral discourse about children, learning, and society. It's time to reclaim a practice that values the heart and soul as well as earning a living. It's time for educational practitioners to think deeply about their work, its purposes, and its worth. It's time to begin the healing our democracy so desperately needs. And the place to begin healing is the school.

References

Bloom, L. (2012). *Swagger: 10 Urgent Rules for Raising Boys in an Era of Failing Schools, Mass Joblessness, and Thug Culture.* New York. Vantage Point Press.

Bugbee, M. (2006, October). The Gift of Mentorship. Principal, 86 (1), 22-26. Retrieved June 20, 2012, from Wilson Web database.

Connelly, G. (2010). *The best of ideas will never come from Washington, D.C.: A conversation with Arne Duncan.* Principal (November/December). Retrieved from http://www.naesp.org

Cottrell, C.A., Neuberg, S.L., & Li, N.P. (2007). What do people desire in others? Asocial-functional perspective on the importance of different valued characteristics. *Journal of Personality and Social Psychology*, 92 (2), 209-231.

Darling-Hammond, L. (2011) *The Flat World and Education: How America's Commitment to Equity Will Determine Our Future.* New York, NY: Teachers College Press.

Davis, S., Darling-Hammond, L., & Meyerson, d. (2005). School Leadership Study: Developing successful principals (review of research).

Doyle, M. E., & Rice, D. M. (2002, November). A Model for Instructional Leadership. *Principal Leadership:High School Edition, 3*(3), 49-52.

Duke, D., & Salmonwicz, M. (2010). Key decisions of a first year 'turnaround' principal. *Educational Management Administration & Leadership*, 38(1), 33-58.

Duncan, A. (2011). National Association of Elementary School Principals. Retreived from http://www.naesp.org

Fullan, M. (2000). The three stories of education reform. *Phi Delta Kappan*, 81 (8) April, 2000. Pg. 581.

Fullan, M. (2003). *The Moral Imperative of School Leadership.* Thousand Oaks, California: Corwin Press, Inc.

Fullan, M. (2008). *The Six Secrets Of Change: What the Best Leaders Do To Help Their Organizations Survive and Thrive.* San Francisco, California: Jossey-Bass Publishing Inc.

Fullar, Ed. J (2009). "Turnover in Principalship Focus of Research". *Education Week.* October 28, 2009.

Ginsberg, R. (2008). Being boss is hard: The emotional side of being in charge. *Phi Delta Kappan*, 90 (4), 202-297. Retrieved June 12, 2012, from http://www.jstor.org/stable/20446093

Goodlad, J. (1984). *A place called school.* New York: McGraw-Hill.

Horng, E., & Loeb, S. (2010, November). New Thinking About Instructional Leadership. *Phi Delta Kappan, 92*(3), 66-69.

Jones, M.G., Jones, B., & Hargrove, T. (2003). *The unintended consequences of high-stakes testing.* Lanham, MD: Rowman and Littlefield.

Leithwood, K.A., Harris, A., & Hopkins, D. (2008). Seven strong claims about successful school leadership. School Leadership & Management, 28(1), 27-42. Retrieved June 5, 2012, from doi:10.1080.13632430701800060

Louis, K.S., Leithwood, K., Wahlstrom, K.L., & Anderson, S.W. (2010). Investigating the links to improved student learning: Final report of research findings. Center for Applied Research and Educational Improvement, University of Minnesota. Retrieved August 20, 2010, from http://www.cehd.umn.edu/carei/Leadership/Learning-from-Learning_final-Research-Report_July-2010.pdf

Lunenburg, F., & Ornstein, A. (2004). *Educational administration: Concepts and Practices* (4th ed.). Belmont, CA: Wadsworth/Thompson Learning.

Marzano, R., Walters, T., McNulty, B. (2005). *School Leadership that Works: From Research to Results.* ASCD, Aurora, Colorado.

Mendels, P. (2012). The Effective Principal. *Journal of Staff Development, 33*(1), 54-58.

Miller, A. W. (2001, December). Finding Time and Support for Instructional Leadership. *Principal Leadership: High School Edition, 2*(4), 29-33.

Millikan, B (2007). *The last dropout: Stop the epidemic!* Carlsbad, CA: Hay House Press.

Nichols, S. L. & Berliner, D. C. (2008) *Testing the Joy out of Learning: School cultures dominated by high-stakes tests are creating more and more reluctant learners.* Educational Leadership / March 2008 Vol. 65. No. 6. ASCD Publications

Orfield, G., & Kornhaber, M.L. (Eds.). (2001). *Raising standards or raising barriers? Inequality and high stakes testing in public education.* New York: Century Foundation Press.

Orfield, G., Losen, D., Wald, J. & Swanson, C. (2004). *Losing our future: How minority youth are being left behind by the graduation rate crisis.* Cambridge, MA: The Civil Rights Project at Harvard University. Contributors: Advocates for Children of New York, The Civil Society Institute.

Palmer, J.P. (2007). Heart at Work. *Christian Century.* Reproduced with permission from the October 2, 2007 issue of the *Christian Century.* Retrieved June 2, 2012, from www.christiancentury.org.

Palmer, J.P. (2011). *Healing the heart of democracy: The courage to create a politics worthy of the human spirit.* United States: Jossey-Bass.

Powell, D., Higgins, H.J., Aram, R., & Freed, A. (2009). Impact of NCLB on curriculum and instruction in rural schools. *The Rural Educator*, 31(1), 19-28. Retrieved May 26, 2012, from http://www.eric.ed.gov/PDFS/EJ876130.pdf

Printy, S. M., Marks, H. M., & Bowers, A. J. (2009, September). Integrated Leadership: How Principals and Teachers Share Transformational and Instructional Influence. *Journal of School Leadership, 19*(5), 504-532.

Protheroe, N. (2011, May). What Do Effective Principals Do? *Principal, 90*(5), 26-30.

Stipek, Deborah (2006). Relationships Matter: The key to raising achievement is connecting students with teachers who support them not just as learners, but also as people. ASCD. *Educational Leadership.* September, 2006.

Taylor, G., Shepard, L. Kinner, F. & Rosenthal, J. (2003). *A survey of teachers' perspectives on high-stakes testing in Colorado: What gets taught, what gets lost* (CSE Technical Report 588). Los Angeles: University of California.

Viadero, D. (2009). Turnover In Principalship Focus Of Research. *Education Week.* Vol. 29, Iss. 12. October 26, 2009. Available at http://www.edweek.org/login.html?source=http://www.edweek.org/ew/articles/2009/10/28/09principal_ep.h29

Walker, K.D. (2006). Fostering hope: A leader's first and last task. *Journal of Educational Administration*, 44(6), 540-569.

West, D., Peck, C., & Reitzug, U. (2010). Limited control and relentless accountability: Examining historical changes in urban school principal pressure. *Journal of School Leadership, 20*, 238-266.

Wes-Burhham, J. (2009). *Rethinking Educational Leadership: From improvement to transformation*. Continuum International Publishing Group. New York, NY.

Wimberly, G.L. (2002). School relationships foster success for African American students. Iowa City, IA:ACT.

Wolk, S. (2007). Why go to school? *Phi Delta Kapan*, 88 (9), 648-658.

Dr. Carl Lashley is Associate Professor in the Department of Educational Leadership and Cultural Foundations at the University of North Carolina at Greensboro. He has served as a general and special education teacher, an elementary school principal, Director of Special Education, and Director of Curriculum and Instruction in public schools in West Virginia. Carl's primary intellectual and advocacy interests in equity, justice, and community come from his career long concerns about poverty, equitable opportunity for all children, and the power of schooling as a mode of social change. His research interests are in education law; special education law, policy, and practice; technology; and school leadership preparation. He is the Co-Director of the Smith Professional Development High School, a partnership between UNCG and the Guilford County Schools. On the UNCG campus, he regularly presents and works with faculty and students on matters related to the responsible conduct of research. Carl currently serves as President-elect of the North Carolina Professors of Educational Leadership. He can be contacted at carl.lashley@gmail.com.

Dr. Aaron Woody is principal of an elementary school in a large, urban district. He also serves as an Adjunct Professor in the Department of Educational Leadership and Cultural Foundations at the University of North Carolina Greensboro. In his thirteen years as a public educator, Aaron has served as a teacher, coach, assistant principal, and principal in various urban, rural, and transitional schools. In addition to serving on a variety of district and community committees, Aaron has been a trainer and presenter at regional and national education conferences. In 2010 he was selected as the Randolph County Schools Principal of the Year. That same year, UCEA recognized Aaron with the David Clark National Graduate Student Research Award in administration and educational policy. His research interests include the strategies and effects of community partnerships within schools, as well as the processes that lead to transformational leadership. He can be contacted at amwoody2@uncg.edu.